Acclaim for Sam Heughan's

WAYPOINTS

"If *Waypoints* were merely about Heughan's walk, it would be delightful, instructive, and enticing. But this is a memoir, after all, and it is his reflection on his life and work, interspersed with the challenges and discoveries of the Way, that lend his story heft and grit."

— Priscilla Kipp, *Bookpage*

"Full of personal revelations…The memoir contains many insights into Heughan's life, from his relationship with his late estranged father to his early days in the theater, but he also packs it with Hollywood near-misses, including the time he auditioned for James Bond."

— Maureen Lee Lenker, *Entertainment Weekly*

"A pleasure for fans of the author, whisky, and Scotland."

— *Kirkus Reviews*

"In many ways, the physical journey that Heughan details in the book parallels his life journey: full of ups and downs, moments of hesitation and determination, and a pretty satisfying ending…Scotland is more than just a backdrop: It's almost like another character, one that continues to challenge, shape, and inspire him."

— Chelsea Greenwood, *Shondaland*

T0371921

"As the title suggests, *Waypoints* is a rewarding mix of markers, both personal as he reflects on his life and geographical as he leads the reader along the West Highland Way."   — Janet Christie, *The Scotsman*

"A deeply personal and warmly entertaining memoir that fans of Sam — and Scotland — will have a joyful time devouring."   — *Heat*

"From both his walk and his career, the common lesson is the power of persistence."   — Stephen McGinty, *The Times* (London)

"With disarming asides and humorous accents, Heughan's narration reveals the fun-loving yet thoughtful man behind his acting roles ... Bookended by scenes with Heughan's estranged father, *Waypoints* is a companionable and inspiring memoir that encourages soul-searching and mindfulness."

          — Mari Carlson, *Bookpage* (audiobook review)

WAYPOINTS

My Scottish Journey

SAM HEUGHAN

VORACIOUS

Little, Brown and Company
New York   Boston   London

Voracious / Little, Brown and Company
Hachette Book Group
1290 Avenue of the Americas, New York, NY 10104
voraciousbooks.com

Originally published in hardcover by Voracious / Little, Brown and Company, October 2022
First Voracious paperback edition, September 2023

Voracious is an imprint of Little, Brown and Company, a division of Hachette Book Group, Inc.
The Voracious name and logo are trademarks of Hachette Book Group, Inc.

The publisher is not responsible for websites (or their content) that are not owned by the publisher.

The Hachette Speakers Bureau provides a wide range of authors for speaking events. To find out more,
go to hachettespeakersbureau.com or email hachettespeakers@hbgusa.com.

Little, Brown and Company books may be purchased in bulk for business, educational, or promotional
use. For information, please contact your local bookseller or the Hachette Book Group Special Markets
Department at special.markets@hbgusa.com.

Photography credits appear on page 281.

Page 101: excerpt from the new verse translation of Jean Racine's *Phaedre*, translated by Edwin Morgan.
Published by Carcanet in 1992, © Edwin Morgan Trust.

Page 133: *Monty Python and the Holy Grail* written by Graham Chapman, John Cleese,
Eric Idle, Terry Gilliam, Terry Jones and Michael Palin.

ISBN 9780316495530 (hc) / 9780316495639 (pb)
LCCN 2022944762

Printing 1, 2023

LSC-C

Printed in the United States of America

To Owen, a patient, kind man and proud Scotsman, who enjoyed a walk, a blether and a good whisky. Thank you.

And to anyone who feels alone on their journey, or in need of some company, come with me. I promise you'll not be walking alone and I'll buy you a dram at the end.

Sláinte. x

It's a dangerous business, Frodo, going out your door.
You step onto the road, and if you don't keep your feet,
there's no knowing where you might be swept off to.
(*The Lord of the Rings*, J.R.R. Tolkien)

CONTENTS

FOREWORD

Sam walks into the room. The first thing I notice about him is how open his face is. Nervous, I guess, and alert, but open to the world, trusting. The formality and potential stress of the encounter – a director auditioning an actor for their first professional theatre role – has not dimmed his eyes or upset his equilibrium. It's not always like this. The audition process can be grim for all concerned, but more especially for the actor (Sam testifies to this a number of times in the pages of this book), and they naturally withhold a part of themselves out of, well, self-preservation, I suppose. But Sam isn't wearing armour today, only a cloak of silent charm.

It's late spring of 2002, and Sam is still a student at drama school. The play is *Outlying Islands* by David Greig for the Traverse Theatre, Edinburgh, to be performed at the Edinburgh Festival in the summer of that year. The role is John, a young Scottish ornithologist in the 1930s from a background of privilege. Sam opens the script at the page I suggest and speaks the lines. He gets it right first time. He doesn't try too hard, the classic rookie error. Instead, he marks all of John's qualities; shy, tentative, easy-natured, loyal, right-minded – a gentleman, a gentle man. To me, Sam *is* John, and that's it. I don't think I've ever told him this, but we never auditioned anyone else for the part.

When he leaves the room, I do a private little punch in the air. Not only have we got our John, but this guy doesn't seem to have any idea how good he is.

I think it's fair to say that *Outlying Islands* was a success – it won awards, transferred to London, and toured internationally. (You can imagine how much hilarity ensued when it featured in the *Daily Telegraph*'s 'Top Five Theatrical Sex Scenes' of all time.) But equally it might have proved a disorientating and unrealistic beginning to any young actor's career. *Waypoints* outlines, fascinatingly but often in painfully explicit detail, the snakes and ladders of an actor's working life. I've always flattered myself that I've kept in touch with what Sam has been up to over the years, but now I realize I haven't known the half of it.

Sam's journal of his trek along the West Highland Way and its daily challenges reads as a parable of the longer journey to become the leading actor that he is today. It's an unusual privilege to get this much detail and insight into what creates an actor in the first place, and then follow them as they negotiate the shark-infested waters of the theatre and film industries. The more difficult the challenge, the higher our lone ranger rises to it. This applies whether he's describing a reckless yomp up Conic Hill by Loch Lomond in the gloaming, or the experience of filming the formidable, torturous scenes (scenes that still haunt me) at the end of *Outlander* season one. The story of his journey is so immediate, so resonant, we walk it with him in our heads, in rain and shine (more rain than shine). And we marvel at how often the landscape of Scotland looks like the ups and downs of Sam's life, as an actor but also just as a man.

What do I learn about Sam that I didn't know twenty years ago when we first met? That he is fiercely loyal, disarmingly self-critical, questing by nature – yes, even when he's not entirely sure what the quest is for – and above all, determined never to be someone who lets other people down.

Outlying Islands is set on an unnamed Scottish island that we learn during the course of the play is the intended location for the Ministry of Defence's experiment with a new breed of biological weapon, one that will destroy the island's ecology. As part of our research for the production, four of us in the company decide to go on an expedition to North Rona, an island that matches the level of remoteness that the playwright has in mind. North Rona lies approximately 40 miles further north than the northernmost point of the Isle of Lewis in the Outer Hebrides, and the only way of getting there in 2002 is with an extreme sports adventure company. And, so it is that Sam – the 'lad o' pairts' from Galloway – finds himself strapped to a RIB (rigid inflatable boat: think dodgem car riding the tops of the waves) in the middle of the North Atlantic, with squalls chasing the rainclouds, plunging of gannets, and sudden shafts of piercing light as at a rock concert.

In the middle of this tiny deserted island (North Rona gives St Kilda a run for her money in terms of sheer stubborn remoteness) lies the ruined chapel of the 8th-century St Ronan and his adjacent hermit's cell. Sam eyes up the saint's accommodation and looks satisfied. I hope he doesn't think we're staying here. He grins, and we both laugh. But now that I've read *Waypoints* – in which Sam tells us 'I like to occupy that outside edge' (p.37) – I look back and think he might have seriously entertained the prospect. Sam Heughan: Lowlander by birth, Highlander by inclination. And now islander?

The skipper herds us back to the RIB earlier than we hoped, appearing genuinely concerned about the forecast for our two-and-a-half-hour trip back to the Butt of Lewis. And so it proves: the reality of the return journey distorts the memory of the outward as a breeze. Now each wave slaps the vessel back down on the water with bone-jangling force. Despite being lassoed (or so it feels) to our saddle-like seats, we cling on for dear life. And – you've guessed right – Sam is the only one of us without fear. He shouts, he screams, he cheers. This is his natural environment.

Philip Howard
Edinburgh
August 2022

PROLOGUE

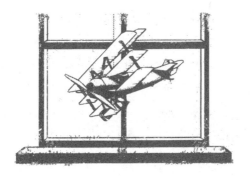

British Columbia, Canada

I have come a long way to be here. The cabin sits at the edge of the wood. Constructed from hand-split logs and timbers, it's partially hidden by tall, majestic trees and dense foliage. Upon reaching the door, I look around and realize it has an inspiring, beautiful view of the valley and mountains beyond.

This is a good place to live, I think to myself. I can understand why someone would want to settle in such a remote, secluded spot. It's my kind of home.

The cooking area is outside, spread out under an extended porch. A row of saucepans and a colander dangle from hooks fixed to the exterior wall. A large knife rests across a butcher's block, while onions and chillies hang from strings to dry in the sun and intensify in flavour.

In front of this area, dappled by sunlight, a large bench table suggests our host is someone who enjoys preparing food for others. I picture a group of friends on each side of the table, swigging from bottles of beer as they laugh and joke and swat at midges. At the threshold to the cabin now, I allow my gaze to linger on what could be a stage set for an open-air theatre production. It suggests a life very different from mine. There's a hesitancy on my part to step inside.

'Let's do it,' says my older brother, Cirdan, who has accompanied me on this journey.

We are here by invitation of the woman who has stepped inside before us. She met my brother and me at the airport, and shared the driving overnight in the car we'd rented for our stay. Neither Cirdan nor I know her beyond a few telephone conversations. She's a very nice lady – in her sixties, I would say – and yet an air of quiet formality governs how we relate to each other.

'Come in,' she says, on realizing we are still on the porch.

I feel my brother gently press a hand to my back.

Inside, out of the sunshine, I am greeted by the smell of woodsmoke, tobacco and coffee grounds. I wonder if I detect a hint of weed as well, but now is not the time to comment on it or even swap a look with Cirdan. As our host closes the door behind us, I let my eyes adjust to the interior. There appears to be just one main living area, plus a wooden staircase leading to a bedroom and bathroom. Looking around, my first impression is of a comfortable, cosy, if notably basic, space.

Books line the shelves in no particular order, their spines fractured in a way that tells me the owner is a passionate reader. A desk stands in the corner. Whoever sits there likes to work by candlelight. I find myself looking at a sprawl of sketches and lists in hurried handwriting. Sifting through the sheets with my fingertips, I find an astrological chart spread out underneath. Ashes sit in the cradle of an open fire, and also dust the hearth. With a crackling blaze on the go, I imagine this is the kind of place that brings respite from the outside world. The worn upholstered armchair suggests it's a been home for quite some time. A place to finally come to rest, I think, which reminds me of the purpose of our visit.

As our host leaves us for a moment to pad upstairs, I am struck by the fact that we are surrounded by the markers of a lifetime. My brother seems to sense this as well. He looks up and around, arms clasped behind his back like a museum visitor. A model aeroplane hangs from a length of fishing line in front of a window. With three wings in glossy vermilion, this First World War-era aircraft is caught in a barrel roll as if preparing to attack. Immediately I recognize the Red Baron, a character who fascinated me as a child. Someone once told me that the owner of this particular model loved to fly. The plane has been both crafted and painted by hand. The detailing is impressive, and reminds me that a creative urge can take people in very different directions.

I move a little closer to the shelves, interested in what titles I might find, only to register not a book but a DVD that's all too familiar to me. I pinch it free with my thumb and forefinger, though I know exactly what the cover looks like because I play one of the characters in this movie. Without a word, I show the case to my brother. He raises his eyebrows in what could be surprise that it's here at all, or confirmation of something we should've expected all along.

I return the tape to the shelf, mindful now that the owner has been following my journey from afar, before running my finger along the books beside it. I don't have to go far to find a library copy of the first title in a series that's about to be adapted for television. I've read them all, as I'm about to star in the show. I pull out the tome just to check it's not overdue. Judging by the date, it's a recent selection. Then I wonder if the person who withdrew it from the library will have time to read it, and try hard not to feel sad. It's an odd take on a familiar emotion. There is little weight to it, as if it's just a prompt for how I should be responding, rather than the real thing.

I go on to pick up clay models of hobbit dwellings and a felt wizard's hat with a floppy fringe. Each item defines a point on a journey through life; from the old cigarette lighter to what must be a favourite mug. Collectively they should lead me to the person who lives here. I'm just not sure if what I find will match my expectations. All I really have are vague early memories and a handful of second-hand stories, but if I'm honest, over the passage of time I just haven't given it much thought. Until now.

The sound of footsteps descending the stairs prompts me to step back, turn and smile politely.

'Your father isn't feeling well enough to see you just now,' she says apologetically. 'We can come back later.'

TIME OUT

Glasgow, Scotland, (almost) a decade later

'I've got to go!' From my bed, I sit upright so forcefully that the duvet lifts and crumples at my feet. 'I've got to do this . . . NOW!'

I'm not talking to anyone but myself here. In fact, I'm alone at home. I've only been back for a few days. After months away due to a bunch of filming commitments, as well as promotional work and business projects, I should be content with lying still. In just the last four weeks, I've hurried through departure and arrival zones in airports from Mexico to LA, New York and Chicago. Not that it's a chore. I love being busy. But by rights I should be happy loafing around in my sweat pants doing absolutely nothing. Instead, thanks to jet lag and a little hangover from a date with my whisky collection the night before, I can't stop my mind from roaming.

'I could just do it,' I reason with myself, as if I know the rational part of my mind needs to get on board with the plan. 'Couldn't I?'

Since I unlocked the front door and dumped my bags in the hall, I've found myself aimlessly killing time. I feel restless. I can't sleep at night, only to doze through the day. Frankly it feels like I've forgotten how to live without a work schedule. All I've been doing is drifting from one room to another as if reminding myself that I actually live here. Mealtimes have merged into snacking sessions. I've experimented with porridge toppings, though nothing beats frozen blueberries, peanut butter and a pinch of cinnamon, and dared the salt and pepper pots to judge me for enjoying eggs with ketchup and hot sauce. A wee trip to the gym towards teatime has been my sole reason for getting dressed – albeit in a random collection of clothing, spring meets autumn/ winter collection, circa 2009. After that, I tune in to reruns of *Back to the Future* and low-budget police chase documentaries. What should be quality downtime just feels like one dull blur. *SssssscccccCCCCCCrrrrrrrackKK!* The new coffee machine I've struggled to learn how to use finishes dispensing some spectacular atomic black liquid into my favourite porcelain mug. Two cups are enough to get me out of bed. Three would be ideal.

I'm annoyed at myself because I'd been looking forward to this break immensely. I considered myself fortunate in that I was in an industry that had found a way to function through yet another pandemic year. The whole world had been affected, and we were no different. Shooting films and television had become potentially limiting in lots of ways, but I was so grateful to be in one of a few sectors able to continue. Now I had a break, and yet I found myself struggling to rest for more than a day. I'm not hyperactive, I crave down time, but I feel guilty if I'm not grafting and pushing myself in some capacity. During this last year, we finally managed to shoot season six of *Outlander*. It was shorter, but more intense and with a darker tone. In my role as the Highland warrior Jamie Fraser, the cast and crew have become like family to me since the show first went into production in 2013. Even though this latest season contained just eight episodes, it proved to be one of the hardest. With the new guidelines and restrictions in our lives, we pulled together like never before to make it something special. It had left me feeling exhausted and looking forward to this short break.

Our base for the production of *Outlander* is Wardpark Film & Television Studios, which is north-east of Glasgow in Lanarkshire. We had to operate in a bubble, and saw very few people outside it. On the first day of filming, which fell in the teeth of a traditional Scottish winter, I found myself in the company of my faithful and ever reliant driver, Davie Stewart. Davie's nickname is 'Hollywood', because he's chauffeured big stars in his time. I like to think he considers me to be an ordinary fare, because he's always relaxed and great company on our rides. We share a passion for bad techno music, and a Friday night in the car home can be pretty wild. Despite my fluid approach to call times, I can guarantee that he'll always get me there on schedule.

That morning, even though I had been uncharacteristically ready and waiting for him, we were cutting things fine on account of the snow. It dusted the landscape, crowning the Campsie Fells as we made our way along the M80 to Cumbernauld, but slowed us down considerably by tumbling across the road in flurries. Fortunately, the traffic was light. This wasn't just down to the weather conditions, but also the fact that the world had pretty much stopped turning since the virus had set in. We took the empty roads for granted now, and while Davie focused on driving, I dwelled on how the pandemic had touched every aspect of our lives. Quite literally, there was no escape from it. I had only just returned to Scotland, having finished work on a movie called *It's All Coming Back to Me*, with Celine Dion and Priyanka Chopra. With social distancing measures in place throughout the shoot, it had been challenging. They had implemented some rather strict rules during the prep period: 25 minutes max spent together in the same room, masks worn at all times, and so on. I felt it important to create a sense of intimacy with Priyanka as we were supposed to be starstruck lovers, so the two of us and the director made sure we spent some time together socially. In some ways the restrictions forced us to raise our game in order to deliver our best work. Mindful of this as we swished through the slush and melting snow surrounding the gates at Wardpark, I sensed fresh challenges ahead.

'All I need is some kit.' I am out of bed now and pacing the floor as I think out loud. 'A tent . . . waterproofs . . . boots . . . *crampons?*' I pause for a moment, aware that even though I don't know the answer, I will need to start from scratch, and then dismiss it as a minor concern.

'I can sort all that,' I decide, even if I'm not entirely sure what else should be on the list.

Yes, I am acting on the spur of the moment. It's an impulsive move, but the adventure I have in mind hasn't just popped into my head. During a location shoot for *Outlander*, in the final week of the schedule, we trekked out from the studio to Glencoe. This magnificent Highlands destination is home to peaks, valleys (or glens), trails and waterfalls. It's also an iconic location in cinema, tailor-made for wide screens, with pivotal scenes filmed here for *Skyfall* and the Harry Potter films. In what had been a hard winter, the landscape looked both serene and savage. Whenever I was away from the camera, I'd find myself drawn to just gazing out at the views. Standing there in Jamie's tattered rags and ill-fitting boots, shooting a flashback sequence from Ardsmuir prison (season three), I'd breathe in the crisp, still air and long to lose myself in this vast, glorious wilderness. Much of my passion for *Outlander* stemmed from the fact that the story went deep into Scotland's history of the struggles and triumphs of the Highlanders. It's an honour to play Jamie, a fierce, loyal, strong and stubborn braveheart, and yet I'd never truly explored what was effectively his homeland.

So on the last day of the shoot, I arranged with another actor who shared my love of running to get up long before our call time and lace on a pair of trail shoes. The cold air woke me as we jogged towards the Buachaille Etive Mòr (The Great Herdsman of Etive), the iconic, imposing mountain that protected the glen. We were following a path well travelled by hikers and backpackers; an iconic walking route called the West Highland Way. This broad thread cut across the landscape, snaking around foothills, disappearing into dips and cresting folds. It drew my eye as far as I could see.

'Glasgow to Fort William,' Jack, my running companion, said, as if inviting me to consider the sheer length of the route. 'What's that? About 100 miles?'

'It's a long way,' I offered, my brain still asleep under the tartan covers back at the hotel. I was unsure of the exact distance but aware that we were briefly following a path that formed a gateway to rugged, elemental country. 'I think it starts close to where I live,' I added.

'Wow.' My companion glanced across at me, barely out of breath. 'It must be an amazing adventure.'

I didn't reply. We were beginning to find our stride, but mostly I focused on my feet because I was reluctant to reel off all the excuses as to why I wouldn't know. The West Highland Way was one of those things on my to-do list. I'd just never got round to ticking it off. It was on my doorstep, quite literally, and yet I always seemed to be too busy to do anything about it. Ironically, I loved being outdoors. I had even founded a charity dedicated to encouraging people to take on challenges and enjoy happy, healthy lives – and yet here I was, too embarrassed to admit that I had yet to walk one of my country's great trails.

Plodding along as the sky brightened at the edges, we passed a camper van parked alongside the path. The curtains were closed. Beside the vehicle, just away from the awning, the remnants of a campfire surrounded by folding chairs and tin cups reminded me why my head was only just clearing. The van belonged to Wendy, a fellow Scot and my wonderful make-up artist, who preferred her mobile creature comforts to the hotel occupied by cast and crew. Wendy had dragged her husband along for the trip. The night before, they had invited some of us to join them for a drink. We had gathered around the warmth from the fire, eating posh Fortnum & Mason biscuits, drinking whisky, petting her two overweight chihuahuas and sharing stories from the shoot and beyond, her infectious laugh regularly piercing the crisp evening air.

Wendy was a marvellous host, with a great sense of humour. I was tempted to bang on the side of her van to wake her. As much as I liked to make mischief, though, especially as we were effectively on our last day of term, it was still very early. Plus I didn't think my running buddy needed to learn from Wendy's vast lexicon of Glaswegian swear words. I could imagine the response: 'Gonnae no dae that! Yer aff yer heid, runnin' at this time, ya bawbag.' So we passed the van quietly and pressed on with the loop we had planned. Leaving the path, we descended across moorland to the River Etive. The banks of this fast-flowing waterway were boggy and somewhat challenging underfoot, but it felt so good to just get out and switch off and feel a little free. This was the last day of the hardest season of shooting. My heart lifted and I felt excited to escape the COVID protocols and the tough schedule that had dictated the days, weeks and months of the shoot.

By the time we arrived back at the hotel, I had just enough time for a shower before rushing out to find 'Hollywood' waiting for me behind the wheel of his car.

'Cutting it fine again,' he said jokingly.

Even with the mud from the riverbank still fresh on my running shoes, I wondered whether he assumed I'd just been sleeping in.

'Always,' I said all the same.

The final day of the production was no less intense than any other. The last scene we had to film would be the one that opened the season. We had actually shot it in the studio six months previously, but the producers thought it wasn't dramatic enough, and decided it needed this epic location to kick the season off. Acting can be a topsy-turvy experience in this way, and so as I set off back to Glasgow on my motorbike, I was looking forward to some normality returning to my life. I could unwind at home, I thought to myself on the long journey back to the city. With no other work commitments for a week, I planned to simply sit back and do nothing. I decided to celebrate my new freedom and took the longer route home, through Stirling and past Loch Lubnaig, a stunningly beautiful loch near Ben Ledi and the secret location of Fraser's Ridge and 'the Big House'. I gave it a wave as I passed. 'See you next season!' I shouted from under my retro motorcycle helmet.

'It's only ninety-six miles,' I say to myself on consulting a map of the West Highland Way on my laptop screen from bed. Just then, it feels as if the absence of those four extra miles I expected to find makes all the difference. In front of me, I study a line that crosses and follows contours on a journey north from my home city to a town at the foot of Ben Nevis; a mountain I have always longed to climb. Ever since my running friend and I set foot on this celebrated path, I have not been able to forget about it. It felt like I had sampled a couple of hundred metres, and now I want to experience every moment from start to finish. And to climb Ben Nevis at the end – what a challenge! Established over 40 years ago, the route is intended for people to immerse themselves in the Scottish landscape. Beginning in Milngavie, a northern suburb of Glasgow, it follows the eastern flank of Loch Lomond for nearly 30 miles. From there, it strikes out across the glens towards Inverarnan and Tyndrum, Kingshouse and Kinlochleven. The route cuts across increasingly wild and wonderful terrain before climbing to the rise that reveals the magnificent peak of the UK's highest mountain.

Scribbling on a scrap of paper, I attempt to calculate how much time it would take me to reach the finish at Fort William. I am in good shape physically, thanks to my passion for working out and the occasional run, and also blindly optimistic (or naïve).

'Easy. Five days,' I conclude, having figured that 20 miles each day would be a breeze. 'It's on.'

I only have a short time available, but it's just enough. If I parked the idea, I don't know when such an opportunity might arise again. In that moment, as I close the laptop, it doesn't feel like a rash decision. It's destiny, pure and simple. With two days in hand, which is enough to get home again by train and prepare for my next work commitment, I could *smash* it.

Partly inspired by Wendy's charmingly boujee, nomadic lifestyle, I figure camping would be the most efficient and fitting way to travel. I could pitch a tent as the sun went down, cook my supper over an open fire, and then turn in under canvas beneath the stars. I hadn't properly camped since my cub scout days (I just loved collecting the badges), apart from a gruesomely muddy experience at T in the Park, Scotland's traditionally waterlogged music festival. This would be different, I decided. It would be the real deal.

'West Highland Way, I'm coming for you,' I declare, sitting back to address the map on the screen. 'Tomorrow we ride! Well . . . walk.'

Before climbing into the metaphorical saddle, I have to assemble all the kit I'll need for my week in the wild. Having made a spontaneous decision, I know I have to act fast. Not only do I intend to set off at dawn the next day, but I am also short on time before the shops shut.

'Will this be all, sir?' The young man behind the till tries hard to maintain eye contact and not gawp at all the gear I've dumped on the counter.

'I believe so,' I say, hoping to sound both casual and confident, acting the hardened hillwalker, hoping he won't call my bluff.

In truth, from the moment I started browsing, I felt completely unprepared. I wasn't just after a few items of kit; I needed *everything*, from a hat and outdoor jacket to hiking boots, and all the bits in between. I quickly found my basket filled, and began loading my free arm as well. I grabbed a tent, a sleeping bag, a big old rucksack, a portable gas stove, and food in pouches to fuel my journey. I even picked out an AeroPress coffee maker, because I worried I wouldn't function without my multiple morning caffeine hit. Touring every rack and aisle, basically panic-buying, I finally navigated my way to the counter for the simple reason that I couldn't carry any more.

'Planning a trip?' asks the store assistant as he begins to ring through the items.

'The West Highland Way,' I say

'Nice! In the spring?'

'Tomorrow,' I tell him. 'First light.'

The guy pauses in scanning barcodes. I am well aware that it's raining hard outside, as it has been for days. The shoulders of my coat are wet from hurrying through the high street to get out of the gale. The weather isn't unusual. This is Glasgow, after all. At the tail end of October.

'That should be . . . interesting,' he says, almost tripping over his own tact. Just then, a gust of wind attempts to gain entry to the store through the gap in the glass doors. 'Most people tackle it in the summer.'

I nod as if that is an option insufficiently challenging for a great outdoorsman like me, only to drop the pretence when it strikes me this guy might know what he's talking about.

'Am I crazy?' I ask, levelling with him now. 'Be honest.'

For a second I can see him drawing breath to tell me what I want to hear. Then, as I hold his gaze, he sighs and gives me a reassuring smile.

'I think it could be amazing,' he says, before offering to review my haul and help me select what I really need. 'And hopefully memorable for all the right reasons.'

That evening, having returned home confident that I possess everything I need to be self-sufficient in the face of a zombie outbreak, I set up my tent in the front room. My pitch is somewhat constricted, not by rocks and trees but by the sofa and my coffee table. I don't bother with the tent pegs, because that would involve punching holes in my floorboards. Afterward, assessing my work from the armchair, I am glad that I have tried it out. Not only did I avoid an argument with myself over the placement of poles and canvas, it helped me to feel like I'd made the most of the short time available since I'd committed to this. As an actor, juggling projects in the pipeline, I'm used to long-term planning. It means that often I know what I will be doing months in advance. So my decision to just get up and go for a very long walk is both unusual and refreshing for me.

Tucked up in my warm bed that night, my eyes starting to close, I find my excitement tinged with a note of self-doubt and uncertainty. Since I decided that the West Highland Way was a walk that couldn't wait, this is the first time I have stopped rushing around to get ready. The dreaded doubt begins to creep in. Now that I have a moment to dwell on it, I ask myself what I'm thinking. Is this really wise? I spend a great deal of time travelling from one shoot to the next, and here is a rare chance for me to just be still. I am home at last. A place I sometimes long to be when it feels as if my life is missing a pause button. Instead,

I am set to become Sam the Wanderer; a frontiersman guided by the sun and the stars (not to mention the foldaway weatherproof map of the West Highland Way that my friend at the store insisted I take). In my mind, I've cooked up an epic odyssey. Just then, however, I feel a bit foolish.

Listening to the relentless rain outside, shortly before I nod off, I wonder whether I should just disarm my alarm. Then I could at least wake up late, with not enough time left to seize the day beyond taking my gear back to the shop for a refund.

DAY ONE

INTO THE WILD

The West Highland Way was opened in 1980. I was born the same year, to the south-west of my starting point, in the county of Dumfries and Galloway. My earliest memory as a child still feels like a mystery in my mind that I've yet to solve. I'm sitting halfway up the stairs in the cottage we lived in for the first few years of my life. A former inn, and listed building, on the old drove road from Edinburgh and pilgrim road to Whithorn and St. Ninians. My father stands at the top of the stairs, while my mum is elsewhere, the kitchen perhaps. There is a sense of distance between them, and though I would have been too young to take in the bigger picture at the time, I recall feeling torn. I can't say if there had been conflict or if I had done anything wrong. It's just something that has stayed with me for more than 40 years now.

One thing I can be sure about. That single moment was no reflection of my upbringing. Despite circumstances that would see my parents part company when I was just 18 months old, I experienced only love.

My mum and dad got together in 1970. They met on Brighton beach, which is where my father, David, picked up a nickname that stayed with him for life: Pebbles. Chrissie, my mother, has a deeply artistic streak, and she formed a connection with this free-spirited young man of (supposed) Scottish descent. His background was always a little vague; though it was a fact that he had lived in a squat on the Strand in central London. When police came to evict the illegal dwellers, a photograph of my dad in the heart of the drama made the front page of *The Times*. According to family folklore, this was the reason his strict military parents had disowned him.

Early in their relationship, my parents lived in various places in the south of England – once including a house boat – while earning a living as local gardeners. Eventually the couple made their way to Scotland, settling over the border and to the south-west in a small village in Dumfries and Galloway called Balmaclellan. There they had two sons: my elder brother, Cirdan, and me. My father was a huge fan of *The Lord of the Rings*, naming my brother after an Elvish character from that epic fantasy odyssey and I believe at times referring to me as 'Samwise', though not officially, thank God! It feels fitting that I'm about to embark on my own quest here, though at six foot three, I'm hardly a hobbit. I always loved the books, however. My mum had a treasured special edition that I'd read and reread as a child; its embossed cover and wafer-thin pages made it feel like a spell book from Gandalf's personal library, or some stolen piece of Smaug's treasure.

According to my mother, I was an adventurous little boy who could also be quite sensitive. I could happily lead the charge when left to my own devices, but in company I preferred not to be the focus of attention. I wasn't shy. I just felt more comfortable observing from the sidelines. We're shaped by so many influences as kids, but I was too young to remember the one that quite possibly had a formative impact on me. For when I was 18 months old, my dad left home and never came back.

I have no recollection of this time. I don't remember the shock he must have left behind, as well as the uncertainty, because for a long period his whereabouts was a mystery. As I grew up, and switched on to my surroundings and the people in it, I became aware that our mother did everything to create a family for my brother and me. Being five years older, Cirdan might have had a better understanding of why she sometimes seemed to carry the weight of the world on her shoulders. My Mum was very hurt by what had happened, and yet she responded to it by making every effort to raise her boys in a safe and loving environment.

* * *

'Snood,' I say to myself from behind the wheel of my car the next morning. '*Snoooood*.'

I have no reason to repeat this word. I just like the sound of it. Ever since the sales assistant at the camping shop assured me that I would be thankful for a snood on my adventure, it's become an earworm I can't shake out. The item itself is currently banded around my neck. Until the blowers stop trying to replicate the bracing conditions outside, I am thankful for the warmth it provides.

A gale has swept through overnight. It's left a carpet of tree debris along the lanes I follow to reach my destination. Flooding is also an issue, forcing me to crawl tentatively in places and hope like hell that I'm not set to return home that morning on the back of a breakdown truck. In less testing conditions it's a 20-minute journey from my house at most; so close it's almost criminal that I haven't walked the West Highland Way before. I'm looking forward to getting started, but also feel a little apprehensive. Barely 24 hours have passed since the idea of walking all the way from Glasgow to Fort William popped into my head, and now here I am with all the gear and no idea of what I might expect.

Slowing to negotiate a fallen branch, I note that I've been gripping the steering wheel a little tightly. Nerves are something I know how to manage, I remind myself. As an actor, it's something I've learned to do before delivering any kind of performance. Then again, I'm not heading for a film set or theatre. There will be no director calling the shots or audience in the circle and stalls. I am about to set out into unknown territory. A solo act without a script, improvising as I go along and hoping I don't get lost.

When I think about it like this, I figure a little anxiety is natural, and nothing compared to my sheer excitement.

'Ach, it's going to be great,' I tell myself, as if that might overcome the feeling that I have accidentally left the fridge door open at home. 'Everything will be fine.'

I switch on the radio, just to distract myself, and select a local station. I want to hear some chatter as I consider the trek I face before pitching camp. I am aware that daylight is not on my side at this time of year. I have perhaps eight hours before darkness settles, and 20 miles to cover before I stop for the night. Mindful that I could run a marathon inside three and a half hours, which is six and a bit miles further than I need to go, I reckon I'll be comfortably pitching my tent around mid-afternoon. I have plenty of time in hand, I decide, even if I intend to waste not a single second along the way.

For a mile or so, I relax in the driving seat and just return to my snood mantra. It's only when I hear the radio presenter mention my name that my knuckles tighten around the wheel again. Recently I tweeted my excitement at being involved in the creation of some *Outlander* Lego figures. I love Lego. As I child I spent hours with my medieval castle, and fashioned a guillotine to send poor Lego men to their death. The presenter, however, is simply sharing the news, if that's what you can call it. Ever since the show found such a passionate worldwide audience, I've never quite got my head around the fact that people would pay so much attention to the cast behind the characters. Still, as I spot the sign for the car park at Milngavie, which marks the starting point for the West Highland Way, I switch off the radio and remind myself that nobody knows about this venture but me.

For the first time in ages, I have an opportunity to walk away from being that ginger Scottish guy from *Outlander*. I don't resent the spotlight that has come to follow me around, but as I park the car,

I realize how much I miss just being part of the scenery. So it is with some sense of ceremony that I check my phone one final time before switching it to silent. For the duration of this walk, I want just one connection, and that is to the ground beneath my feet.

'This is it,' I say to myself as I haul on my rucksack. 'There's no going back now.'

The car park is tucked away behind the town's railway station. While the sun has yet to break through, I have high hopes that on such a blustery day, the clouds will soon clear. I didn't mind the few spots of rain that kept my wipers on intermittent. Zipped into my brand-new coat with the hood, I am ready for anything. OK, so the rucksack feels heavier on my shoulders than it did when I tried it on back home. Yes, I went on to squeeze in a few extra bits and pieces, from spare socks to the gas canister without which my portable cooker would be pointless. Even so, as I leave my car behind, it feels like someone has jumped on my back for the ride.

'Not a problem,' I mutter, mindful that a tall, broad-built Scotsman like me should be seen to be taking something like this in his stride.

At the far corner of the car park, a sign on the station wall points me in the direction of the official start of the West Highland Way. A pedestrian underpass is hardly the gateway to the wilderness I imagined, but just now it seems quite fitting. I am about to leave behind the modern world, which feels drab and unexciting in view of the adventure that awaits me on the other side. Striding towards the entrance, ignoring the weight of my pack, I feel a surge of adrenaline.

Frankly, I cannot wait to get started, even if my first-night nerves about such a vast undertaking have yet to fall away.

'Be cool,' I say quietly. 'Let's head north and conquer Nevis.'

A few people are milling around outside the station. I keep my head down, clearly looking like a man on a mission, only to perform an about-turn at the underpass and hurry back to my car to check I really have locked it.

* * *

As a family of three, we left Balmaclellan for the area's main town called New Galloway. There, my Mum worked for a clog maker to support us. She was an artist at heart, but providing for us became her priority. While she never talked about my Dad, who became a closed chapter in our lives, she did everything to create a new start that would allow us to put down roots. I was too young to remember that brief time in town, but when we moved to what would be our lasting family home it became a formative part of my childhood. I was five when we relocated a few miles south into the countryside. My mum had found a place in a converted stables complex just outside New Galloway. With a courtyard in the middle, and people coming and going, it had a strong community atmosphere. People left their doors unlocked. They looked out for each other, and that felt both natural to me and welcoming. Celebrating New Year for the first time in our new place, neighbours and friends from various villages in the area would just come and go, while we were free to visit people and help ourselves to food laid out for everyone. It was a network built on trust, and in the wake of my dad's departure, we valued that. I was surrounded by families in some ways. Ours might not have resembled them, or the kind I saw on our black-and-white TV, but I never felt anything was missing. My mum made sure of that. More immediately, given that I was a little boy who liked to explore, the place I now called home was situated in the grounds of a derelict castle.

The ancestral seat of the Gordons of Lochinvar, whose most famous occupant, William Gordon, was executed for his role in the 1715 Jacobite rebellion, Kenmure Castle is steeped in history. It's said to be the birthplace of John Balliol, King of the Scots from 1292 to 1296, and was certainly the perfect playground for a wee lad in the eighties lost to make-believe.

The castle, atop a steep mound, had been abandoned in the middle of the 20th century. Since then, nature had laid siege. The roof had collapsed and the walls were crumbling, while brambles, thorns, grasses and saplings sprang from every crack and fissure. All the windows had been broken long ago, and the entrances blockaded with heaps of masonry. Naturally, we were forbidden from entering, which served as a siren call to a kid in search of a stage so he could become King Arthur or Robert the Bruce.

On a few occasions, I dared to venture inside. The only realistic access was a spiral staircase, which was both dangerous and deeply creepy. Naturally, ghost stories swirled around the castle. I never encountered the headless piper who was said to be the star of this show, but I was certainly scared off numerous times by my own shadow. Climbing those steps, I just held my breath in anticipation. The state of the interior, combined with my imagination, quickly got the better of me, but I look back with fondness at my early attempts to test boundaries. Mostly I played outside the walls, overlooking the shores of Loch Ken, or in the garden where we laid our faithful canine friend Meg to rest. Under brooding skies, I'd swing my imaginary sword and shield at enemies from my country's history. Sometimes other children from the stables would join me for a battle, but above all I was happy striking out for Scotland on my own. If anything, that ruined old fortress was responsible for encouraging me to explore how much fun it could be pretending to be other characters.

* * *

Today is Halloween Eve. I don't know if that's a thing, but the pumpkins are out in force. They watch me from doorsteps and inside windows as I make my way towards the official start of the West Highland Way. There, I stop to take a selfie with the stone obelisk and the steel arch that mark this starting point. It's quite a busy street, and though it's impossible for anyone to take a picture of themselves without attracting attention, I try to do so in a low-key way.

'Excuse me. It's Jamie, isn't it? From *Outlander*?'

I pocket my phone to see a woman approaching. She's looking at me intently, as if I might be an old friend but she can't be sure. Ever since the show took off, I've become used to people approaching me in this way. It's still a weird experience, because they don't know me as Sam. I just represent a character in a story that they've become involved in. Still, over time I've learned to give them what they want. On the whole, fans are kind, lovely and genuine, and if I can chat for a moment or pause for a quick picture, then I've made people happy and can press on with my day.

'Hey, how are you?' I say, aware that she's now registered my rucksack.

'Are you doing the walk?' she asks. 'Oh, it's beautiful. You're going to love it. The views are amazing!'

We chat for no more than a minute. She tells me that she's completed the whole route herself, and notes that I'm brave to be attempting it so late in the year. Then she wishes me the very best of luck, and with that I'm on my way. It's a short, sweet exchange that actually helps me to feel less daunted in that moment. I remind myself that I could so easily have lifted the snood over my face and just beaten a retreat when she spotted me. As much as my preference is to be invisible, often I find these small connections meaningful for all involved. It's not a problem being nice to people. While sometimes I'd like to be invisible, I'd also hate to be that guy who disappoints.

The first mile of the walk takes me through a local park. It's populated by kids on swings, clusters of parents with prams, and people out walking their dogs. It's not exactly the wild glen I imagined, but I'm aware that's all ahead. With nothing particularly to admire, I put my head down, pick up my pace and just aim to put this stage behind me. Within minutes I've worked up a sweat. My back feels hot and slick from the pack I'm carrying, while the weight of it also presses on my mind. I try to guess its weight. Twenty kilos? Thirty? It had felt fine when I slung it onto my shoulders in my living room. Now, as I leave the park behind and follow a river path towards open countryside, I try to ignore my load and tune into my surroundings.

'You'll find your stride,' I tell myself, only to pause a few minutes later where the path has flooded. Not just flooded; it's like a bloody great river! It might be a dry but blustery day today, but the recent rainfall has left the ground waterlogged. In my brand-new walking boots, which I'm keen not to test quite so soon, I tiptoe around the water's edge. As I do so, I hear a series of splashes in quick succession moving towards me from behind. I turn just as a trail runner strides through the flood as if it didn't exist. I nod, feeling like a bit of a lightweight, and then realize I should just follow in his footsteps. Within seconds, the water seeps into my boots. 'Great start,' I mutter to myself. 'Way to go, Sam.'

Once I've stopped feeling annoyed that it's so wet, I find I quite enjoy just sploshing through the water. It reminds me of being a child. I loved my green frog-eyed wellies as a kid. *Splash!* Nothing can stop me now, I decide, even if my socks are starting to squelch.

For the first hour or so, I walk with my phone in my hand. I've no intention of checking my emails or messages. It's just I keep wanting to take photographs of things I find interesting. I turn the lens on bracken and tree trunks, and then stop for a few minutes to take pictures of the cows that wander across to greet me. These are Highland cattle, with horns like the handlebars of the bikes in Easy Rider and shaggy, salon-grade hair. 'Awright, lads! I'm moooving on!' I'm just so charged up and excited, as if I'm an explorer uncovering a whole new world. After months of film shoots, and shuttling from airports to hotels, I feel liberated.

What really grabs my attention is the carpet of fallen leaves all around me. The wind has swept so many from the branches to the ground in the last few days, and I quickly fall in love with the colours. I'm looking at russet reds and yellows of every stripe. It'll be a week at least before they lose their vibrancy, and yet I find myself taking one shot after another, as if this moment might just vanish.

* * *

As a child, a difference of five years in age can seem like a generation. I looked up to my brother, and still do. In some ways he became a father figure to me. He's always been very practical – building dens or mending bikes as we grew up – which is a quality I really admire. I wanted to be good with my hands like him, and though I tried, he just seemed to have a natural gift. I'm rubbish at mending stuff and don't have the patience. Ultimately I just preferred to stand and watch him do it for me. Even though we could squabble and fight at an early age, we still played games together like table tennis and pool. Cirdan also had a passion for cycling, which would become central to his adult life. He was always pedalling off on adventures, which seemed so exciting to a kid like me.

I'm guessing Cirdan's experience of our Dad's departure was very different from mine. He was more aware of what had happened, whereas I just grew up with no memory of what life was like with two parents. Once, when I was about seven, someone at primary school asked me where my father was.

'I don't know,' I said earnestly. 'I don't have one.'

I wasn't hurt by the question. I just had no answer.

Once, around the time I turned 10, my Mum answered the phone and handed it to me.

'David wants to speak to you,' she said. 'From Germany.'

I had no idea who it was. I just took the phone, thanked the man for wishing me a happy birthday, and then listened to him tell me that he'd witnessed the fall of the Berlin Wall. It was only during this story that I realized who was on the other end of the line.

'Do you know who this is?' he asked, just as the penny had dropped for me.

'It's David,' I said, suddenly feeling uncomfortable about calling him anything else.

A pause came down the line.

'I'm your dad,' he said eventually.

'OK,' I said, which set the tone for the short, polite but awkward conversation that followed.

Sometimes I wondered about my father, but at home nobody ever went there. My mum pressed on with working all hours to provide for us, while Cirdan just didn't talk about it. He could be incredibly laid-back, seemingly not fazed by anything, which was both a winning quality and also, I think, a protective mechanism. In some ways it forced me to deal with the emotional side of family life. I could see that my Mum never stopped, at work or at home, and I wanted to help.

There was only so much I could do as a boy, of course, but it certainly switched me on to feeling the need to please people.

* * *

The opening miles of the West Highland Way take me near the Glengoyne Distillery. As much as I'd like to pay a visit, I'm on a mission here. Whisky is a great passion of mine, and it's been a thrill in recent years to get my own variety off the ground. My rucksack is currently digging hard into my shoulders, but I'm not sorry about the fact that I managed to squeeze in a solid steel flask among my provisions. I enjoy my first wee nip around lunchtime, along with a protein bar, when a shower sweeps through that's strong enough for me to seek shelter under trees.

'*Sláinte*,' I say, raising my flask to the path in a traditional Scottish toast. 'Here's to a grand adventure.'

After the rain comes sunshine and then rainbows. Glasgow feels a long way behind me now, even if it's still only a short journey by road. The landscape has opened up to reveal rolling hills with rugged edges, but I just can't stop looking at the arches of coloured light that materialize and then fade against the sky. It's magical, and also distracts me from the weight on my shoulders. When the path begins a gentle but long ascent, however, I really have to get my head down. I curse myself for not properly trying out the rucksack after I'd loaded it at home. In my mind, I review the list of what I've packed. If there's anything I can jettison when appropriate, I won't hesitate to lighten the load. My café press comes to mind, a portable means of making fresh coffee, but when I consider the possibility of starting the next few days without caffeine, I know it has to stay. The tent, my sleeping bag and cooking equipment are all vital, as are my waterproofs and change of clothing. I have a map, but that doesn't weigh much, and a baseball cap that I carry on my head. There is only one item in my possession that suddenly feels like it should face the firing squad, and that's my walking poles.

'You'll need these,' the sales assistant advised me back in the store.

'Why?' I asked. 'I can walk just fine.'

The poles folded into three. The guy was holding them across his hands as if presenting me with some precious holy relic.

'Trust me,' he said. 'On any trek there will come a time when these become the most vital piece of equipment in your pack.'

I eyed them dubiously. Still, the young guy had made it his mission to equip me for this walk, and so I took them anyway. Even folded, they were cumbersome to pack, but with no bins in this remote spot, I'm stuck with the horrible things for now.

After what feels like an age, the ascent levels off and takes me along a winding ridge. To my right I see the prominent Dumgoyne Hill, and behind it, Earl's Seat; the highest hill in the Campsie Fells but hardly a third of the size of Ben Nevis. Below, a country road looks like a ribbon. I watch a car follow the twists and turns, the sun glinting off the windscreen, but it's so far away that all I hear is birdsong in the breeze.

It's then that I realize there is one thing I can cast off here, and that's the tension I've been carrying. I've come out here just so that I can breathe freely and feel at peace. I'm supposed to be enjoying myself! All I've done for the last few months is work, and fantasize about what it might be like to do something like this. Now I'm here, and yet I've just trudged up a hill in such a brooding stew about my stuff that I didn't look around until I reached the top. I smile to myself, adjust the straps so my rucksack sits more comfortably (well, until they don't threaten to draw blood), and press on with my head held high.

As soon as the opportunity presents itself, however, I'm dumping the stupid sticks.

* * *

Living in the heart of the Scottish countryside, my brother and I certainly made the most of being outdoors. We both loved to fish. I would try to go with him whenever possible, and not just so we could spend time together. As much as I adored the whole angling lifestyle, I just wasn't cut out to deal with one important practicality. Removing the hook. Despite playing the character of a fisherman, I knew deep down that this was something I couldn't face. The whole idea of removing a barbed piece of wire from a fish's mouth made me feel giddy and weak. It was the only aspect of the role I couldn't face, and I relied on Cirdan to do it for me.

To this day, I don't know if my Mum was wise to my reluctance to get to grips with a caught fish so I could return it to the water. Maybe my brother had privately put her in the picture, or perhaps she had worked it out for herself. Either way, it says a great deal about her character that she still happily agreed to transport me on solo fishing expeditions. She would drop me off at the shore of Loch Ken, making sure I had enough to eat and drink to see me through a few hours on my own. I'd unload my rod and tackle box from the car, looking like an experienced junior angler were it not for the fact that one vital piece of equipment was missing: the bait.

'I'll dig some up later,' I'd tell her.

Unwilling to hurt any living thing, it meant I could fish to my heart's content knowing that my bait-free hook and line was in zero danger of attracting a catch. When it came to angling, I just loved pretending to be the genuine article. Sitting there in my wellies, watching the float bob on the water, I could lose myself in quiet dreams about landing killer pike, enormous perch and perhaps the occasional fresh-water monster. I didn't have to deal with the reality, and I adored it.

In some ways, it was my first taste of acting. I learned how to look like an authentic fisherman, and even how to think like one. It allowed me to be myself by pretending to be someone else.

* * *

At this late time of year, the afternoon feels like one slow fade towards darkness. As the sun retreats and contours deepen across the landscape, I'm determined to reach my destination before nightfall. According to my activity watch, I've covered just over 15 miles. In the distance, beyond the vanishing point of the path, I glimpse a sliver of Loch Lomond. My destination lies another 5 miles from here, low on the eastern shore of this 39-kilometre-long body of water. I intend to eat a good supper in Balmaha, a village with several pubs and cafés, and also a campsite on the outskirts. Still giddy with the romance of my venture, however, I am planning to make the most of the fact that in Scotland we are free to pitch our tents in the wild. It's a wonderful, romantic and liberating right, and encourages people to be both respectful and responsible. After such a long slog today, I intend to pitch my tent somewhere off the beaten path. I am loving the solitude this day has brought me, even if my rucksack now feels like a companion who is proving to be hard work.

Conic Hill. I glimpsed this wee peak countless times as I advanced on Balmaha. I have an ultra-runner friend who tackles it regularly, but right now I don't even feel like walking, let alone running. It's a short sharp rise overlooking Loch Lomond, and also a slight detour from the West Highland Way. I realize this on reaching a signpost still dripping from a downpour that has only just subsided. It's a welcome waypoint, a faithful guide, bravely standing against the elements. It also marks the last stretch of my first day's journey, and presents me with a dilemma.

According to the signage, Balmaha lies just 2.5 miles away if I follow the West Highland Way around the hill. Alternatively, I can take a longer path that will lead me to the summit of the hill and then wind back down to the village. It would add more than a mile, but promises incredible views from the summit.

'You take the high road and I'll take the low . . . de de de dah dah . . . on the bonnie, bonnie banks of Loch Lomond.' The song lyrics circle around in my brain. 'I just don't know.'

It's almost four o'clock in the afternoon. I have about an hour of daylight left, although my patience with my rucksack ran out some time ago. I shake it off my shoulders, letting it drop to the ground and giving the muscles burning in my back a much-needed break. At the pace I've been going, with the previous 18 miles already wearing on my hips and tired feet, I really should take the easy option. It's flat, and even a little downhill. Ultimately, it would mean that I could be settled in the warm, dry and welcome embrace of a Balmaha pub before darkness fell; tucked away by a roaring fire with a pint and my dinner in front of me.

Then again, how can I miss this opportunity to hike up to the summit and admire the view? It would be like visiting the gift shop at the foot of the Eiffel Tower instead of taking the stairs to the top.

With a weary sigh, I make my decision and haul the proverbial kitchen sink back onto my shoulders. Then, hating myself just slightly, I take the path up the hill.

Flanked by dying bracken and a strengthening breeze, I find myself pushing on one knee after the other in a bid to get this climb done. In response, my rucksack seems to gain weight by the step. Midway up, the hill just feels like an obstacle in front of the view I've come to admire. I have a view of the loch on each side, but it isn't enough. Pausing for breath, I watch a sheet of rain roll off the glen and across the water towards me. There isn't a single soul around, unless you count a few hardy sheep in the distance bracing themselves against the gusts. Unless I hurry up, I realize, my victorious conquest of this summit could be met with a dousing. I press on, listening to the crows cawing as if willing the bad weather to beat me to the top.

'Do your worst,' I mutter to the gods, and get my head down for the final push. 'Let's go!'

I almost double over as I climb the steeper sections of a natural staircase that seems to go on for ever. I'm growling and swearing to myself; staring at the gravel and the rivulets of running water. The sound of my breathing pounds in my head. Surely this isn't good for my heart, I think to myself. My legs and feet are certainly complaining that I'm asking too much of them.

'Where are you?' I demand out loud, addressing a summit that never quite seems to appear. 'Gah, I am going to do this!'

Whether shouting at the hill, the weather, myself or my imaginary enemy, I refuse to give up. I start to use my hands as well as my feet to scramble my way upwards. This is far tougher than I imagined. I know I've been on my feet all day, and making excellent progress. Right now, though, I am done.

A moment later, as if the hill itself is satisfied that I've now given it the respect due, I find that the steep climb softens dramatically. I push off the ground with my fingertips, rising upright in the next few steps, and register that I have done it.

On the crest of Conic Hill, looking out across an unbroken vista that reveals the loch and the range behind it, the weight of my rucksack just fades away.

Rain is in the air. It's on the way for sure, and yet I am greeted by a sunburst through the clouds. It literally stops me in my tracks. Even my racing brain subsides, the calculations and constant time management negotiations silenced by this beauty. It sparkles on the loch and brings colour to the forested isles. Yachts and small boats bob on the water, excited by small waves whipped up by the wind. *This* is the Scotland I have come to see, and in that moment I feel like the king of all I survey.

I'm exhausted, sweat and rain dripping from my baseball cap, but also fired up at the thought that I am set to wander deep into this magical wilderness in the days to come, my journey's end far off on the horizon, hidden by black clouds and brooding mountains.

But first, as I pay the price for this detour and watch the sun sink behind the hills, I must descend into the dusk for my destination at the end of this first day. As much as I'd like to pitch my tent on the summit, I know the wind would make a mockery of any such attempt. I really do need to reach Balmaha, defined from up here by points of light from buildings and street lamps, but not just because I plan to camp nearby. Having walked all day, I am ravenously hungry. I might have the means to cook my supper, but despite hauling the stove and the junk that goes with it all this way, I just want to slump into a cosy pub nook and order from a menu.

* * *

In class, I had four friends: Frankie, Kirsty, Annie and Christopher. That was the sum total of kids in my year group. The entire primary school comprised just 20 children. It was tiny, but not unusual in this rural pocket of Scotland. We got on well. I guess we had to. At weekends, we'd often just hang out at each other's houses. Through my young eyes, it was another extension of the family community forged at the stables. Frankie was a fiery redhead with a freckled face and a wiry frame. Christopher was quite a bubbly kid, whose father was a retired high-ranking naval officer. He was really into army stuff, and we would often go into battle together with our imaginary rifles. Kirsty was tall, willowy quiet and very kind, while I had one best friend among them all, and that was Annie.

Our mothers had been close since we were infants, and so Annie and I had known each other for a long time. I just felt very comfortable in her company. Annie was quite a tomboy. Like me, she enjoyed being outdoors in wellies. We grew up together in so many ways, and that included our first kiss when we were about ten. It was pure experimentation for us, part of a game. Sleeping Beauty and the prince. A king and his queen. We trusted each other. It felt daring, weird, funny, exciting and foolish – a glimpse of a world that awaited us – and then we just went back to being damn good friends.

Even as I began to switch on to my feelings about girls I didn't have much confidence in myself. I was very tall for my age. At a time when everyone is getting to grips with their identity, it made me feel like I stood out for the wrong reasons. I also had poor eyesight. My Mum couldn't afford a decent pair of glasses, and so I wore an NHS pair with thick lenses. They made me feel so self-conscious that I just couldn't bring myself to wear them in lessons. As a result, my memory of the blackboard is just a blur. Combined with being slightly on the chubby side, as well as very sensitive, it meant I retreated to the fringes of the class. Among friends, I was content to hang back a little. I like to occupy that outside edge. Even though things weren't quite in focus without my glasses on, it meant I could watch and take notes.

On one occasion, towards the end of my time at primary school, I found myself the focus of unwanted attention. Having just stepped into the school lavatory, I also had nowhere to hide.

'Get out of my way, freak.'

The boy who'd decided to pick on me was basically just asserting his authority. I knew Frazer was a rowdy, confident kid, and I'd done nothing to upset him. All he did was shove me, but that was enough for me to respond – unaware of my own strength, perhaps – and throw him against the urinals.

'Sorry!' I said immediately, as he picked himself up from the tiles. 'Are you OK?'

Frazer glared at me, in shock and possibly also a little bruised. At first I thought he would come at me. Instead, he grinned as if I'd just missed out on a joke, and from that moment on we became friends. I never saw him pick on anyone again, and I once even trusted him to pull out a wobbly tooth for me. I even pocketed it afterwards knowing it would earn me at least 50 pence from the Tooth Fairy.

I'm not really in touch with any of my old classmates from those early school years. Nothing can take away from that influential time. It's just that the nature of the work that would come to define my life means I'm always moving around. As an actor, I never really know where I'm going to be next. It could be a studio in Los Angeles or on location anywhere from New Zealand to the Arctic Circle. I love what I do, but that has made it hard to put down roots.

* * *

At the tail end of my first day on the West Highland Way, I put up my tent by the light from my phone screen. While I know I've lugged a head torch in among all the stuff inside my rucksack, I cannot find it in the dark. Rain has been falling for the last hour. It's set in for the night. I can hear droplets detonating on the water behind me. I'm preparing to settle on a wee shore by the loch, tucked away from the main road out of Balmaha. I'm so pleased to have found this spot, which is situated within a national park. Despite the rush to get ready yesterday, I went so far as to check the park's by-laws to be sure I wasn't going to be spending my night in a cell. Even though the idea of a dry space is appealing right now, I really want this experience. As I'm here out of season, which raises other issues about my decision-making, I know that as long as I'm respectful of my environment, I am within my rights.

'Who invented this?' I grumble, clamping the phone between my teeth so I can use both hands to finally make the tent stop resisting my efforts and pop into shape.

Earlier that evening, on finally arriving in Balmaha, I had walked into a bar to find myself being served by Darth Vader.

'You look like you've come a long way for a drink,' said the Sith Lord and Supreme Commander of the Imperial Forces. 'What will you have?'

It took me a second to register the candles and the pumpkins on the bar, and the fact that the barman wasn't alone in fancy dress. I ordered a local beer and found myself a seat among the living ghosts and ghouls. There, as I dried out and warmed up, I enjoyed a really good vegetable curry with my pint. Having trekked all day, I was tired and hungry, but also very happy to be there. On the descent from Conic Hill, I had found my path obstructed by a herd of Highland cows. Earlier that morning, I'd been quite relaxed about snapping photos of a whole bunch from over a fence. This lot were roaming freely, and though they seemed quite docile, I didn't like the look of their military-grade horns.

'Coming through,' I'd announced on approaching them. 'If that's OK.' Chiselled across the flanks of the hill, the path was quite clearly the only sensible option open to me. If I tried to cut out the cows and barrel down the slope, I risked either breaking an ankle or face-planting into thorny undergrowth. By this point, in the late light, the hairy beasts had tuned into my presence. I felt like they were waiting for me to produce papers before letting me pass, but I stood my ground all the same. 'Let's be reasonable here,' I tried again. 'Don't you have barns to go to?'

The cattle didn't respond. They were too busy sizing me up to see what they could mug from me while turning over wads of chewing tobacco in their mouths. At least that's how it looked. Briefly I had thought about turning on my heel and retracing my steps all the way over the crest and then back to the signpost on the other side of the hill. I dismissed the idea, partly as I knew that I would hate myself, but also because just then I heard voices behind the herd. The cows turned and then gravitated expertly on to the bank to reveal a small group of elderly hikers approaching. These guys were so busy chatting it took a second for them to register me. I don't think they even cared about the great beasts now waiting for them to pass.

'Evening!' I said breezily, and pressed on in the hope that they thought me 100 per cent Bear Grylls and hadn't witnessed my stand-off.

By the time I left the pub, the rain was drifting down in sheets again. It was also dark, with no street lights or moon to guide me. I'd consulted the map before leaving. A local campsite would have been the sensible option for the night, but it was still quite a walk away. With my sense of adventure revived by food and a pint, I had set my sights on a secluded section of shoreline nearby.

OK, so the tent takes me far longer to put up compared to my practice run in the living room, but once I get inside it feels like a palace. A cramped one perhaps, but my blow-up mattress provides some comfort.

For an hour, I just sit cross-legged at the entrance and look out into the downpour. Occasionally car headlights blink from the road that runs alongside the other side of the loch. Having found my head torch at last, I pick out spots on the water and the beach and watch the raindrops hammering. I find it really quite relaxing, and decide that I should end my evening with a nip of whisky from the flask. I also have a cigar with me, which I fire up briefly. A minute later, having been forced to evacuate my smoke-filled tent, I realize that perhaps I should have considered the stiff breeze sweeping in through the flaps.

Extinguishing the cigar on a stone, I brush the sand from the soles of my feet in turn before retiring for the night. After just one day on the West Highland Way, aching, soaked through and exhausted, I am ready for a long, uninterrupted sleep.

DAY TWO

THE WAKE-UP CALL

Picking a path through my teenage years, I began to see life with more clarity. It wasn't just about growing up and switching on to the feelings and needs of the people around me. Mostly it was down to the fact that I started wearing contact lenses.

After years of me feeling too awkward to wear my milk-bottle-top glasses, my Mum took me to the optician to try out alternatives. The contact lenses felt like a miracle cure. A revelation! They literally changed the way I viewed the world. I no longer had to choose between blurry vision or feeling self-conscious in my specs, and in turn I felt liberated. It didn't boost my confidence as such. I was never shy, but my poor vision had definitely contributed to my tendency to hang back from the action somewhat. By the time I started wearing contacts, however, that place I occupied had become second nature to me. Now it meant I was able to watch what was going on with pin-sharp vision. I could see people's faces clearly and read expressions. I felt like a late starter in life, but one with a new-found confidence and keen appreciation for detail.

* * *

At the break of day, I surface to the sound of low-flying waterfowl and dripping water. I take a second to register that I'm in a tent and not at home facing some kind of awful plumbing emergency. Then I trace my thoughts back to the moment I decided that walking the West Highland Way in late autumn was a good idea. I mean, it still *is* a good idea. My first day was an adventure, and even though it proved far tougher than anticipated, I unzip the front of my burgundy and blue cocoon with a sense of optimism and excitement.

'Hmm, good morning,' I say to the world outside. The loch reaches across to forested shores that are rich in autumnal colour. Low, ragged clouds drift across the sky like smoke after battle. I stretch and perform a deep lunge, my right hip tight and achy. It feels good to work out the tension while admiring such a dramatic view. It isn't raining. At least it isn't right now. The dripping water is coming off the trees behind my pitch. The air is moist and cool, but so fresh that I inhale through my nostrils and close my eyes. I'm just happy to be in the middle of nowhere; surrounded by nature and cut off from the wider world. 'It's time for breakfast,' I remind myself, aware that I need fuel for another long walk ahead of me.

Having cursed the weight of my rucksack throughout the previous day, I'm thankful that it contains the means for me to prepare a nice hot porridge with cinnamon and peanut butter, and even make fresh coffee using water from a nearby stream, which I boil, as the water source runs through the surrounding fields, and God knows what might have fallen in. I eat my breakfast perched among the roots of a tree on the bank. The ground is soaking wet from so much rain, which looks set to return at any moment. Listening to the birds, I suspect that now is the time for activity before the heavens open once again. So, I set about packing my tent before it pours. With no time to let it properly dry out, it feels heavier now than when I set it up, but I put that to the back of my mind. I wash my pan and the cup in the loch, brush my teeth, and have everything bundled and ready for the day before the first drops pepper the water.

'Here we go again,' I mutter to myself. I'm fired up by the prospect of another day on the West Highland Way, though, and the rain doesn't bother me. It's the damned rucksack that weighs down my spirits. I shrug it off once more, determined not to let it cast a shadow across my day. While my stove, pan and café press have earned their keep, along with my tent and sleeping bag, I pull out the walking poles.

'Who thought this would be a good idea?' I ask, holding one aloft while I quietly curse the helpful guy from the outdoor store.

I decide to keep them in hand while I make my way along the lane and pick up the path once more. There's bound to be a bin, I tell myself, or maybe even a bus stop. I'm thinking about leaving the sticks for a stranger as a random act of kindness when I find myself deploying them as intended. What am I doing? This feels . . . good?! It takes a moment for me to realize that the tapping of the carbon tips on tarmac has started to accompany my footsteps. It's quite a pleasing rhythm, I find. What's more, the poles ease off some of the weight on my shoulders.

* * *

Shortly after my life came into sharper focus, at an age when my brother and I were finding our feet, my Mum applied for a place at Edinburgh College of Art. Having devoted herself to raising her two sons, the time had arrived for her to pursue her first love once more. It was such a thrill for her to learn that she had been accepted to study fine art, as well as drawing and printmaking, but it meant we had to move from our rural home to the bright lights of a big city.

After years of living in a quiet community, my mother, my brother and I packed our belongings for what felt like a whole new world. Swapping the stable and the castle ruins for a suburban street in Edinburgh, we set about settling in for this new chapter in our lives. It was a big change, but also hugely exciting for two young lads like Cirdan and me. I had just finished at my little primary school, so I started high school at the same time as all my new classmates. There were just so many of them! It was a little overwhelming to begin with, but since I could now see without the dreaded glasses, I soon started to make friends and feel comfortable in a crowd.

James Gillespie's High School was very strong on rules and discipline. With so many teenage pupils cramming the classrooms and corridors, I guess it had to impose a sense of law and order to stop the whole place descending into anarchy. As a boy who was happy just to fit in, rather than stand out in the crowd, I got my head down and worked hard. I've never liked to get into trouble with authority, even if it was quite easy to invite. A tie at half-mast could earn attention from a teacher for all the wrong reasons, while lateness was just not tolerated. For many pupils, detention became the last lesson on the daily school timetable. Mostly I avoided the warnings and reprimands. On one occasion, however, I came very close to getting into trouble from the top.

Our head teacher was a petite woman. She compensated for this with her uncompromising commitment to pupil discipline and adherence to the rules. At the time, I had just been made a school prefect. It wasn't a great honour, because everyone had a shot at it at some stage. Still, by wearing that badge I was expected to conduct myself by example, which I didn't.

The incident began with a milk carton. I had been tasked with helping to dish them out at break time to pupils who were part of a milk-in-schools scheme. On finding one left over, I decided to join the scheme for one break only, and pierced the carton with a straw as I ambled back to class. It didn't seem like a huge deal, which was what had persuaded me to help myself. A moment later, like a gunslinger in some two-bit town, the headmistress stepped out at the far end of the corridor.

My eyes went wide with horror. In a blink, I hid the carton behind my back. Then, gripped by sheer panic as I felt sure that she had seen it, I seized an escape route in the form of the door to the toilet block.

Had I been a little more collected, I might have hidden the carton in one of the cubicles. Instead, I took one look at the open window and lobbed it out. The block was on the second floor. I didn't even think to check that it was clear down below, where pupils often congregated. I simply threw that carton like I'd just removed a pin.

'That was close,' I muttered to myself, checking my reflection in the mirror to be sure I didn't look too flustered before heading back into the corridor.

'Ah, Heughan. I thought it was you.' The headmistress was waiting for me outside the door. I had practically walked straight into her. 'Where's the carton?'

It took me a second to process what she was asking me here. She had quite clearly seen me drinking the milk, and yet her focus wasn't on the highly illegal act but on the whereabouts of the evidence.

'I, ah, put it in the bin,' I said, with as much confidence as I could muster.

She looked up into my eyes as if to see what was lying behind them, and then into my soul. I held her gaze, determined to convince her that I was telling the truth.

'Then go and fetch it,' she said after a moment, before making a little revolving gesture with her finger. 'Empty cartons should be returned to the recycling area. They do not go in toilet bins!'

Back inside the block, it felt like my lungs had tightened considerably. I just stood there, frozen with indecision, then stuck my head out of the window. The carton lay two storeys below; its contents splattered across the ground. Then my attention locked on a pedal bin beside the sink. Kicking up the lid, I tore through the contents, half wishing the container was big enough for me to climb inside and hide.

And then, near the bottom, I found the one thing in the world that I needed more than anything else at that moment. I could only think that another pupil had been spotted doing the same thing as me, and had stashed their carton responsibly rather than randomly milk-bombing the courtyard below.

'Here it is,' I said, emerging back into the corridor with a triumphant smile.

The headmistress considered the carton in my hand, her mouth tightening at the edges somewhat. Once again she seemed to be searching my expression for cracks. The face-off only lasted for a couple of seconds, but it felt like a lifetime.

'Go and put it in the appropriate bin,' she said. 'And hurry, or you'll be late for your next lesson.' She spun on her heel and stormed off down the hallway, students scattering before her.

It was perhaps the first occasion that I'd got into character, and it wouldn't be the last. It was certainly a test of holding my nerve and creating a story. Ultimately it showed me what was possible if I delivered with conviction.

* * *

By the time I rejoin the West Highland Way, having passed a bus shelter with a bin beside it, the walking poles have become a vital piece of kit. Quite simply, they're a revelation, providing just enough support to make the weight on my back bearable. I'm not even sure how I managed to get this far without them.

Less than an hour into the second day of the walk, I lose patience with the rain. I set out feeling quite at peace with the fact that it was likely to pelt down all day. Now that the weather gods are delivering on that promise, I feel like shaking one of my sticks at the sky and pleading for them to give me a break. My baseball cap and waterproofs are doing a decent job, but so much water has turned the ground beneath my boots to a quagmire. It makes for slow going on a day when I really intended to pick up the pace.

It doesn't help that after yesterday's undertaking, my hips have begun to hurt. I give thanks once again for my walking poles, which have quite possibly become a permanent feature in my life. Not only do they take the edge off my rucksack, but I also find they provide me with a confidence boost in slippery mud. I am just thinking about traction as I pick my way towards a country lane, only for a shriek of surprise to stop me in my tracks. I look up to see two women in swimsuits rushing towards a small unoccupied car that has started rolling slowly backwards.

'Whoa!' I cry, as if it's a horse and not a hatchback, and rush to their assistance.

Just as I clatter through the kissing gate, the car nudges into the hedgerow at the front of the lay-by and comes to a safe halt. The drama was so fleeting and uneventful that the two ladies are just standing there laughing.

'We've locked the keys inside,' one tells me, which seems like a cue for an awkward scene, given their attire. 'With the handbrake off.'

'Well, that's not good, I suppose.'

'We were planning on a wee swim in the loch,' her companion says. The shore is only a 100 yards or so from where we're standing. 'Ach, what a bother!'

'Is there anything I can do to help?' I ask, and then immediately wonder whether my walking poles could save the day. 'If you need me to break the window, I can do that,' I offer.

'Oh, that's kind, but no need.' The first lady draws my attention to another car parked further along the lay-by. 'We can take mine and pick up a spare set. Lucky we've got some towels to wear home.'

With that, the pair turn and pad away. They're still giggling as they climb into the car. I watch them drive off still wearing their caps and goggles, and decide that I could do with a dose of their relentless positivity.

'So what if it's raining?' I say before continuing on my way. 'It's still a beautiful day.'

Even with my spirits lifted, I can't ignore the fact that my progress is bordering on pitiful. With the shore of Loch Lomond away to my left, the path takes me up through woodland and down slippery sloping paths where I have to watch my footing. After two hours of walking,

I have covered just 5 miles. With 15 miles more to go before I pitch my tent once more, I'm beginning to worry that the daylight will give up on me because I'm just taking too long.

'Where's a nice stretch of flat tarmac when you need one?' I ask, though I don't really mean it. As much as the path is testing me, I can't deny that it's leading me through an enchanted landscape.

I'm walking under towering oaks. Some have toppled over the years, providing me with plenty of places to rest and enjoy a quick snack. I'm carrying a few protein bars, but by lunchtime I'm down to just one. I really didn't plan this out. Nor do I have time to set up my stove and cook a meal. Thanks to my map, I also know I can't peel off the path and find a shop as there aren't any villages for miles. I push on with my trusty sticks as the climbs become longer and more challenging. It's knackering, but I'm rewarded with stunning views across the water.

As I move north, the loch tapers considerably. I keep one eye on the far bank as it appears to close in. Eventually I'll pass the point where the River Falloch feeds into the loch, bringing water down from the Highlands. Then I'll know my destination for the night is close at hand. I'm aware that moment is a long way off, however, and try not to think too far ahead. It's hard, though. One moment I'm gazing at the ground beneath my feet. The next I'm wondering if I could make it into the record books as the fastest person in history to complete the walk. If that's a stretch, then perhaps the fastest actor. Failing that, I am confident I could become the quickest member from *Outlander*.

* * *

I spent only one year as a pupil at James Gillespie's High School. I wasn't unhappy there by any means. It was just that my mother was keen for me to explore my creative side. She pitched the idea to me that I might thrive on a Steiner education. It was basically a normal school, as she sold it, but with a focus on developing pupils' artistic and practical skills. I went for a week to try out the Edinburgh Steiner school, and never looked back. Instead of feeling like a prison inmate, with teachers ordering us to hurry from one lesson to the next, I felt relaxed and liberated. There was no uniform, and so I wore a pair of jeans and a very fashionable tie-dyed T-shirt. I thought I looked so cool, and hoped it might help me to fit in with these alternative, artistic kids. I also wanted to make an impression on the girls, who seemed smart, gifted and grown-up.

With a boldness that came from not peering through glasses, I quickly made friends. Steiner children really did seem different, open, kind and inclusive. They protected each other fiercely, and welcomed any newcomer into their circle. After a short while, I realized that it wasn't a question of adapting to fit in. I could just be myself, the same as everyone else, and that both surprised and delighted me. I'd never considered myself to be a loner, but that first term I realized that perhaps I had always tended to be self-contained. Now, I found myself making firm friends that I still have to this day. Thanks to my mother, that new school felt like my second home.

Alongside the standard lessons in subjects like maths and English, we did everything from sketching to sculpting, and gardening to astronomy. The teachers were referred to by their first names and everyone seemed approachable. We were encouraged to discipline ourselves, so there were rarely any detentions or punishment for being tardy or badly behaved. Best of all, the school encouraged pupils to immerse themselves in drama and theatre production. I'd never experienced anything like it. As someone who felt content with standing in the wings of life, all of a sudden I was under the spotlight, and it just blew me away. I'd never thought I would be comfortable on stage. I'd assumed I would feel too tall and awkward, which wasn't uncommon for me in my everyday life. To my surprise, I just felt completely relaxed. Why? Because I was playing a role. Even as the centre of attention, I could hide behind a character. From there, I was able to express all sorts of emotions I'd normally hold back, from outright rage to raw passion and despair, and I loved it.

I was well aware that I had a lot to learn, but among all the opportunities available to me at school, performing felt something like a calling.

One of the first plays I got involved in was Molière's *The Prodigious Snob*. It's a satire about social status, and I played the lead role. In his doomed bid to climb the social ladder, my character makes decisions that bring him nothing but mockery. It's very funny, and I worked hard in rehearsals to make the most of the script. In the first performance, I hit my marks, delivered my lines and went with every emotion and impulse. I felt free and alive, with no restraints. What I hadn't anticipated, and had almost forgotten about, was the response from the audience. They laughed in all the right places, and even in some I didn't know were there, which was an incredible feeling. It was like I had a connection with these people; we were all in it together, laughing at the foolishness of my character. As the play progressed, they were watching every move I made, and listening to each line so closely that I found it quite exhilarating.

And that was when I completely forgot my lines.

For one heartstopping second, I saw myself standing on stage with the audience watching me. A prompt from the wings brought me back into character, though it was hard to recover or feel as tuned into the play again. Faltering like that was a rookie error, and frankly not the last time it would happen to me, but I could not forget that thrill when everything had gone right. I was a young teenager, but I had found something I could be passionate about. Just as my older brother came alive on a bicycle, I found the same connection to acting. I enjoyed it, and crucially, I didn't suck. I had a lot to learn, but that was all part of the appeal.

* * *

Long after my lunch lochside, which amounts to half of my remaining protein bar, I pass a remote youth hostel. Despite the relentless rain, I've no plans to call it a day here. I'm feeling good, if a little hungry, and trudge on by. Out of the corner of my eye, I spot a wee stall made from crates outside the building. A handwritten sign offers water and cakes, which is enough to draw me closer. Unfortunately, there are no cakes. Nor is there any water. The only items on display are two canisters of butane and a plastic bottle of Diet Coke. The sign invites me to take what I need, providing PayPal details underneath in what is an impressive update of the honesty-box concept. Unfortunately there is zero phone reception. So, I make a note to pay for the Coke as soon as I reach civilization. It isn't something I drink by choice, but I'm thankful to whoever has performed this random act of thoughtfulness. I imagine urban kids coming here and being initially aghast at the remoteness, lack of Wi-Fi and sheer silence. Over time, I know they'll grow to love the woods and forest as I do, kayaking in the loch and hiking the local Munro.

The next section of pathway proves to be the most challenging of the day. I encounter a lot of drops and climbs as I negotiate the lower slopes of Ben Lomond, the most southerly of the Munro mountains. I'm also aware that this is the vicinity of the Highland Boundary Fault; a geographical feature and natural barrier that separates the Highlands and Lowlands of Scotland. It's tough going, with jagged rocks lining the route, and in such wet conditions, the run-off from higher ground means the many small streams that cross the path have become torrents. Sometimes I have to divert to clamber over slopes and ridges rather than find myself ankle deep in water. I pass waterfalls that look like perhaps they have only recently come alive. It's very beautiful, but I'm having to pick my way so carefully that it's not just slow but also really tiring.

The Coke gave me a little energy hit. One hour later, however, that sugar high is threatening to turn into a crash. Several times I imagine consuming the last half of my chocolate raspberry protein bar (tastes like Turkish Delight – delicious, but I'm bored of them now I've eaten so many). I've chewed it over in my mind but find myself incapable of stopping to eat what I have left because it feels like a waste of time. Eventually, as the path rises out of the woodland, I spot an outcrop of rock some distance ahead that looks purpose-built for me to sit on for a final snack break. Just for a minute and no longer. From where I'm standing, the path snakes over several folds thick with bracken before climbing up to my designated rest spot. It'll take me a few minutes to navigate my way there, but when I arrive, I plan to savour every meagre mouthful left of my bar. The rain breaks off for a moment as I press on, and if the sun finds a way through, then I'll know that someone is watching over me.

When I clamber up the last rise to the rock in question, I find there is indeed a pair of eyes observing my huff and puff. Somehow, in the time it has taken for me to get here, I find that what looks like a mountain man has claimed my spot.

'Afternoon.' The man observes me intently. He's sitting on the rock overlooking the loch, leaning back against a tree trunk with exposed roots that practically serve as armrests. With his long, thick beard and a kind of mohawk/topknot hybrid, I get strong Viking vibes from him. Like me, he's dressed head to toe in outdoor gear, and has a rucksack at his side. It's just none of his stuff looks like it was sporting price tags 24 hours earlier. 'Wit a day, eh?' he grumbles, eyeing me from under his thick brows.

On the inside, I am boiling over with the injustice of the situation. This guy just appeared out of nowhere to squat on a rock that quite clearly has my name written all over it. I saw it first, I reason with myself. Out here, even between fellow Scots, is that not nine-tenths of the law?

Despite my disappointment, I note that the man is stockily built. He strikes me as someone who has spent time serving in the forces. Unwilling to fight him for the seat, I agree that it has been quite a day before pressing on with my trek.

'I didn't want to stop anyway,' I remind myself very, very quietly. 'There's no time to waste.'

The endless rain is not making my life easy. Nor is it making my adventure that enjoyable, I concede, as the reality sets in that at this rate I'm going to run out of daylight. I just cannot make the progress I intended. Even with my poles in hand, my rucksack feels more cumbersome than the day before. I wonder if it's letting the water in, but the prospect of stopping to check seems unthinkable. I'm tired, hungry, annoyed and a little stressed now. It's a far cry from how I felt when greeting the day from my wild campsite.

I pause to check my map. I'm on track – there's only one path through the forest ahead of me, so I can't get lost. It's just the loch beside it that I can't seem to put behind me. Until I do so, it's hard to feel like I'm making proper progress. Tracing my finger along the map, I attempt to figure out how much further I have to go. Within a couple of squares, I find myself lost in mental arithmetic and eternal recalculations as I consider what pace I need to set to get this done before nightfall. I try to make the numbers work. It's just I'm painfully aware that anything but one unbroken sprint for the next few hours would lead me to the same outcome. As the wind strengthens, and I face another lengthy clamber, it feels like my long walk is beginning to go downhill fast.

* * *

With my interest in acting kindled, my Mum encouraged the fire by taking me to see plays at the Royal Lyceum Theatre in Edinburgh. Money was still tight, but sometimes the theatre offered free preview nights. We'd have to queue early in the hope of getting tickets, which earned us the chance to watch a play as the cast and crew smoothed off the last rough edges, and as the house lights faded, I'd find myself transported by the story unfolding on stage. I loved the darkness, as if the world around had powered down, only for the stage manager (or the director, if things got really bad) to halt proceedings every now and then to fix a piece of set or adjust a sound cue. It would come as a jolt, but an enlightening one for a boy with aspirations to become an actor, allowing me to peek behind the production. I got to see the inner workings, and appreciate the fact that when everything came together, it had the power to transport the audience to another place and time.

During my teenage years, I saw all sorts of plays in the making. My favourite had to be a modern Scottish adaptation of the legend of King Arthur. It was called *Merlin*, but it swapped out the swords and sorcery for an urban backdrop featuring burned-out cars and fires burning in braziers. With the cast in army fatigues and the production underscored by beautiful, dramatic live music, I was completely blown away. It was just so passionate from start to finish.

I was completely lost in the moment, wide-eyed in wonder – and then the director walked on with his script in hand.

'So sorry, ladies and gentlemen, we're just going to run that scene one more time.'

I didn't have a particular passion for musicals, but I had the opportunity to attend a production of *Phantom of the Opera* with the rest of my classmates from school. By then, I'd seen enough plays to know that my heart would skip a beat when the curtains opened. On this occasion, when a scream preceded the moment that a chandelier swung into view and cued the music, I was literally left shaking in my seat. I was captivated from start to finish, even with the occasional pause in production, and experienced such a wealth of sensations that when the time came to head for the exits, I felt completely exhausted. I'd sweated through my trusty tie-dye T-shirt, but I didn't even care. For me, the theatre had become a playground for the emotions. A good production could bring me to tears or make me laugh out loud. Either way, it was a safe place for me to express myself, and I loved spending time there. So when I spotted a part-time vacancy for an usher, I jumped at the opportunity.

For a teenager with a love for theatre, it was a perfect job. My shifts took place in the evening and at weekends, so they fitted around school. I was also in my dream environment, which meant it never felt like work. Even though I could end up watching the same show repeatedly, having helped to settle the audience in their seats and served them various ice creams and chocolate at the interval, I would always be captivated. It didn't matter what production was being staged, even if it was a pantomime matinee, I just felt happy to be involved.

As well as working at the theatre, I enjoyed hanging out with my friends. We were into riding mountain bikes and playing video and board games. Fantasy was the genre that bonded us together. If the weather stopped us from hitting the trails, we would spend hours at each other's houses playing *Doom/Quake* or *Command & Conquer* on my friend Andrew's computer, or Warhammer at the kitchen table. I had a mighty High Elf army that would regularly conquer my friend's lesser army of Undead. I also enjoyed painting the figures, perhaps my only artistic streak similar to my mother's chosen profession. From riding out together to battling orcs on quests for mythic scrolls, we were all drawn to a sense of escapism from the ordinary world. The ability to lose ourselves in a story is something that stays with us all to a certain extent. At the time, I had no idea that it would become central to my working life.

I was certainly interested in theatre. Even so, I didn't quite have the confidence to set my sights on drama school. Nor was I entirely convinced that acting was what I wanted to do. Instead, as one term after another took me closer to leaving school, I found myself applying for university courses that were the closest I could find to my passions.

Academically, I did enough to get by. I really enjoyed English, but subjects like maths and science never truly engaged me. I just coasted in order to get the passes I needed, and then hoped I'd done enough to follow everyone else into higher education. It came as a relief when the University of Aberdeen offered me a place on their English and film studies degree. I just wasn't really fired up about it. Once the initial excitement had dimmed, I began to question where my life was heading.

'Why don't you take a gap year?' my mum suggested when we talked it over. She had gone to art school as a mature student. During her studies, I'd watched her come alive with enthusiasm for the subject. She'd seized her opportunity, having spent years raising two sons, and I wanted that same clear-eyed commitment to my next step. So, having deferred my place at university, I left school intent on spending the next 12 months figuring out what I really wanted to do with my life. It was an exciting moment, like facing a horizon in the belief that I would find my true identity waiting for me on the other side.

* * *

'Ah saw yer last movie. The SAS one. Wit a load of rubbish!'

I glance up with a start to see my mountain friend once more. He's looking down at me from a mossy bank and a backdrop of pine trees.

'Oh,' I say, taken aback not so much by his film review as by the fact that he's managed to steal an advantage on me so stealthily. From where I'm standing, in a gully, I note that the yellow treads of his walking boots provide the only flash of colour in this dark, forbidding pocket of forest. We are in the wilderness here, but only one of us seems comfortable with that right now. 'I guess if you're ex-special forces, it must be a little weird to watch.'

'Special forces?' The mountain man reaches for the end of a long drinking tube. It snakes over his shoulder from what must be a water bladder in his rucksack. 'Nah, pal, ah work in IT.'

'Oh, right,' I say, feeling slightly relieved that I have misjudged him, and yet still unnerved by his plain speaking. 'Well, it was a fun movie to make. I learned a lot.'

'Ah'm just saying ah did nae like it at all,' he says, as if this should be the final word on the matter. He clips his drinking tube away. As he does so, a sparkle comes into his eyes and he finally grins at me. 'But ah like *Outlander*, that's real drama, and mah wife likes it too.'

My new friend's name is Graeme. He too is attempting to walk the West Highland Way from start to finish, having set out from Milngavie on the same morning as me. While we've covered the same ground, Graeme tells me that he's being dropped off and picked up each day so he can go home and sleep in his own bed. It may not sound as romantic as camping under the stars, but just then I experience a small pang of envy. It's compounded by the fact that without a tent and all the gear that goes with it, his backpack looks notably lighter than mine.

'Pal, why would you camp at this time of year?' he asks me, as if no answer could undermine his incredulity.

I want to tell him that I can call upon my military training to survive in all conditions, but think better of it. Instead, we chat politely for a couple of minutes, during which I realize that after our initial encounter, he must have checked out my social media and seen my recent posts. He seems to know all about the spirits brand I've just launched, as well as my charity encouraging people to get outdoors. I hope he doesn't expect me to be some kind of poster boy for hiking, because right now, I'm suffering. My muscles ache and I really need to make the most of the daylight before it fades away. Despite falling belatedly in love with my walking poles, I realize that my palms are feeling quite raw from grasping them. Graeme is also rocking a pair, and having discussed the finer points of the best carbon tips for this terrain, I must begin to look quite restless.

'Well, ah'll be on mah way,' he says, as if perhaps solitude is the default mode for any traveller on this route. 'Maybe see yous later, pal.'

It's a brief encounter, and I decide to give Graeme a chance to get ahead of me. I really do want to be alone with this trek, although as I spend a few minutes finishing what's left of my protein bar, I realize that I welcomed our chat.

As soon as I push on once more, I find myself following my fellow traveller's fresh footprints in the mud. I'm alone, but somehow it feels comforting to know that another human being is out there. With yet more rocks to clamber over, streams to negotiate and tracks to slip around on, I find that the challenges I considered to be part of the adventure are becoming tiresome. I know I haven't eaten enough to conquer the soggy shores of Loch Lomond. I'm running on empty, with nothing left to throw in the tank, and a good few hours left before I reach the staging post that will mark the end of a challenging day.

* * *

With school behind me at last, I joined my core group of four friends to go travelling. We had moved on from board games and mountain biking and were beginning to look for real adventure (with the prospect of meeting some local girls and drinking a crisp European beer or two). First we visited Latvia and Estonia, staying in bunkhouses and drinking in cheap bars. From there, we decided to venture across the Russian border to check out St Petersburg and get some culture.

We had all the correct documentation, but it still felt like we were heading out of our comfort zone. Among a group of lads, of course, any sense of unease I felt was quickly forgotten amid the banter and bravado. We occupied a four-person compartment in the train carriage, chatting and laughing while quietly taking in the chilly landscape outside that represented the Soviet superpower of our childhoods. I put it to the back of my mind as we settled down for the overnight leg of the journey, only to wake to find myself in what felt like some Cold War movie.

With the train pulled into sidings, large searchlights strafed the carriage windows. Shouts and slamming doors marked the arrival of armed soldiers, some of whom had boarded the carriage accompanied by dogs. The sound of ferocious barking filled the corridor, yanking us all from sleep. A soldier entered our compartment, shining a light in our faces and shouting something aggressively in Russian.

'Ticket inspection.' one of my friends suggested, who didn't sound half as terrorised as I felt.

Blearily we rose to our feet to retrieve our papers. I kept mine in a pocket of my backpack, which I'd stowed in the overhead rack. As my turn came, I reached up for it, only to dislodge one of my boots, which I'd also stuffed up there. The boot came down before I could grab it, hitting the soldier square in the face.

My eyes widened in horror.

'Oh my God, I'm so sorry,' I mumbled, raising my hands as if that might defuse the situation. The soldier didn't even blink. He just waited for me to present my papers.

This time, I retrieved my passport and ticket. I had to stop the rucksack from tipping over the rack's guard rail as I tugged both from the outside pocket, which meant my hands were occupied when something else slipped out and clattered to the compartment floor. I glanced down, and to my horror saw the Swiss army knife I was carrying with me. I'd only packed it because of the gadgets enclosed alongside the blade, and had pretty much forgotten it was there, but in that moment it represented a weapon and a threat to my liberty. Without hesitation, as the soldier examined the visa stamps in my passport, I placed my foot over the knife and eased it under the bench.

As I did so, the soldier looked across at me and glowered. He only broke eye contact when another object dropped out of the rucksack, which I was still holding back somewhat uselessly. He might have missed the knife, but his gaze followed the stuffed toy lion as it flopped onto the seat. It was travelling with me as a kind of joke mascot. Just then, though, nobody was laughing.

'Puh . . . Americans.' The soldier handed me my documents, then left us with what sounded like a curse in his mother tongue. Nobody dared to correct him. We were just a group of young Scottish boys who had been forced to grow up fast.

Within minutes, as the train resumed its journey towards St Petersburg, we were joking about the incident. Even so, it was one of those brief moments in time that has always stayed with me. Despite my love of theatre, and vague ideas about pursuing acting as a career, I still liked to be the sort of person who slipped under the radar. Admittedly, nobody enjoys being shaken from sleep by a soldier brandishing a rifle. Even so, my moment in the flashlight did little to persuade me that I should dare to dream.

* * *

In order for me to complete the walk as planned, and tick off the West Highland Way in less than a working week, it's vital that I don't fall behind. My destination is Inverarnan, a small hamlet about 3 kilometres upriver from the loch. On my map, it doesn't look far, and yet it feels like it's taking me forever to cover a few miles. I find myself struggling to make any meaningful progress, because the rain is turning the ground into a treacherous mire. I begin to feel sluggish, tired and frankly quite depressed. This is not how I envisaged my grand adventure. As a romantic wander amid the rocky crags and sweeping glens of my ancestors, it's kind of sucking hard right now.

Throughout the afternoon, I've grown used to the sound of water rushing across the path ahead. Normally it gives me a few seconds' warning before I encounter the full extent of the cascade coming off the hills thanks to this seemingly endless dismal downpour. It means I have to watch my footing as I navigate the torrent. One slip and I would likely break a bone or two as well as receive a thorough drenching. The streams and burns are completely saturated. All I can do is cross them with great caution and cling to the distant memory of what it felt like to walk with dry socks and boots. On this occasion, closing in on the sound of water gushing down from the *cruachan* (which is Gaelic for 'formidable mountain peak'), I round a bend fringed by great ferns to discover a wooden bridge awaiting me.

'What a result!' I declare to myself, upon which I realize that a figure is leaning against the rail on the far side. The bridge spans just a few metres, allowing walkers to cross what is clearly an established mountain waterway. As for the figure who turns around on hearing my arrival, with his striking hairstyle and epic beard, I can't help thinking Graeme looks like some kind of fabled gatekeeper set to warn me that I am about to enter a realm of lost souls.

> You cannot pass. The dark fire will not avail you, flame of Udûn. Go back to the Shadow! You cannot pass! (Gandalf, *The Fellowship of the Ring*, J. R. R. Tolkien)

'We picked a challenging day all right,' he calls across to me, and I don't disagree. 'Shall we walk together for a while?'

Having felt low since our last encounter, I am really quite pleased to see him. After I've crossed the bridge, Graeme tells me he's not finding this easy. I'm heartened by his honesty, and respond in kind.

'It's harder than it looks,' I say, as we turn together and crack on, 'but I'm not giving up just yet.'

'Yeah, ye cannae do that.' He looks across at me, as if perhaps he can sense that the thought has entered my mind.

We talk as we walk. Or should I say, Graeme talks. A lot. A really easy, friendly patter that accompanies our waterlogged footfall. He tells me he's getting picked up at the Drovers Inn, which is pretty much the only place for travellers to stay in Inverarnan that doesn't involve having to pitch a tent. Just then, the prospect of sleeping under canvas for a second night seems deeply unappealing. I'm soaked through and hungry, and I really need to rest. Within a short space of time, I decide that if we make it to the inn for the night, I will book a room. And if they're full, I'll sleep in the stable. I really don't care. This weather has got into my bones.

* * *

Apart from a couple of minutes of sheer terror in a train siding outside St Petersburg, I really enjoyed travelling with my friends. It was one of those adventures I didn't want to end. I spent a short time back at home feeling flat and wondering how to fill the rest of my year out. Within a short space of time, I had called upon the last of my savings from working at the theatre and was on a plane bound for San Francisco.

I had just turned 18 years old. To a young man raised in the Scottish countryside, America was the promised land. I had caught the travel bug from my first adventure by rail. This time I planned to explore the USA like the free spirits did in the movies by riding

Greyhound coaches. Some lonesome cowboy travelling on his silver steed, albeit driven by someone else. On my first day, I left the hostel where I was staying so I could lay eyes on the Golden Gate Bridge. With mist wreathing the strait, it seemed to be floating on air. It looked magnificent, and having found a good viewpoint, I stayed there for hours, listening to my cassette tape of Otis Redding singing '(Sittin' on) the Dock of the Bay' on repeat. In that city, I tasted my first Mexican food, feeding myself once a day on a five-dollar veggie burrito filled with beans, queso, avocado and hot sauce, with a side order of corn chips. *Que ricos tacos!*

As the days and weeks passed, dreaming became central to my travelling experience. I was alone with my thoughts, reflecting on my future, and constantly on the move. Having explored San Francisco, riding the tram and walking the steep hills, I headed south-east and stopped at the Grand Canyon on the way. I checked into Las Vegas, losing 20 dollars on a game of blackjack in a casino before being thrown out for being underage. From there, I dropped down to the Mexican border for a crazy night in El Paso, and then frequented bars in downtown New Orleans, drinking Hurricane cocktails and making friends with bartenders. I had very little money, but it felt like I was living the American dream. I met a lot of fellow travellers, on the road and in bunkhouses. Sometimes people would ask me about my plans. I would just shrug and smile as if hoping the answer might come to me at the next destination. One time down Florida way, I fell in with an Australian guy who was travelling in the same direction as me. It was hot, and so we had hit Pensacola Beach to go swimming.

The water was as clear as the sky. It was idyllic, which made the next few moments jar for us both.

'What's that?' I said as we floated in the water far out from the beach. 'Do you see it?'

It took a second for us to process what we were looking at. The fin sliced between us and the beach, some distance away but near enough for us both to fear we had come onto the radar of a predator.

'Stay still, mate,' my friend said, though I could hear the fear in his voice.

At once, I felt as if responsibility for my fate had just been taken away from me. I thought about shouting to the beach for help. I just couldn't find the courage as if perhaps this underwater threat would pick up on my voice and zone in on me. When the fin sunk out of sight, all I could think was that my journey was about to come to an unwelcome end. We looked around, braced for the worst, only for a splash to turn our attention towards what turned out to be not a shark but a dolphin. The pair of us breathed out hard, exchanged a look as the fear that had gripped us washed away and then laughed out loud.

'I thought it was all over,' my friend said as we swam back to shore. 'Life is precious, right?'

Relieved to be alive and able to enjoy a beer, we sat and talked about our respective plans for the future. What money I'd been living on was about to trickle out, and I knew it was time I headed home.

'I guess I'll go to university,' I said, gazing out to sea, and I must have sounded less than enthused.

'What do you really want to do?' asked my Australian buddy.

I told him about my interest in theatre and acting, and my hopes that an English and film studies degree might touch upon it. In response, he looked across at me and waited until he had my full attention.

'Mate, if acting means that much to you, go for it,' he said. 'Otherwise you'll just look back and feel you missed an opportunity.'

I finished my beer, reflecting on his advice as the sun dried the salt water from my shoulders. When we finally drifted back to the coach stop, preparing to go our separate ways, the next chapter in my life had become clear in my mind.

* * *

Graeme talks as fast as he walks. I am grateful for both qualities, because it forces me to pick up my pace while being distracted from the endless rain by good conversation. We stop in front of the Arklet Falls on the north shore of the loch. I've seen plenty of waterfalls today, most of which were quite possibly trickles until recently, when the heavens opened. This one is well established, and also really impressive. It crashes over a series of rocks to the loch below, spitting white water on its final journey from the Highlands. We stand on the bridge that crosses it so Graeme can take a picture of us both on his camera phone.

'Smile!' he barks playfully, knowing full well that's the last thing either of us want to do, but it serves to lift my spirits.

I like my new friend. He's great company. Since joining him, I haven't felt quite so adrift in the wilderness. Even so, I note a lack of conviction in his voice when I ask whether he thinks we'll make it to the inn before nightfall.

'It's only 6 miles,' I say, which doesn't sound like much.

'Aye, but ye can fit a lot of ups and down into that distance, Sam.'

As the light weakens, I discover that this final stretch of my second leg on the West Highland Way is by far the most challenging. Had I known we'd face bog, flood, rocky ascent and slippery descent, I'm not sure I'd have been so quick to muster that smile for our photo at the bridge. In the twilight, I begin to feel quite weak. I don't want to admit this to my friend, however. I know Graeme is also struggling, but he's impressively stoic. I want to follow his example as much as his footsteps. His cheerful anecdotes and questions about my life and career keep us occupied as we plug on. I'm equally interested in his background, and learn that he has a wife who has sensibly decided to skip the walks. I only break out of the conversation at one point because I am convinced I can smell cheese.

'Do you smell it too?' I ask. I'm aware that I'm ravenously hungry, beyond tired and close to hallucinating, but I know I'm not mistaken. 'It's cheese, Graeme. I swear it's in the air. Like . . . a goat cheese, perhaps?'

My friend stops to look around. I watch his nostrils twitch before he grins and then gestures with one of his walking poles. 'Ah think these guys may be responsible.'

Just feet from where we're standing, three wild mountain goats observe us from an elevated rocky platform in the hillside. They certainly smell quite funky, in an unpasteurised way, and Graeme laughs at where my senses have just taken me.

'So, I'm hungry,' I protest, smiling all the same. 'Though I couldn't eat a whole one.'

Rounding another bend on the loch side, the path leaves the shore for a short uphill section. Graeme tells me that in 1306, the infamous Scottish outlaw Rob Roy MacGregor hid in a cave near here whilst on the run. He became a folk hero, a real inspiration for young children aspiring to be just like him whilst dabbling in a little treason, banditry and theft. What a guy! On reaching the top, we glimpse lights twinkling in the gloom. Since joining forces, it feels like Graeme and I have been walking for hours. Now, we are quite sure that we're within sight of our destination. There's still a mile or so to go in sweeping rain, but those lights represent hope.

As we plod towards the hamlet, we pass the ruins of ancient outlying dwellings as well as several unoccupied, boarded-up cottages. I'm well aware that if I still had plans to camp, I'd be pitching my tent around here. We walk past another haunted ruin, and I promise myself that if there's a room available, I'll check in at the Drovers Inn. When I first set off on this adventure, I might well have considered it to be cheating. Right now, I can't help thinking that camping should be banned by law outside of the summer months.

'It's time for the head torches,' says Graeme, which is when I realize just how dark it has become.

We take a moment to find our equipment. At the same time, Graeme produces a thick chocolate bar and offers me half. It's a small act of kindness at a time when I feel drained and overwhelmed. We fell in with one another by chance, both tested by the elements, and I realize now that I would not have got this far without him. Even before we switch on our torches, I consider him to be a beacon.

With our beams silvering the rain, our march becomes progressively slower. We slip and fall into puddles and mud, which on one occasion causes Graeme to break from his good-natured rambling to curse loudly. I'm thankful that it doesn't spell an end to his stories. All I'm really doing is trying to keep moving, my sense of balance affected by limited visibility and the loss of depth perception. My field of vision seems to narrow and retract. I see shapes form in the dark and wonder if I'm imagining things.

At one point, where the loch has breached its banks, we lose sight of the path. It forces us to traverse a deep bog. Sinking up to my knees, I question whether I can do this any longer. As soon as the notion enters my mind, I feel like a failure. This comes as quite a shock. I'm used to putting my mind to a challenge and getting it done. What's more, I'm struggling with what is basically a countryside walk. Jamie Fraser wouldn't be troubled by a wander through the glens, but here I am close to hurling myself to the ground like a toddler and refusing to get back up again. My hips ache sharply, my back is never going to forgive me, and my neck is screaming from walking all this way with a loaded rucksack on my shoulders. I thought I was fit, but now I'm painfully aware that pumping iron in the gym is a very different discipline to the demands this long trek presents.

When Graeme falls silent as we take one hillock in the dark after another, I wonder if he's wishing that he'd never fallen in with me. I check my watch again. It's only just gone seven o'clock. In homes across the country, small children are enjoying bedtime stories. More importantly, adults are curled up on the sofa, eating delicious food and perhaps enjoying a stiff drink by the fire. It's not late, and yet it feels as though we're in the heart of darkness. Normally I can call upon reserves of strength and determination. I have faced many endurance challenges and enjoyed them. Yet this one really hurts, psychologically as much as physically, and makes me long for things I take for granted. I start to think about the people I love. I fantasise about how it would feel to enjoy a good hug and a warm smile.

Then, out of nowhere, I decide that I'm going to quit. The thought floats into my mind without warning, and then sinks its claws in deep. I set out with high hopes, but now I'm stuck in such a low that I really don't want to be here. I'm beginning to wonder if the Drovers Inn is a figment of my friend's imagination, but I know I wasn't mistaken when we saw those lights from the ridge a while back. Even if it's just a handful of crofts on an isolated lane, I will ring for a cab and head for home. It's been emotional, mostly in unpleasant ways, but at least I didn't make a big song and dance about my departure. It means I can slope back to my life and nobody will be wise to the fact that I failed to conquer the West Highland Way. I had set out to smash it in record time. Two days in, thanks to the rain, the mud and the fact that I acted on impulse, this hike has transformed into a horror show.

'There! There it is, my friend.'

'Huh?' I almost bump into Graeme as he stops for a moment, jolting me from my dark thoughts and deep claustrophobic stupor.

'There. Ya see?'

I look up as he points towards a vague illumination beyond a line of trees. My heart leaps and I march on with revived enthusiasm. Turning off the path, we pass between wood-panelled huts that are part of some sort of farm camping site, closed for the winter. With the beams from our head torches sweeping through the rain, we then follow a drive towards a main road. It's deserted at this time, and takes us just a short hop to the source of the lights we saw. Flanked by parking spaces and fronted by picnic benches, the Drovers Inn strikes me right then as the most inviting place in the world. The stone walls are bathed in external lighting, while the warm glow through the windows makes it look so welcoming.

'We did it!' I declare, as if this is a snow-capped mountain summit and not an easily accessible hotel. 'Thank God, Graeme, we survived!'

I have been limping for the last few miles, as a result of one of my many slips and falls, plus my soggy socks have rubbed my toes raw. Now, I don't even feel it as I pick up the pace with Graeme towards the main doors. In that moment, all I want is four simple things: a beer, a hot meal, a bed, and the opportunity to completely give up on this bloody walk.

THE GREAT REBOOT

I am a Taurean. Born at home under a full moon. According to my mum, my parents had a friend in Dorset who read the ephemeris and said I would see things they couldn't see... like UFOs! My star sign dictates that I am bullish, stubborn, dedicated and determined. I certainly didn't feel that way on limping through the doors of the inn on that fateful second leg of my West Highland Way adventure. Even so, I still consider myself to be highly competitive at heart.

Unlike many of my friends, I grew up with no real passion for football. I just never engaged with it. With the exception of rugby, which I love as a spectator, team sports were for other people. When it came to going head to head with anyone, I tended to do that with myself. I have always liked to strive to do my best. I also set myself high standards, and then punish myself somewhat if I fail to meet the mark.

Growing up, the closest I got to any kind of competition was in judo. I was a club member for years. During my time on the mat, I worked my way towards achieving a blue belt, which is just two colours away from the black belt we all aspired to. I was taller than most boys in my age category, and my frame meant I often outweighed them as well. I like to think that gave me an advantage when face to face with an opponent.

Once, I came third in a regional competition. It boosted my confidence no end, but when I look back, I realize that perhaps the adjudicators had just taken pity on me. At the weigh-in, I stood on the scales to find I was slightly over the limit for the category I intended to fight in. Strictly speaking, the adjudicators should have placed me in the category above. As that meant I would have faced much older and stronger competitors, and no doubt received a pasting in the process, they instructed me to step up onto the scales again, but only once I'd taken off my heavy robe and stripped down to my shorts. Unfortunately, it was the first time I'd chosen to wear bright blue budgie-smuggler-style underwear, so as to protect the 'crown jewels' during the various bouts. The judge looked me in the eye the whole time, as my coach sniggered from behind the scales. But at least I got to stay in a category that meant I wouldn't get destroyed within seconds.

That podium finish became a defining moment for me. I had to fight hard for the position, but it showed me the rewards that came with hard work, commitment and a tight pair of pants. Had I found myself facing competitors who were older and stronger, I wonder if the inevitable crushing would've steered me in a different direction in life. Without doubt, it would've taken the edge off the sense of drive and determination that steered me through my early attempts to break into acting as a career.

* * *

Emerging into the morning light, I feel reborn, if slightly stiff and sore. It's the day after Halloween, which has roots in a Celtic pagan festival that's all about death and new beginnings. Following a restorative sleep in a warm bed at the Drovers Inn, it certainly seems like I'm making a fresh start. My clothes have dried overnight, slow-baked on a radiator, and I've stood under a hot shower and washed away the dirt, sweat and tears of the last two days. As I set out to continue my northbound trek along the West Highland Way, all memory of the sodden, dispirited and wretched traveller who stumbled in the night before has been cast from my mind.

Before I go any further, however, there is one thing I have to do. I've just left the hotel's main entrance, retracing my steps along the pavement beside the main road to the campsite drive. My rucksack continues to weigh me down, as if every item inside it has mysteriously turned to stone, but it won't be a problem for much longer. Oh no, your days are numbered, Mr Sack. For I have hatched a plan, and right now there is no going back. With no sound of traffic from either direction, I leave the pavement and cross a strip of rough ground bordered by a low stone wall. There, crouching before a sprawling wild rhododendron bush, I shrug off my rucksack and open the drawstrings. I then haul out a bin bag that is straining to contain everything I've stuffed inside. After slogging relentlessly from the outskirts of Glasgow, I have determined what is essential for my journey. Everything else is surplus to requirements. Quietly, almost ceremoniously, I plant the bag beneath the bush, out of sight of the road, and cover it up with leaves and twigs. I'm well aware that I look like a man furtively burying stolen valuables or body parts. If anyone is watching and dares to investigate, they'll find nothing but the sad trappings of an outdoor explorer who bit off more than he could chew (along with a rather lovely AeroPress).

Once my journey is complete and I'm safely home, I plan to ride out on my motorcycle and collect the bag. For now, knotted tightly and with no food inside to attract wildlife, it's safe and out of sight. Without my tent, the cooking equipment, my beloved café press and a whole bunch of spare clothes, my rucksack feels like it has ended its rebellion. It feels good now, in tune with my body. Later, when I pull out my walking sticks – which will accompany me to the end of the West Highland Way and quite possibly even to my grave, because I love them so much, my pack will seem so light I'll forget it's on my back at all.

* * *

Fresh from my travels across the USA, I returned to Scotland to follow my dream. Declining the university offer awaiting me at the end of my gap year, I had set my heart on going to drama school. A degree in English and film studies just wasn't for me, I realized. I had only ever been lukewarm about it, whereas the desire to become an actor was now burning strongly in my heart. I wanted to tread the boards, speak in iambic pentameter and dazzle the crowds. By then, I was committed. I could see no other future.

In terms of timing, I had missed the window of opportunity to apply to drama schools for the next academic year. To my great surprise, and also delight, one school in Glasgow, the Royal Scottish Academy of Music and Drama (which later become the Royal Conservatoire of Scotland) offered me the chance to overlook the standard application procedure and audition privately. The school was run by a theatre director I really admired called Vladimir Mirodan. The thought of learning from a man with a formidable mastery of acting psychology filled me with high excitement and also dread. Immediately, I felt out of my depth, but attended the audition all the same.

And it was a disaster.

My instincts had been right. The opportunity to try out in front of Mirodan was incredible. It was just I did not have enough stagecraft under my belt to impress him. I was nervous. I stumbled over my lines. I couldn't find my way into the character I'd prepared to play. I winged it to the best of my abilities, which didn't amount to much. Before Mirodan even stopped me and said he'd seen enough, I pretty much knew I had blown it.

'Get some experience and then try again next year,' he advised me in his deeply resonant voice, and I knew that I would spend the next 12 months getting as much time on stage as I could.

I had failed to get into drama school, but that served to incentivise me. I was quite prepared to go into competition with myself. I needed to prove that I could do it. So, having given up my place at university, I set about doing everything I could to earn one the following year as a student of the great Vladimir Mirodan. I joined the Royal Lyceum Youth Theatre, which brought me together with really creative young people both on stage and behind the scenes. Its tutors, Colin Bradie and Steve Small, both charismatic and really engaging guys, quickly become people I considered friends. We would sit after workshops drinking spicy rum and Coke in the theatre bar, discussing current actors and plays that inspired us and bonding over our love of war movies. It helped me to feel like I was moving in the right direction, and I made lasting friendships with the other students too.

It was inspiring to be involved in productions on the main stage. Knowing that I had another chance to follow my dreams at the end of the year, I was hungry to learn and improve at all times. I also fell for a girl in my class, called Emma, a talented and charming actress, and wished to impress her too. I was infatuated. I looked forward to going to the acting sessions and would always try to arrive early and leave late in the hope of catching her eye. In some ways my rejection from drama school was a humbling experience, and that fed into my desire to prove to myself that with hard work and dedication, I could make it.

* * *

I feel great this morning. It's a fresh start, and in sharp contrast to the fact that I had come close to admitting defeat. The night before, as I followed my fellow traveller through the entrance of the Drovers Inn,

I just wanted to sink to my knees and weep. Closing the door on the downpour, I had shut my eyes for a moment. The second day of my journey had been frankly hideous. It had poured with rain every step of the way. I was soaked to the bone, starving hungry, dehydrated, exhausted both mentally and physically, and ready to give up.

'We have one room available,' the receptionist told me after Graeme had ambled through to the dining room. I'm not sure what my response would have been had she informed me they were fully booked. It probably would've had me arrested. 'I'll take it,' I said, and that's where my dreams of wild camping under starlight collapsed forevermore.

After supper, the plan was for Graeme's father to give him a lift home for the night before bringing him back at first light for the next leg. It was a sensible plan, and the sort of support system I should've considered had I not been so impulsive about just throwing myself into this journey. I also figured this would be the last time that I saw my new walking companion. I had no intention of continuing with my own trek. I was done. The West Highland Way had defeated me. It had coaxed me in with a promise of a romantic hike through the wilderness, only to spit me out for lacking due respect for the reality of the undertaking. It was tough, far harder than I had imagined, but all that was behind me now.

We found Graeme's dad in the dining area. He had saved us a table by a roaring fire. Just then, there was nowhere else on earth I would rather have been. Having ordered a large glass of water – I was so thirsty! – as well as a pint of lager and a hot meal so I didn't have to get up again, I flopped into a chair and set about doing damage to the delicious food on offer.

Graeme's father was sweet; a lovely guy who asked all about our day. Mostly I let his son answer for me, even if he did flatter my efforts considerably. The room was decorated with fake cobwebs and plastic vampire bats to mark Halloween. Though they didn't need to add many, as the Inn is famous for its 'olde worlde' feel, and there were likely plenty of cobwebs in places no one could hope to reach! I love it that way. The staff wear kilts and it is decorated with stuffed animals, including a life-size bear who, tonight, appears to have made friends with a dancing skeleton and some plastic vampire bats. I felt about as lively as that old grizzly as my new friends carried the conversation.

Many of the guests around us had dressed up as witches, ghouls and skeletons. Perhaps one or two regulars dress like that year-round? It was hard to tell in the firelight and the hangover of my boggy hallucinations. It seemed as if I had come as the corpse of a lost hiker, to sit alongside the contents of the local graveyard. It was only when dinner arrived that I came alive somewhat. With a steaming bowl of Scotch broth in front of me, I just spooned it metronomically into my mouth. It wasn't pretty, but it felt like I had slipped into survival mode. By the time I had followed it up by polishing off a delicious pie with mash, and finished with a nip of whisky, I was ready for bed.

Before the door to my room had even shut behind me, I dumped my hated rucksack on the floor, banishing it to the corner. Then I visited every radiator I could find and turned each of them up to full. The last thing I wanted to do was head home with wet, heavy clothes in my pack. Within minutes, having stripped down and laid all the wet stuff out to dry, a warm fug filled the air. I even opened my tent and spread it over the door of the shower. It began to drip enthusiastically, which left me wondering just how much rainwater I had lugged through the day: half the loch by the look of it.

'What a disaster,' I muttered to myself. 'I'm done.'

Lying in bed with the lights off and my face illuminated by my phone screen, I unwrapped a fistful of trick or treat sweets I'd picked up at the bar. The simple pleasure of a strawberry and lemon fizz sugar rush helped lift my mood further. As I chewed, I messaged a few close friends. Having set off on this trek in secret, I wanted to confess to those I trusted, as if hoping they might offer comfort and advice to make me feel better.

Yr quitting? This was the first response that came back. *WTF, Sam?* (Harsh, but a fair point.)

Don't be a loser lol. (Rude.)

OMG, lol, I walked it last year no problem! (Thanks, friend.)

I knew they meant well. At any other time I would've laughed with them. I was just so tired, and also somewhat shocked that I had been beaten. Even when one of my friends read between the lines, reminding me that at least I had given it my best shot, it didn't make feel any better. All I could do was thank them for their kind words, even if some had resorted to banter, before shutting down my phone and finding some escape in sleep.

* * *

In order to fund my year out, living at home with my Mum after my brother had moved into his own place, I found work in Edinburgh as a manager at an internet café called Cyberia. At a time before broadband was piped into every home, these places were crazily popular and humming with life. People flocked in to sit at computers with dial-up connections and explore this liberating new dimension we called the World Wide Web. It meant my shifts were as busy as they were entertaining, and my customer care skills tested like my rudimentary technical know-how. I would sign clients up to Hotmail, launch Internet Explorer (RIP) and serve them cappuccinos and the odd hazelnut latte. In my downtime between shifts, my friends and I would compete in the occasional online gaming competition and hang out in chat rooms talking rubbish to strangers. My online pseudonym was 'Shokkie' and I loved the alternate universe and characters online.

Later, I switched jobs to become the duty manager at the most unconventional café, Ndebele. It boasted great African food and loyal, artistic clientele, and I loved the sense of community. It was next to the King's Theatre in Edinburgh, and our customers included actors, stage crew, comedians, musicians and even strippers from the local club. Everyone was warm and friendly, and we would all convene afterwards in a bar round the corner that boasted the best jukebox in Edinburgh. We blasted The Doors, The End, Bob Marley and Oasis loudly all night, while drinking beers and discussing anything that came to mind.

That year, I also took on some work as part of the stage crew at the Royal Lyceum Theatre Edinburgh, and at another theatre called the

Traverse. I'm not too proud to say that I was terrible in the role. On one occasion I dropped a piece of set onto the hand of the assistant stage manager and sent him to hospital for several stitches. Another time I was charged with making cucumber sandwiches for a Noël Coward play that the poor unsuspecting actors would have to consume on stage. I cut the bread so thick the poor guys struggled to deliver their lines between mouthfuls. I tried my best, but my efforts were lacking. I was just more comfortable on stage than behind it, and that's where I felt I could shine.

In my bid to become a better actor, my love for theatre deepened. I idolized Scottish actors like Tom McGovern, Eric Barlow and Jimmy Chisholm. I watched them in incredible productions, and that just made me all the more determined to turn my passion into a career. While being tall and broad-built had felt like a challenge growing up – it had taken me a while to feel comfortable with the fact that I couldn't just hide in a crowd – it became a virtue as an actor. On a couple of occasions, simply on account of my stature, I even found myself promoted from the youth theatre and put into the main productions, albeit in really minor roles. It was like being a film extra with no lines to deliver, but the experience was incredible. It meant I had a chance to be backstage with actors I considered my heroes.

Once, I picked up a tiny role in a Chekhov play called *Three Sisters*. The production featured Carolyn Devlin, whose work I admired greatly. I was only on stage briefly, which meant I could watch her from the wings. Her performance was powerful and intense. I could sense how the audience were captivated. In one particular silent scene, she – as the character – held it together and then broke down on stage. It felt as if everyone was holding their breath as her character unfolded before them. I was spellbound. When she came off stage each night and saw me watching, my head against the brick wall, partially hidden by the flats, she would smile at me in passing and it would leave me on such a high.

* * *

That morning, I had awoken to the sound of birdsong. Unlike the night before, there was no hint of the gale that had buffeted the windows of the Drovers Inn. I opened my curtains to be greeted by a box-fresh day. Sculpted white clouds presided over a still, serene morning. At the same time, I sensed an air of peace and calm within me. I had slept for what felt like a century, and risen with no sense of the doom and despair that had sent me to sleep.

'I can do this,' I said to myself, with some doubt in my voice until I repeated the words with absolute certainty.

The night before, I had sworn to myself that I had reached the end of the road. Now, feeling rested and with my sense of purpose restored, I was ready to take on the West Highland Way once more.

And so, having checked out in heat-stiffened clothes, fuelled by coffee and a hearty breakfast (porridge and toast with raspberry jam and peanut butter), I set off from the inn. With my phone in hand over breakfast, I had searched for hotels along the way; booking a series of rooms for the next few nights. If I was going to continue on my journey, I needed to make some changes. Wild camping had been wonderful for one night only. It had given me a taste of sleeping under the stars (well, in the rain), as well as sore joints from the hard ground and a knackered back. It was with this in mind that I had bagged up the contents of my rucksack that I no longer required to live that dismal, doomed dream, and hidden it all under a bush just off the A82.

Back on the West Highland Way on this crisp, dry and refreshing day, I feel liberated. I could wrap what's left in my rucksack into a cloth square, tie that to a stick and just walk with my worldly belongings slung over one shoulder. I could whistle if I wanted; skip a little, too. I imagine that if I did so, woodland creatures would pop out on the path to accompany me for a while. That's how happy I'm feeling as I head into this third day of my trek, and my first as a Highlands walker, in no hurry whatsoever.

This is a unique experience for me, and I like the feeling. It's in my nature to be driven; always looking for the next project or challenge. When the idea to undertake this journey first struck me, acting on impulse with no other plans to fill a rare break in my schedule, I intended to *smash* it. In the short time I spent preparing, I figured I could crank out close to a marathon each day, and complete the whole walk in five days at most. I've run the iconic 26.2-mile distance on several occasions, but there's a difference between pounding the tarmac in a road race and navigating the endless ups and downs, floods, rocks and muddy trails that I've come across so far. There's simply no comparison, and my efforts up to this point have shown that I can't sustain this pace.

So now I have decided on a different approach. I am going to slow things down considerably, and reduce the number of miles I need to walk each day. I have no wish to repeat the closing stage of the last two legs, in which I'd been forced to quicken my pace to reach my destination in the dark. With this in mind, I have downsized my ambitions so that I can comfortably complete each day. There's no rush, after all. I have all week if needs be, and this struck me like a revelation because I've always been primed to push myself.

Even now, as I lock into a leisurely stroll, I find my focus has shifted. I'm no longer fretting about how much further I have to walk, or brooding because it feels like my rucksack is loaded with bullion that doesn't belong to me. I don't care about just getting it done any more, because I realize that mindset means I'm missing so much. Instead, I tune into my surroundings and enjoy the here and now.

* * *

In the world of acting, head shots open doors. If I wanted to attract the attention of casting directors, I needed a studio portrait photo. It had to be something that made me look professional, and not just a young hopeful. I found a local photographer to take some pictures and hoped it wouldn't be a waste of money. Perhaps due to bravado, or just sheer ignorance, I strolled into Stewart Christie, a small actors' agency in Edinburgh, and convinced them to represent me despite my lack of experience. Shortly afterwards, I found myself in black tights, a bodice kind of thing, some very large ruffles around my neck and wrists. I had been cast in a TV docudrama as Lord Darnley, a notorious womaniser, syphilis sufferer and extreme boozer who was killed by his wife, Mary, Queen of Scots.

It was one of those shows largely told by talking-head-historians with cutaways to a dramatization. As a result, I had no dialogue with the actress playing Mary. We just had to do a period dance and then stare at each other intently. In theory, it wasn't a difficult part to play. The only challenge, I discovered – and one I would face repeatedly later in my career – was the fact that I had to wear a sword in a heavy leather sheath around my waist. It was huge, and clanked every time I moved. When we came to perform the dance, the sheath kept catching poor Mary or clanked against stage props or floor lights. It was an unexpected challenge I had to conquer quickly to keep the shoot moving, and I found that I really enjoyed it.

I didn't understand much about the filming process. It seemed to me like a whole new level of acting in which the camera was the audience, but I was also keen to do more. At the same time, when the director called 'cut' for the final time, I knew my roots would always be in theatre. That was where I was born as an actor, and even though both film and television have provided me with many memorable opportunities, I always consider the stage to be home.

* * *

Ruadh. Gaelic for 'red'. We Scots (and Irish) love a ginger (you know the ones with pale skin, freckles and sensitive to light), and there are a great number of these in Scotland – among them not only the character that has most changed my life, the red-headed Jamie

Fraser, but also one of my earliest *Outlander* friends, Marina, from the Isle of Lewis. My family also has a lot of gingers: my grandad, uncle and mum are all redheads. But *ruadh* can also describe hills and trees. It's certainly the word on my mind as I admire the colour that governs this autumnal landscape. There could be all manner of ways to describe the different shades and tones of the heather and the hills and the fallen leaves. I just love the Gaelic language because there's passion in the roll of that first vowel. *Rua . . . rrrrua . . . ruaaaahhh.*

As I walk, I think about my travelling companion from the day before. Graeme was striking in appearance and memorable to me for the companionship we formed in the face of adversity. I had set out on my adventure with a view to keeping a low profile. It's how I've come to be since my character in *Outlander* means people look at me like they've seen me somewhere before. Graeme had made the connection, and caught up with me to share his views on my work. I had tried to keep my distance at first, but I'm so glad that he persevered. Not only was my new friend like a talisman as we navigated the remains of that wretched day, but it also reminded me that I didn't always have to shrink from attention. By default, I tend to give fans of the show what they want so they go away happy, but yesterday reminded me that not everyone is after a selfie or a signature. Sometimes people are just interested in people, especially when thrown together in unusual circumstances, and that's how lasting connections are forged.

I imagine that having stayed with his father overnight, and due to his enthusiasm and tenacity, Graeme has set out way ahead of me. He seemed better prepared on so many levels, and I am grateful to have fallen in with him. I don't even want to think about how I might have fared on my own through that last phase of the walk, when despair began to stalk me. It's very likely that I'd still be trudging lochside with just the sound of my waterlogged socks for company. Now, as I drift along in a world of my own, I spot boot prints in the mud and wonder if they might be his. I'm quite familiar with the pattern of his heavy tread, because I saw so much of them while cursing and stumbling along in his wake. I also know he takes shorter steps than me, not because he's smaller in stature, but because he told me it was more efficient. It must be him! I'm quite sure of it, in fact. I like to think we will see each other again on this journey. On setting eyes on yet another print, seemingly emerging from a puddle as if the owner walked around the water, I decide it must be him. Graeme told me that he hates getting his feet wet.

* * *

By the end of that year following my failed drama school audition, which was a kind of 12-month-long work experience, I had immersed myself in the world of theatre. I'd been involved in a string of productions with Lyceum Youth Theatre, discovered I wasn't much of a stagehand, and appeared in a few low-key TV programmes. Most significantly, I had come into contact with several professional actors. They knew all about my hopes and dreams of going to drama school. As the time approached for me to audition once again, they shared their advice on picking out scenes that suited me. Some even helped me to rehearse until I felt completely comfortable with the characters. I chose Sebastian from *Twelfth Night*, and a new piece of writing I'd seen at the Traverse Theatre. It helped me to build my confidence, which was something I had lacked on my first attempt.

I returned to Glasgow's Royal Scottish Academy of Music and Drama with high hopes as much as mixed feelings. I was determined to get into drama school, but in my year out, I had also heard amazing things about studying in the English capital. Drama Centre London had caught my imagination. Some people said that it was really progressive, with actors being required to strip off their clothes to test their commitment to roles. The idea terrified and excited me. Plus my idol and muse Carolyn Devlin had attended the school and encouraged me to apply. As soon as I stepped back into the Royal Scottish Academy, however, it seemed like the place for me. I felt at home, and knew instantly that would be my chosen school. I also really wanted to learn from a master like Vladimir Mirodan, and that was enough for me to feel certain that I had made the right choice to try for a place there.

This time, upon auditioning, I performed with a year's stagecraft under my belt. Along with the scenes I had prepared, we were required to do some voice work, act like animals (classic) and show some movement skills. Everything I had done as an actor in those 12 months had been with this moment in mind, and when Mirodan invited me to start in the new academic year, I felt both thrilled and complete. It meant leaving my mum in Edinburgh, where I had been living, but she was so excited for me. The time had come to spread my wings.

As I prepared to start my first term, news filtered out from the Royal Scottish Academy that there would be a change in the teaching staff. Vladimir Mirodan had taken a new position, I learned, at Drama School London of all places! I couldn't ignore the irony of the situation. It was almost funny, even if I was quietly gutted. Still, I had a place at a prestigious school, and every intention of making the most of the opportunity. I could have no regrets.

* * *

What a difference a day makes! Only 10 miles or so left to cover. Well under half of what I was grinding out late into the last two nights. I feel like I've dropped into an easier gear. I can breathe freely now, rather than panting and puffing and occasionally cursing. I even have time to stop by a brook, sit back against a rock and eat my lunch. The staff at the inn kindly supplied me with some tuna sandwiches, a packet of crisps, an apple and a granola bar, and I tuck in with the enthusiasm of a schoolkid on an excursion. My rucksack sits beside me, as if it too needs to take time out from the effort of the first two days. We've settled our differences now. I don't hold any grudges against it.

In no rush any more, I plan to walk off my lunch on a gentle descent through the glens to the midway point on this third day of my journey. It's only about an hour from here, according to my map. I just hope that where I'm heading will serve fresh coffee. I don't regret stashing my gear, but I do miss my café press.

Crianlarich is a staging post on my walk that styles itself 'the gateway to the Highlands', though not in neon lights (that would make a pretty eye-catching signage). The village stands in the shadow of Ben More, on the bank of the River Fillan, and the views north are spectacular. The mountain beyond strikes me as a playground for romance and adventure. At the same time, I feel as if I've passed through quite a few places that claim to be this mythical entrance to Scotland's rugged wilderness.

As I approach the outlying forest, hiding the village below, I'm drawn from my thoughts by another kind of gateway before me. Rather than the kissing gate variety – and I have breezed through many of those in the last few days – this is one of the old-school 'shepherd's stiles', ladder stiles that bridge so many stone walls around here. It looks sturdy enough, but once I've committed to the sloped rungs, I have to avoid grasping the barbed wire that appears to have been strung up to test a weary or overconfident traveller like me.

Could *this* be the gateway to the Highlands? I wonder, pirouetting over the top to begin the clamber down the other side. It's not an easy manoeuvre, I discover. My legs aren't just sore from so much walking. The muscles are so tight that I fail to clear the top of the stile with one foot. Instead, I clip it with my heel while my centre of balance moves on. In my mind, I make a cat-like landing. In reality, if this had been a sequence for an action movie, the director would call cut and politely bring in the stuntman to do it with more grace and conviction. As a final humiliation, I realize I have stepped down into something squishy. Sheep shit, it seems, judging by the flock in the middle distance now glaring at me like I should take my boots off in their house. With just one field to cross before I reach tarmac, I walk on without making eye contact. The sheep continue to watch me. Like the cows I have passed, these guys also sport formidable horns. I wonder if it's confined to livestock around here, and hope I don't find myself coming face to face with a squirrel or a rabbit that looks like it's in league with the devil.

'Nice sheep,' I say soothingly, as if this will make a difference. 'Good sheep.'

* * *

Moving from Edinburgh to Glasgow was a happy time for me. I made good friends at the Royal Scottish Academy, and really felt like I was being treated seriously as a young actor while also finally living independently. I moved in with two girls from my course, Helen and Flortjee (from Shetland), and another student actor we never really saw. I think he just committed to living the student life as much as possible. Like any first-year students, we had a riot. We got high and wandered the streets looking for the best Sunday roast to curb our munchies. We went out and danced at the Arches, the infamous nightclub venue, or hung out at Trader Joe's during karaoke night. We also slept very little, with weekends becoming a blur until Monday morning.

By then, almost two years had passed since I'd left school. I was a little older than my cohorts at drama school, and maybe even wiser about the Scottish theatre scene from having met many of the players whilst working in Edinburgh. I also understood a little of the professional world I'd be entering. I liked to have a good time as much as everyone else, but by then I knew when it was time to work and not squander the chance to do something with my life that I might not get again. So every lunch break, without fail, after consuming whatever snack I could rustle together, I'd find one of the numerous empty rehearsal rooms and work for half an hour on my voice. 'Gallop apace, you fiery-footed steeds . . . The raven himself is hoarse . . . But, soft! what light through yonder window breaks? . . . Is this a dagger which I see before me . . . Haa, haaa, hooooo, oooooooh . . .'

I felt driven. My voice work paid off. I entered and won the Elaine Gullen poetry-speaking competition and also the Duncan Macrae Scots-speaking competition. My favourite piece was from Edwin Morgan's *Phaedra*, in full Scots. It was a play I had watched while working as an usher, back at the Lyceum Theatre, when the auditorium had been turned into the theatre-in-the-round to replicate the traditional Greek theatre. I would stand in the wings, ready to guide the audience to their seats, but also to allow access for the actors to pass through. One of these was Carol Ann Crawford. She had a terrific speaking voice and a dexterous grasp of the language, and our paths were to cross again some 20 years later, as she now works as the accent coach on *Outlander*. It's a play I watched repeatedly, and I would love to be in a revived version, perhaps as Theseus. This particular speech (worth seeking out in full) about the demise of Hippolytus moves me even now, the language rich, visceral and deeply poetic:

A tairrible cry comes yellochin fae the sea-bed
Tae brek an wrack the lown dowf atmosphere;
A vyce as fearsome answers it, gowlin
Fae the wame o the yird tae thon hoo fae the sea.
Oor bluid rins cauld intae the hert's root;

I was passionate and ambitious, and among people who shared my interests and values. I also knew that I had a lot to learn, and knuckled down to make every moment count.

I know exactly when I learned how to act. That moment occurred in my second year at the Royal Scottish Academy during a production of *Romeo and Juliet*.

'Sam, you just don't seem to have what it takes. Acting is all about being in the moment, and I just don't see you there.' It was one of my tutors who had taken me to one side in rehearsals and all but crushed my dreams. Even though she was no doubt challenging me to up my game, this view came as a blow.

'I am in the moment,' I insisted, but I knew it wasn't enough. I couldn't simply tell her. I had to prove it. Not just to my tutor, but also to myself. I knew I had to let go.

I had in my mind an idea of what it meant to be an actor. It was something we'd explored at length at drama school. I was familiar with the idea of being in the moment. To me, it meant existing in the present as I played a character, and liberating myself from any sense that I was acting. The key to Shakespeare, I learned, is to allow the text to live. It's the punctuation and poetry that guides the actor, which makes breathing key to delivery. Honestly, it seemed like magic to me. If the actor's body is open, a vessel, then the character is literally in the words and the play comes to life. Well, in theory it made sense. When I listened to feedback, it seemed I hadn't found it on stage. With my tutor's view still burning in my ears, I returned to the rehearsal. I was playing Romeo. We were running through the banishment scene, in which my character is distraught at the prospect of living without his beloved. This time, I was determined to show that I had what it took.

'Free yourself,' she advised me from the wings. 'Don't think about the audience, your lines or even what your character should be thinking. Just let it all go.'

I understood what she was driving at. I also thought I really did know how to be in the moment. It seemed like something that perhaps we could all find instinctively. At the same time, I could think of many incidences where I'd found myself focused on the fact that I was on stage. In that frame of mind, well aware that it was just a performance, I'd forget my lines or become completely unconvincing.

The previous year, I had been invited back to my old youth theatre to take part in a version of *A Midsummer Night's Dream*. I was playing Theseus/Oberon; a really powerful and commanding character. I had a big final speech to make, but midway through I registered the audience and thought, 'wow, this is cool!' and everything fell apart.

'Now, until the break of day,
Through this house each fairy stray.

To the best bride-bed will we,

Which . . . Which . . .'

Silence. The audience shifted uncomfortably. Then my classmate playing Bottom the Weaver hissed at me: 'Which by us shall blessed be!'

Yes! I woke, my brain released from its frozen state.

'Which by us shall blessed be;

And the issue there create

Ever shall be fortunate.'

Applause. I sighed. I couldn't allow that to happen again.

Back at drama school, in the scene we were rehearsing, Romeo is in despair. So I called upon my tutor's frank opinion of my performance to light the touchpaper. Somehow I had to stop feeling conscious. I needed to be at one with the role.

The moment it happened will stay with me for ever. I lost all sense of self-awareness and allowed my character to take over. In a sense, I stopped being me, and that set Romeo free. It was intense, like a jazz musician taking flight with a song, knowing he can bring it back. The text is so robust and versatile; suddenly I realized there were many ways to play it, but once you commit to the words, the rest takes care of itself. On finishing the scene, I only needed to look at my tutor to know that her words had always been intended to push me to that place.

I often think back to that time, but not just because it was an epiphany for me. It showed me that even though I was learning to feel at home on stage I would always have a lot to learn. In particular, I remember one performance of the same play in which I just had to improvise or risk everything unravelling. At the moment in which he threatens to commit suicide, Romeo holds a dagger to his throat. On this particular occasion, however, I realized I had forgotten to pick it up off the prop table in the wings. Other than throw myself off the stage to my death, the only other way I could demonstrate my determination to kill myself was by trying to strangle myself with both hands. Anthony Bowers, my flatmate and friend, was playing the priest, who is supposed to rush over to stop Romeo from killing himself. While we managed to pull it off, Anthony nearly choked himself to death trying not to laugh. 'O hohoho deadly sin! O ruuuuude unthankfulness.'

I often think back to those early days, because it's one thing to be in the moment on stage. In film and television, there is often a great deal more to consider. An actor has to be aware of the camera, find the best light, and operate in what can sometimes feel like an artificial environment. Details become important, like not setting a cup on a table while delivering a line, because it can make a noise and mess up the sound. I had to learn to speak around any noise, or raise my voice over external interruptions. Over time, I feel like I've learned to disappear into a character with one half of my brain, while the other remains conscious of the technical things I need to remember.

Losing myself to the moment as an actor isn't something that comes naturally. I had to learn to let go. There are times when I wish I could do the same in life, but somehow I've always been primed to keep looking ahead. Even before I've completed a climb, I'm searching for the next summit.

* * *

Crianlarich crossroads. According to the sign, this is the halfway point on the West Highland Way. It also marks a dramatic change in the landscape. The route will now begin to climb and fall as I tackle the true Highlands. The placard sits in the centre of a fir tree copse. Once upon a time, centuries before the sign came into existence, drovers would pass through here, steering their cattle between the brooding mountain peaks in search of fresh pastures. It could be a dangerous journey. Rustlers, bandits and the steep decline a mile or so down to the village must have left them in need of some nerve-calming refreshments on arrival. I have no cows in my care, but I could murder a good coffee.

Today, I hardly notice the uneven ground, energized by the freedom and lack of time pressure. A trip down to the village would be a detour from the path and probably add on an hour or so of walking. However, my spirits and load lightened, I decide the diversion will be worth it if it results in some roasted java beans, ground and brewed in hot water, served black and strong. Ooh, the caffeine! My body is definitely craving it. At work, I drink a huge amount; I've normally had three cups by the time I leave the make-up chair to go on set.

I feel a sense of pride in getting myself back on track after the wheels fell off so unexpectedly, and then shifting into a gear that has brought me a sense of peace. I have also come far enough on my own now to be struck by any signs of human life. So when the forest opens out and I spot small houses and a railway station below, I pause for just a moment to peer at the scene. On deciding that there must be a shop down there, and aware that I now have plenty of space for snacks in my rucksack, I leave the path and head down the hill. Even my walking boots can't hold me back as I leap off tree stumps, relying on the pine needles and moss to cushion my steps.

Foresters have been hard at work on the outskirts of Crianlarich. Peeling off the pathway for the village approach, I pass clearings carpeted in sawdust with log piles in the centre, and smell the scent of sap in the air. Surrounding the clearing, lichen-clad trees stand defiantly. Cobwebs glisten in the sun. It feels like each tree has a character of its own. Some lean in, as if seeking a closer look at their fallen comrades, surveying the waste with a unified sense of puzzlement. Like an ancient kirkyard cemetery, the chopped logs have lain there for some time and begun to decay. I spot mushrooms, joyfully balancing on the dead bark and moss. The peace and presence of the trees excites me. I feel as if I'm in a crowd, protected by the masses, like walking towards Murrayfield stadium, the sense of anticipation and anonymity a blanket around me.

At a promontory, now cleared by the tree-eaters, yet more peaks reveal themselves to me: I recognize Ben Lawers in the distance, on the north shore of Loch Tay; a large Munro I have still to climb. A lone tree stump, half cut, forgotten by the forestry machines, stands pointing out to the views beyond. Disc-like slices of trunk have been placed on top of the stump to create a kind of spiralling staircase to nowhere. With each step ornamented by white marbled stones, it could be some strange altar to a pagan god. Carefully, I add a smooth stone that I picked up from the shores of Loch Lomond. Is this just a recent act of whimsy created by walkers, I ask myself, or a tradition older than the hills?

I hop and skip down what's left of the path into the village before it turns into a tarmac road. Crianlarich doesn't appear as exciting or interesting as the red-needled grey-green forests I have just walked through. Still, if I can find a shop, that will put the two worlds on a level pegging.

Ahead, I spot an underpass that will take me to the high street.

'Attention, trolls!' I shout out loud as I run downhill. 'Incoming!'

The tunnel cuts through a bank under the main road, out of sight and mind of drivers. I find my phone and look for a spot to prop it up for the obligatory selfie. As I do so, I notice a mound of bags, cardboard boxes and rubbish inside the tunnel, just out of reach of the daylight. It's a mess, and as I head inside, I voice my disapproval with a tut.

It's then that I realize I am not alone in the underpass. There, in the middle of the trash, is a figure. Bent over, cross-legged, the outline of a cowled hood barely visible in the gloom of the dark tunnel. I blink and look again. My mind plays tricks in the dark. A troll? My imagination runs wild, my breath caught in my chest. A goblin king, sitting on his vaulted throne, wretched and bent over, his spine outlined up the back. I stop my imagination before it gets out of control and hold my breath. My excited muscles and the momentum of the run keep me moving forward as I pick my way through the tunnel, avoiding the broken glass and discarded trash. A wisp of smoke snakes its way up to the ceiling of the cave, like a sorcerer's wand – a burnt cigarette held in a blue finger and thumb. I'm struck by shame that I can't speak. The figure doesn't move, as if waiting. The air tense, the sound of my steps echoing all around.

'Hi...' I say, breathlessly, picking my way through the gloom, but receive no answer.

Out of the tunnel and back into the modern world, it feels like I've passed through a gateway. It gives me shivers. A railway station, cars, a village shop... the modern world, not my foolish imagination. I burst into the shop, my mind racing. 'What an idiot! So stupid! Why didn't I say hello properly? That person needs help.' I look for something to give them – sandwiches, fruit, smoothies or anything sweet. I'm determined to help.

* * *

As a student actor, learning to lose myself in a role proved to be a turning point. It became my 'safe place'. Hiding behind a character or immersing myself in a fantasy world meant I didn't have to face the real one. During the production of *Romeo and Juliet*, I was approached to audition for a lead role in a play called *Outlying Islands*. Written by David Greig, it's a moving and compelling story about two young ornithologists pushed to extremes on a remote island on the eve of the Second World War. Even though I was a student, the director, Philip Howard, was impressed by my performance as Romeo, and after I auditioned, he offered me the part straight away. As the play was due to be staged at the prestigious Edinburgh Festival, I couldn't turn it down. First, however, I needed the blessing of the Royal Scottish Academy to put my studies on hold. Fortunately for me, they recognized that a professional production of this calibre could be an invaluable schooling. They agreed to let me take time out, and in some ways it was my chance to fly.

In 2002, as part of the festival, the company debuted the play at the Traverse Theatre in Edinburgh. From there, we set out on tour, travelling to small theatres on Scottish islands such as Shetland, Lewis and Skye. Sometimes we performed in tiny rural venues and it felt like everyone had come to watch. We visited isolated places like Easdale Island, which had a population of about 60, and that made the show particularly memorable. Everyone was crammed into the little hall. I could hear seagulls sitting on the roof as if they had gathered for the occasion, and it felt like we were bringing the whole community together.

The play did well, and we transferred to the Royal Court Theatre. It was an incredible opportunity for me, not least when we went on tour. Me and my co-stars, Laurence Mitchell, Lesley Hart and the legendary Bob Carr, travelled widely. We even took the show to Toronto in the height of winter. Bob was very unimpressed, but did find a good bar for us to drink local beer in. The show has so many themes – coming of age, the war, island life, identity, suicide, growth – and great Laurel and Hardy humour.

It was an honour to perform the play so widely, especially at prestigious theatres, and yet the smaller Highlands and Islands venues were the most rewarding. These little places were rammed and the atmosphere intense for all the right reasons. It was such a privilege, like being part of a shared experience. It also reminded me of my childhood in New Galloway. Touring productions sometimes visited our community, and my mother would always take me along. Through my eyes, it felt like the wider world had knocked on our door. In bringing the play to the stage across pockets of Scotland I had never visited before, I hoped that youngsters in the audience would be inspired as I had been.

By the time the run ended, I had just a few months left at drama school. I returned to the Royal Scottish Academy for the end of my third and final year, and they allowed me to graduate. It was highly unusual, but I am so grateful for the support and understanding of my tutors. It had been an unconventional schooling, and in some ways a fast track to becoming a professional. I have been able to repay my school and help encourage new students by recently setting up a scholarship for several students each year to have their fees paid. I also created a playwriting competition, which has cash prizes and support for the students to develop their ideas.

I just learned so much on the job, but I also missed my fellow students. They spent time experimenting as actors, staging their own productions and just having a great time together. It was so good to rejoin them, but I did feel like I'd missed out on that shared experience as young actors on a learning journey. It was a small price to pay, of course, and I value the friendships made. I've just always been aware that in those three years I spent my time on the edge of things once more; whether I was away with the play – which was about being in

18 months old, my first hike? Mullwharchar hill, Galloway. Must be where I got my passion for it. Especially when someone is carrying me.

On top of the Merrick, Galloway. My favourite sweater. I think it had a Lego schematic on it. Best part, it had an actual Lego figure that attached to the shoulder (clearly missing).

Age 5. I hadn't started school yet. Probably why I'm smiling. Above the Steadings. Looking down to Kenmure Castle and Loch Ken.

Right: I imagined that warriors, knights and some gruesome beasts had climbed (or slithered) up these stairs in Kenmure Castle. The owner of the castle must have been right-handed (due to the stairs circling anticlockwise).

My first time on the main stage at the Royal Lyceum, Edinburgh, in *Three Sisters*, by Chekhov. Some of my idols were in the same production and inspired me to audition for drama school. I think I had maybe one line in the entire play but loved every second.

Sam Heughan
Usher/would-be actor
Brings contentment to the mind.

As an usher working at the Lyceum Theatre. 19 years old. I don't remember what play I was describing, but I was clearly trying to be clever (between selling ice creams).

Philip Dorr, *Island at War*. Recently graduated. My first major TV production. We shot on the Isle of Man for a number of months. Living the dream, being paid to act!

Hamlet makes his friend(s) uncomfortable. I played both Rosencrantz AND Guildenstern. As one character…'Rosenstern'?

Manchester Royal Exchange, playing Tom Veryan in Noël Coward's *The Vortex*. Tom was suffering from PTSD from the First World War, masking it with music, dancing, alcohol, cigarettes…and an affair.

Romeo and Juliet, 2002, Royal Conservatoire of Scotland (formerly the Royal Scottish Academy of Music and Drama). Alana Hood was my beautiful Juliet.

'Look, love, what envious streaks

Do lace the severing clouds in
    yonder east:

Night's candles are burnt out,
    and jocund day

Stands tiptoe on the misty
    mountain tops.

I must be gone and live, or stay
    and die.'

The Pearlfisher, directed by Philip Howard. Traverse Theatre. My brilliant co-star, Elspeth Brodie, who beautifully captured the audience (and my heart, on and off the stage).

Right: *Outlying Islands*. Circa 2002–3. Premiered at the Edinburgh Festival then transferred to London's Royal Court. I think this scene was an addition to the original script. John is trying to develop photographs…but is distracted by the alluring island girl!

Back at the Royal Scottish Conservatoire (formerly the Royal Scottish Academy of Music and Drama), on the Athenaeum stage, where several decades earlier I got my first break as Romeo. I enjoy going back and have created several scholarships for new students.

Knives In Hens, TAG Theatre, 2005. With the brilliant John Kazek and lovely Rosalind Sydney. Ros drove us in her car as we toured around Scotland. I couldn't drive then, I learnt when I was 30! My character was ultimately crushed to death by the miller's stone. Painful.

Self-taping at my digs in Los Angeles during pilot season. Some friends and castmates from *Batman* joined me in LA and we helped each other film, work out, BBQ and drink cheap beer every day.

Bondi Beach, Australia. On the press tour for *Outlander* season 2. I brought my friend Luke Neal, former actor and playwright, with me. He made me eat uni (sea urchin's roe) in Japan and I was violently sick (but not from all the Japanese whisky, ahem).

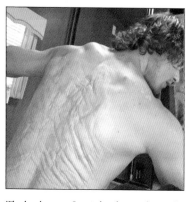

The back scars. Jamie has been whipped around 200 times. Initially it took over three hours to put it all on, plus his frontal scars and wig/make-up, etc. It's quicker now. Can take around an hour to remove, and wearing it is a very odd sensation, especially when you start to sweat! Ugh.

My first Comic-Con, San Diego. Marching through the main floor with a procession of female pipers, it felt very dramatic and like nothing the attendees had ever seen. Scotland had arrived at Comic-Con!

Ah, 'the Governor'. Tim Downie and I are reunited on the *Outlander* set. We had worked together before for several years, in the Tennent's lager commercials. In our story, he was my long-suffering butler (and the real genius behind the Golden Brew).

My long-suffering make-up artist/groomer/ counsellor/music guru/friend and confidante, Wendy Kemp Forbes. Life and soul on set, she keeps me going and I couldn't do it without her (and her random chat!).

When the Starlight Ends. An independent movie I shot on hiatus with director/writer Adam Sigal – who used to be a PI and took me out on secret surveillance missions in his car. Would be hard not to notice us in this truck!

On the red carpet for *The Spy Who Dumped Me*. 2018, Los Angeles. With my brilliant, compassionate and discerning agent, Ruth Young. I love how she operates, inspires and works fairly and honestly. I have learnt a lot from her. She's been a great ally and friend.

On location with Hannah John-Kamen in the Hungarian vineyards, winter 2018. Even psychopaths get cold, it appears.

My brilliant stunt double, Nathan Barris, on the set of *Bloodshot* in Cape Town, South Africa. Such a cool character to play, but the green 'frog legs' didn't do anything for our street cred on set.

My first Golden Globes. I'd just arrived from Thailand and had been very ill with a virus. Dosed up with drugs and some whisky, I managed to walk the carpet without falling over.

Men in Kilts crew shot, on Islay, peat bogs. Fuelled by adrenaline, whisky and good humour, the road trip was a success, and the next island(s) we would go to was New Zealand.

Left: Honorary doctorate from Glasgow University, awarded in Dumfries, near my home town. My uncle Trevor Leat (basket maker and wicker sculptor) and Owen Scott (dear family friend) both kindly attended and posed with me dressed as Harry Potter.

Tequila Town, near Guadalajara, Mexico. I can't remember the name of the horse, perhaps due to the copious amounts of delicious Tequila consumed.

On with your heads! The *Men in Kilts* dream team. The bearded one, co-creator Graham McTavish; the one with the funny accent, exec producer Alex Norouzi. Clearly the power has gone to our heads (and headdresses).

remote places – or catching up with classmates who had formed strong bonds in my absence. Even so, I didn't look back. It was just one more experience to remind me that as much as I love to bring a character onto the stage, as Sam I will always be happiest just to be in the wings of life. I like to be on the sidelines looking in, whether I'm watching my brother as he fixes a bike when we were kids or undertaking a long walk along the West Highland Way as far from the spotlight as possible.

* * *

If this was a Wild West movie, Crianlarich would be one of those one-horse towns in which the man with no name arrives to find the place seemingly abandoned. He rides through the dusty main street, tumbleweed blowing across his path, knowing full well that he is being watched from every window. At least that's how I feel as I head for the first store I can find. In fact, it's the only store.

Inside, having been greeted by the nice lady behind the till, I browse the shelves and pick a sandwich, a soft drink, a smoothie, a packet of granola bars and something sweet. At the counter, as the lady scans my stuff, I find myself eyeing the tobacco products behind her. I keep thinking about the person in the underpass with the smouldering roll-up. In cities like London and New York, the homeless are so engrained into street life they go unnoticed. We're all so wrapped up in our own lives that often we just walk on by. Out here in the middle of nowhere, I can't ignore it. I only slept out for one night, but that was enough for me to know how meaningful small comforts can be. I return to the shelves and pick up another sandwich. When I go to pay, I ask to get some cashback. 'Sorry doll, your card's been declined'. I'm desperate to give the nameless person some cash and then realize, with some relief, I'm not out of funds, they just don't accept Amex. Guess it hasn't made it to Crianlarich quite yet. I try another card, this time with more success.

I used to be a smoker. I look back at that time as one I wish I could change. So as much as a pack of cigarettes might be welcomed by the underpass dweller, I feel that food is the better option. I had found myself with a nicotine habit thanks to *Outlying Islands*. My character was a pipe-smoker. I lit up on stage for the sake of authenticity, learning to overcome the coughing until smoking became second nature. By the time the touring production came to an end, I was burning through 20 roll-ups a day. I now realize I was probably showing up at auditions reeking of nicotine. When I finally faced up to the fact that it could be harming my work prospects as much as my health, I found quitting to be quite a challenge. Today, I might smoke a cigar now and then, but always make sure that it's through choice and not habit. With this in mind, I head back the way I came to continue on my walk, clutching an alternative gesture that I hope might be appreciated.

Returning to the underpass, I feel strangely uneasy about who or what I might find. I even begin to wonder if that silent figure in the shadows is some kind of gateway guardian. As I drop into the tunnel, I find myself silently rehearsing what I might say. It's only when my eyes adjust to the lack of light that I realize my friend is nowhere to be seen. Empty carrier bags and boxes, all from the village shop, are stacked neatly against the side wall. A bowl containing empty cigarette butts is positioned next to a laid out camping mat with a makeshift seat at its head. There is no sign of any creature of my imagination. This is clearly someone who has taken some care. There must be other people visiting or supplying gifts. A few bags hold groceries and are thoughtfully stored next to the mat. This is someone's home... I can't tell in the dark if I am completely alone and don't wait to look around. I place my meagre offering and move on. The resident has seemingly vanished, or perhaps is waiting for me to leave. I think about how I have been alone and craved the silence of the hills. But also how, in my darker moments, a friendly hand has helped me. I long to speak to this person, at least hear their story or offer them some warmth. Or am I being a fool, thinking this person cares or even wants my help? 'Stupid Actor', I scold myself as I begin to climb back up the pine needle path to the crossroads above, letting my imagination get the better of me. As I pass the ancient forest and silent trees, who have witnessed this whole episode, the hairs on the back of my neck vibrate. I still wonder if I am alone. I hope the woods at least provide some comfort to the tunnel resident. I vow that I will do something more to help upon my return – I will look to support homeless projects – and I wish him, or her, some peace and comfort.

* * *

Fresh from the Royal Scottish Academy of Music and Drama, I set out to build on my experience. This meant auditioning for roles, which was competitive and testing when it came to resilience. I also wasn't very good at it. I didn't really know how to prepare, and would often find myself not being able to deliver what I felt the casting director was looking for. Before the audition, I'd spend ages researching my character. I'd fill journals with cut-outs, timelines and history notes, and study the costumes and the director's past productions. I'd look into the era in which the character lived, or their motivations in the story, and forget the key point to auditioning: learning the lines. I'd go in, armed with all the background information on my role, imagining we would sit down and discuss the character at length, but that rarely happened. The casting director just wanted to see me deliver a performance, only to disengage as I muddled my way through.

I knew why I wasn't getting the parts I wanted, and quickly changed how I prepared for auditions. I was also keenly aware that it was a cut-throat business. As much as I hungered for a role, I was in competition with actors who knew how to deliver exactly what was required. If anything, it encouraged me to focus on – surprise! – learning my lines and conquering my nerves by losing myself in a character.

In those early years, as a jobbing actor, I discovered that auditioning was a craft in its own right. The more I attended, the better I got at them, and slowly the rejections turned to recalls. The early years were interesting, though. While I sat in a pool of nervous sweat, older, more successful and experienced actors would be given priority, and as they left, they'd embrace the casting director – 'Oh thank you, darling, SOOO good to see you again, we'll speak soon, yah yah, call my people and we MUST go for another drink!' I'd sit, green with envy, only to receive a steely glare and a curt 'Next!' as I walked towards the audition room door as if facing the gallows. I didn't despair, however. I just knew that I had to work on building those relationships.

My very first taste of success came in the form of a television miniseries. *Island at War* was an ITV drama about the German occupation of the Channel Islands, which was in fact shot on the Isle of Man. I played a British spy. It was an exciting time, a chance to work with high-profile actors, but I still didn't quite understand how to act for the camera. All my experience came from reading books. I devoured Michael Caine, Laurence Olivier and a host of other acting biographies and manuals. I was hoping for insight, but nothing beat learning on the job.

A key scene on the first day of the shoot involved a head-to-head between my character and his father, played by James Wilby. It was an intense exchange. I'd read that Michael Caine practised not blinking, as it is important for a close-up not to distract the viewer and makes the take way more powerful. It's a technique I have subsequently mastered, but impossible for a scene lasting 5 minutes or longer. By the end of it, my eyes were watering so hard I could barely see. It was then that the director, Thaddeus O'Sullivan, took me to one side.

'If you blink,' he said in his soft Irish accent. 'It means we can see your soul.'

I understood what he meant straight away. I relaxed and forgot about trying to make an impression. Instead, I allowed the character and action to take over. I didn't need to demonstrate a technique or signal intensity with my eyes for this scene. I just needed to be truthful.

* * *

The clouds, including those that weighed down my thoughts yesterday, have lifted. My oversized pack, now baggy and deflated, bounces cheerfully between my shoulder blades. Instead of fretting about the fear of failure, my brain seems calmer, and I start to enjoy the rhythm and repetition of the day's walk. My decision to abandon wild camping has gone from a reluctant concession to the best decision I could have made. I worried it would put paid to the romanticism of this journey. In reality, it's stopped me from feeling damp and miserable. I wonder if anyone has found the stash from my rucksack, though . . .

I have booked a room for this evening at the Muthu Ben Doran Hotel. When I made the reservation online over breakfast this morning, it looked big enough for me to be anonymous, which is what I crave right now. The hotel is a few miles north of here, in a place called Tyndrum. The village is near the battlefield where the mighty Clan MacDougall defeated Robert the Bruce and his army. Today, Tyndrum is also well known for a classic A-road service station. It's one I'm really keen to visit, but more of that later.

I dive back into the comfort and safety of the trees, the main road lost and hidden some distance away. Deeper into the forest, the wind catches the lichen and throws it into the air like a flurry of snow. The sun that previously warmed me in the glen is now blocked out by the dense forest. It's growing colder and I can see my breath. Like walking through the wardrobe, I have entered a different land. There, from broad beds of dead pine leaves, I find myself under surveillance.

What is it about mushrooms? Since I set off today at a less insane and more leisurely pace, I've noticed them everywhere. They seem to be gathered in legions, under trees and beside boulders. I start to spot different varieties, and though I can't tell one from the other, I begin to think of them as battalions of tiny soldiers distinguished by their helmets. I don't feel threatened by the wee guys, but the sheer number becomes something I can't ignore. It feels as if the forests have sent them out as a show of force. *Ho! You! You're welcome to walk through here, pal. But nay funny business, understood?*

I've taken mushrooms a few times. The first time in Camden, London. It was the last day it was legal to purchase them. My friends and I howled with laughter and I became a gnome, sitting in the hollow of a tree in North London, 'fishing' and at one with the world. The second time was back in Scotland, having gathered about 100 wild capped mushrooms with some friends. We made a thick soup of just water and raw mushrooms, whizzed up. It tasted foul, but we all chugged down a mug each. Sitting in the living room, we watched a friend's self-made horror movie. 'Well, those mushies did nothing', I thought and sneaked into the kitchen for another large helping of our delicious truffle soup. Then, it started... Things became intense, the air got thicker and I started to sweat. The house was organic. It became alive. It probably always was. 'Life' was in the walls. The red room upstairs – I could smell the colour – the walls and ceiling a mass of naked bodies, moving and pulsating as one. The sounds of Leftfield's *Leftism* was the heartbeat. We all breathed and sighed in time to the pulse of the music. Outside, we delighted in the world: an ocean, the solid ground and trees, now a hexagonal sea, a regular smooth wave. Everything was alive; fractal. I smelt colour and marvelled at the sensation of touch and heat. I was having a blast. Though my staring at the ceiling and walls for hours made the other guests at the house – who had not consumed the powerful concoction – begin to worry. After I finally came back to a more stable reality, I was put to bed on the couch. My dreams featured fantastic colours and I explored the centre of the universe, from my temporary resting place. The come down was horrific. I was paranoid and fragile. These mushrooms are powerful wee blighters. They are definitely watching me now, in the woods, or perhaps they are paranoid themselves, concerned that I might consume one of their own. Maybe they recognise me? I think anyone who has dabbled in some sort of powerful hallucinogenic is never the same again. Their neurons slightly altered, or their mitochondria more connected to the universe.

I stop at a wooden footbridge, simply because the river it crosses is seductively slow-moving and I fancy playing Poohsticks. I haven't done this since I was a child. In fact, I've forgotten what a simple pleasure it is to drop an object from one side and then cross to the other to watch it sail away. Looking around for something suitable to float, I spy an advance guard of mushrooms on a tree stump. I show them my hands, as if signalling that I mean no harm, then pluck an acorn from the ground.

'Well, that's no good,' I say in disappointment, having dropped the acorn into the water and watched it promptly sink.

Next I try a fern, which seems to reach out to the bank for purchase and refuses to float away. Figuring I should perhaps play by the rules, I look around for a stick. I know I'm being lazy, but the easiest thing for me to do is just grab the end of an overhanging pine branch and select a twig. Being fresh and pliant, it takes a while to come away. As I twist it this way and that, I quickly regret not just picking a stick up from the ground. Finally my prize peels free. I drop it in, run to the rail downstream and cheer as it floats away.

'I win!' I say to the mushrooms, clenching my fists, only to see blood trickling from one hand.

I wash it in the ice-cold stream and see that it's only a tiny nick, which I must have done in wrestling with the pine. It is, I think, the tree's way of punishing me for not using a fallen twig. It's a lesson learned, and I figure I'm now two strikes away from being run out of the wilderness by all the capped little fellas on long stalks who witnessed the scene. I wash my hands in the river, and then press on feeling as if perhaps my claim of victory was a little premature. The mushrooms, I note, are bristling. *All right, big man? On yer way, Sam. Mess with nature at yer peril. We are ALL connected.*

* * *

Knives in Hens was one of the first significant theatrical parts I landed after graduating. Written by the respected Scottish playwright David Harrower, this spare, fierce and moving drama is a story about awakenings and empowerment between a ploughman and his wife, and a love triangle that threatens the nature of their existence. I was invited to play with TAG theatre in the role of Pony William, the imposing, adulterous husband, which was both a challenge and an irresistible opportunity. The play is one that you dream of. One that you feel and don't fully understand until later. It challenges the audience and digs into the human psyche, exposing the dark places. We opened at the Tron Theatre in Glasgow, only for the production to snowball into something far bigger than I could have anticipated. After the initial run, we took the show on the road for what would be an unforgettable experience for several reasons.

Acting gives the opportunity to explore dark places. *Knives in Hens* provided me with one of those roles. Pony William is a belligerent, bullying and bestial husband, abusing and repressing his wife, played by the lovely Rosalind Sydney. She seeks enlightenment and intellect, finding her saviour in the local miller – a man who treats her well. John Kazek played the miller. He is a brilliant stage actor and also happened to be my former drama school tutor's partner. We all got on well and enjoyed each other's company on the long drives around Scotland in this touring production. The miller encourages Pony's wife to think for herself, and inspires her towards artistic and creative thinking. Pony travels in the opposite direction, and fills with anger and distrust. He is eventually killed by the other two, crushed to death by the miller's stone.

In losing myself in Pony's character, I saw a chance to release the power and rage inside me. I was in my early twenties, and though tall and broad, I had found my place on the sidelines, playing nice guys or decent young men. Pony offered me the opportunity to open up in an imposing way. I knew I had learned to convey a sense of power and darkness and could bring the character alive for the audience. Rehearsals had gone well. I got on well with the director, Guy Hollands, and word was beginning to spread that this was a play worth watching. The writer had even brought in a group of TV and film producers to the opening night. They saw potential and I felt confident.

Shortly before that first performance, I went for a long run along the River Clyde in Glasgow. It was something I had begun to do as part of my preparation. I found it helped to clear my mind and relax me. On that occasion, aware that I faced a testing time, I perhaps pushed myself a little harder than usual. It meant I only got back to the theatre with half an hour to spare. I had just enough time to shower and get into costume. In terms of recovering from effectively pounding the pavements for 10 miles, I needed a lot longer.

Pony is a character hewn out of rock. He's solid. Immovable. Unyielding. On that opening night, however, the mix of adrenaline, sweat loss and fatigue meant that the muscles in my legs kept cramping, and I couldn't mask the agonising pain. I could feel the disappointment from the stalls. My leg was shaking; I couldn't stop the muscles trembling. It was an odd sensation, but the more I became aware of it, the less I could concentrate, and the performance suffered, horribly. I wanted to disappear. When the curtain finally came down, I swore I wouldn't act again. I was ashamed that I had let myself down, as well as the cast and crew who had worked so hard towards this moment.

Afterwards, in the bar, I was greeted with empty congratulations and false praise, and that scarred me deeply for some time.

Overnight, having dwelled on what had happened, I resolved that I could not allow this to defeat me. I needed to let the character I was playing lead the way.

The next night, Pony returned even more forcefully than he had in rehearsals. He was steadfast, and the show brought the audience to their feet. From that moment on, I swore to myself that I could never allow my personal life to undermine or disrupt my character on stage. If I went for a run or a workout before a performance, I would allow enough time to recover. Nothing could be permitted to spill over, I decided, though it wasn't long before I would find that put to the test.

We had brought the show to the Macrobert Arts Centre in Stirling, in the grounds of Stirling University, where some ten years later I would receive an honorary doctorate. Reviews had been really positive, and with every performance it felt as if we were building on a collective energy. I still felt quite new to the idea of being a professional actor, but I was enjoying the process immensely. Things were going well for me. I was earning just enough to get by – or at least to pay the rent – but it wasn't about money. I simply loved being on stage playing a character like Pony William. He wasn't me, but he allowed me to express emotions I would normally hold back or bury.

Then, midway through that run, I received a message out of nowhere. *I'm in the UK*, it said. *I'd like to come and see you.*

My dad wasn't just in the country. He was staying close by. So one hour before going on stage, I met the man who left my life before I had any real memory of him.

I had no idea in my mind about what my father might look like. What's more, any feelings I might have had about his sudden reappearance just didn't have time to solidify in my mind. So when this man with wild long hair appeared, wrapped up in a big Tibetan-style scarf and a fusty but familiar-smelling jacket, it felt like I was meeting an old acquaintance from a time so long ago that I'd lost all emotional connection.

With little time available to me before the performance, I suggested that we go for a walk. As we followed a path around the lake on the university grounds, the talk was small, polite and a little guarded, as it would be between two men who were effectively strangers. My brain was half on the experience, soaking up the thoughts and emotions, and half back in the stable with old Pony boy. It was only as we followed the path back to the university buildings that I noted something and almost stopped in my tracks.

We had exactly the same gait. From our easy stride to our pace, we walked in an identical manner. I have a specific walk, long legs and big feet. I'm not saying it's like a clown, or a giraffe exactly, but there's something loping, lumbering, galumphing and a little relaxed about it. His was the same, our legs and torsos operating in the same way. We moved over this planet with the same energy and direction.

It was uncanny, and didn't make me feel entirely at ease. For this was a clear connection, as anyone would expect between a father and son, and yet I didn't feel that bond between us.

My performance that night proved to be challenging. I was determined not to let the events of the day unsettle me, but it was hard to let go. I knew my dad was in the audience, and I couldn't disconnect from it. He'd also asked me to join him for supper afterwards at a local Indian restaurant. I didn't want to go – I was feeling overwhelmed and confused – but I found myself agreeing out of politeness. My father had appeared out of nowhere, someone who had played no part in most of my life, and I didn't know how to react.

'Sam,' he said over his curry as we steered through an awkward conversation, 'will you just relax?'

'I am relaxed. Don't I look relaxed?'

I wondered whether I should be forcing a relationship that wasn't there. As if to create some distance, I found myself thinking this encounter was just so weird that it might help to inform a future role. Like Hamlet . . . though wait, he was close to his father. It did feel like I was sitting opposite a ghost, however. Quite simply, the only way I could process the situation was to take a step back and consider him like a character I might play or encounter. It was hard to know how else to relate to him, because it demanded an intimacy that required all the time he'd been absent. 'I'll try my best to open up,' I added all the same.

I don't let people into my life with ease. Trust is something that takes time for me to establish. I have very few super-close friends. No doubt some of this can be traced back to the fact that my dad just disappeared when I was very young, though I'm not using that as an excuse. I've just learned to enjoy my own company. I crave it. I am somewhat guarded as a result, and that is perhaps why I am drawn to acting. On stage, I need to be the opposite of something that has become second nature to me. As an actor, I've learned to drop those protective layers and let go, and that's when I come alive. Much to my surprise and delight, I find a long trek in the wilderness allows me to do the same thing.

* * *

I am surrounded by the Crianlarich mountains. East of Loch Lomond and south of Strath Fillan, with Ben More being the highest peak, at 1,174 metres. This afternoon, I can confidently say that I am deep in the Scottish wilderness. My path skirts a broad ribbon of water in what is known as a strath, or river valley – hence the Strath of Fillan. But who is Fillan? I wonder. Who am I? I'm nobody out here, and that's exactly what I want to be.

Normally, with my hood up and head down, I'd miss out on details I now find fascinating. The mushrooms have kept me entertained all day, but it isn't just the sights like this, nor the sound of birds taking flight or water tumbling over rock. The scent of pine and wet soil is so rich I can't ignore it, but above all it's the sense of history that captures my attention. This area is magical, and it does feel like I'm entering a very special land as I cross over the water, leaving the forest behind. A sign on the bridge makes me chuckle: *Tyndrum Massage – call or txt Ang*, and the number below. 'Ah Ang, gie's the full body an dinnae hold back on the coconut oil!'

As my path crosses farmland, I pass stone ruins that stop me in my tracks. A small information plaque reveals that this is the site of St Fillan's Priory, which was endowed by Robert the Bruce. I learn that some of the graves, timeworn and clad in moss, date back to the 8th century. I wonder what life they have witnessed passing by, and silently pay my respects to the dead. In the background, the magnificent mountain of Ben More looms large. Though I'm not religious, it's moments like this when I can appreciate a certain spirituality. I finish reading the plaque, which tells me that in the 1870s, another graveyard was established on higher ground. I look across at the foothills, struck by the air of peace and solemnity I have found here.

Just then, submerged in the landscape along with the mythology and wonder of its history, I realize I am doing something I had to learn to do on stage. I have lost myself to the moment. Not in character. As me.

* * *

At the time, moving to London seemed like the right thing to do. It was a rite of passage that so many young British actors felt they had to go through in order to be at the centre of things. The bigger acting agencies were there, plus most of the work was generated out of the capital's West End. It's no longer necessary to be in the big cities, as most of the auditioning is done online now, but back then, being 'in the room' was so important.

During *Outlying Islands*, I had been lucky enough to pick up a new agent. The wonderful Ruth Young, who still represents me, has been a terrific guide, insightful and caring, and I am so thankful that she took the risk. Ruth was true to her word and put me forward for all the right auditions. I was still learning how to perform for the casting director, but with the upswing in opportunities, I found myself improving and learning about the industry fast.

For all the excitement of prospective acting roles, the reality of living in London on a jobbing actor's income quickly began to bite. Unless I landed a role, I had no money. I was living with a bunch of struggling young actors in Golders Green, in the north of the capital. We survived on late-night bagels and cheap Polish beer. Like the others, I needed to support myself financially by taking on casual, and then full-time work. I knew I had to remain available for auditions, and also use any spare time to research and immerse myself in the theatre scene in London, watching as many plays as I could (and hanging out in theatre bars afterwards).

Within a short space of time, I found myself holding down multiple jobs. I worked behind bars, delivered sandwiches by bicycle (in the height of winter!), found myself placed in charge of the entire NHS doctors' rota in south London, worked as a receptionist at a mental health treatment hospital, and even found myself selling perfume, and then Vivienne Westwood clothing at Harrods. In some ways I was playing roles, and I told myself they could come in useful to me as an actor one day. Most of my free time was spent in pursuit of acting opportunities. That meant travelling around town to auditions by bus or train, something that proved expensive, so my bicycle was put to good use.

In London, I joined the legion of young hopefuls who dreamed of a big break while living on the breadline. That ambition became a valuable asset, because as time wore on, it stopped me from just giving up in despair. By now, in my mid-twenties, I had friends who held down proper jobs, with salaries and a sense of security, and yet there I was in my shared accommodation, counting pennies to pay the bills. When I did land roles, they were often one-off gigs for commercials or low-key parts. According to Stanislavski, the great Russian theatre practitioner, 'There are no small parts, only small actors.' That's true, Stan, but the small parts don't pay the rent! I would see some income, but it just served to keep my head above water, and that became a way of life.

Despite the fact that money was tight, I had some great times with my friends, a small group of Scottish actors, who all arrived off the train and settled in north London at the same time. We had shared our time at drama school together and now shared any knowledge or experience with the group. If a friend was in a play, we would all go see it, then sit around with some beers, discussing and dissecting the performance. Living this life could be fun and exciting. We frequented the Groucho Club (a notorious late-night members' bar) and had our friend bring us backstage to the actors' bar in the catacombs of the National Theatre. We rubbed shoulders with the more successful actors and casting directors and hoped that six degrees of separation might help. I had a relationship with a smart and ambitious production assistant at Working Title Films. We lasted a while until we moved in together. A week later, we realized we were so not compatible in any way.

Each day was exciting, not knowing when the next opportunity would arise. I lived in hope, daydreaming as I pedalled the city streets or was rocked to sleep by the Northern Line train. It was also mundane at times, and stressful when it came to cash. One time, things got so tight that the bailiffs knocked on my door. I was out at the time, and my housemates (brothers Matt and Luke Neal, both ginger and over six foot; we looked like triplets when standing together!) refused to let them in. Even if they had invited them in to pick over my belongings, they wouldn't have found much of any value. Frankly, I was skint and somewhat desperate. So, when I landed a part in a soap opera back in Scotland, I seized the opportunity. Even if I had never pictured myself as an actor in a daytime television drama, that had to be more rewarding than flattering customers about the cut of a dress or misting the air with a perfume they didn't need.

* * *

In the closing miles of the third day, with daylight on my side and time in hand to pause and ponder whatever grabs my attention, I pass the Holy Pool, separated into two sections: Pul nan Bain and Pul nan Fear – the pool of the women and the pool of the men. Tradition has it that the waters are imbued with St Fillan's miraculous powers, which can treat mental illness and other ailments. The fast-moving water slows almost to a standstill here, with fresh fallen leaves dotting the surface. As I take a moment, time stands still and I can feel the energy of the water washing over me. I'm tempted to jump in, but the thought of an evening beer and a large portion of fish and chips next to a fire is also reviving. Later, further down the path, I come across a hut painted in bright colours. It's fronted by a little sign, which reads: *If I could dance with my father again.* All of a sudden, I feel very sad. We all know how heartache feels. It's upsetting. Coming to terms with the loss of a loved one is a journey, I think, and often one without end. As I leave the hut behind, I hope that person isn't in too much pain. Eventually, I suppose, we will all be together again. I always feel I carry something. I'm not sure what that ache is, but it's there. A well to draw upon.

Sometimes I think of myself as a loner by design. Perhaps I just like my own company. It's certainly manageable. Or maybe, if I don't forge those meaningful connections, I can't be hurt, right? I know that's not the answer, but it's how I'm wired in some ways. I've always had an awareness that I hold back. It's only now, looking back with all the time in the world to make sense of it, that I start to wonder if this walk might be a turning point in my life. In order to be our best selves, we have to learn and grow, right? Though it may take more than 100 miles to change my habits, it's certainly a start. As I wander on, reflecting on how I've arrived here, I think that perhaps in future I should embrace the outlook I'm uncovering with each step. Today, I haven't even thought about what lies beyond the next rise, or whether I should pick up the pace in case I lose the light. In short, I haven't worried about what is ahead. I've just enjoyed the present, no matter what the future holds, and I like it as a way of living.

This day has been enchanting, and I thank the Irish hermit for safe passage (and the good farmer who has allowed wanderers like me to cross his land). As my walk stretches into the afternoon, the river serves as a returning companion. Sometimes the path leads me up into woodland, only to drop back down to the reassuring sight of the waterway glistening under a low November sun. I feel like I've had time to start setting my world to rights. Before setting off, there was no way I could've pictured myself ambling along with no wish to set a land-speed record. It just isn't me. At least that was how I saw myself until the elements beat me to a pulp and forced me to question what really matters here. I know I don't have far to go before reaching Tyndrum, but rather than counting down the miles, I half wish this day would stretch on for ever. I'm weary, but that's no surprise after yesterday's endurance effort. It's all the more reason to just drift along and immerse myself in a landscape steeped in history.

Lochan is a Scottish term for a little loch. I wouldn't dare describe them as ponds, or even small lakes. They are what they are. I come across one on my walk, just outside the village of Tyndrum, though I question if it's big enough to be a lochan. This pool, I feel, has some size issues, though it's the quality of the legend it contains that makes it notable. For this is the Lochan of the Lost Sword, which is said to be the final resting place for Robert the Bruce's legendary weapon. We're not just talking about any old sword. By all accounts, Robert wielded one that was upwards of 9 feet in length. The guy was either a giant or superhuman in strength, and that one fact earns my full respect. According to the story, this is where he stopped with his men while attempting to evade the English. Keen to pick up the pace to outrun them, he threw his weapon into the lochan and encouraged his men to do likewise.

Yet some men say in many parts of England that King Arthur is not dead, but had by the will of our Lord Jesu into another place; and men say that he shall come again, and he shall win the holy cross. I will not say it shall be so, but rather I will say: here in this world he changed his life. (*Le Morte d'Arthur,* Thomas Malory)

As a boy, I was obsessed with Robert the Bruce. Known as the King of the Scots, and responsible for wrenching independence from England in the early 14th century, he was a hero in my eyes. In the shadow of those castle ruins where I grew up, I would stand with a stick held aloft and yell, 'Rally to me, Scots!' Right now, I'd love to roll my sleeve up, fish around in the murk and clasp that sword of destiny. I can only imagine the headlines I would make if I returned from the wilderness to claim my right to the throne.

I stand at the edge of the water and attempt to focus on the bottom. The lochan is quite murky. It's almost a bog, in fact. I dare say many, many walkers before me have dropped down to prod about under the water. I imagine closing my fingers around the handle and then raising it from the surface; with both hands if it's as hefty as they say. Wouldn't that be amazing? Then those mushrooms watching me right now would have to bow their caps and recognize me as their king. I could command them to follow me, in fact. Together we would face down anyone who dared to suggest that an actor and his fungi forces could not lay claim to the throne.

'What do you say, boys?' I ask, addressing the mushroom clusters over my shoulder. 'Who is with me?'

Their silence speaks volumes. With a sigh of resignation, I rise back to my feet. Then I chuckle to myself, pick up a stone, smooth and flat, and skim it hard across the water.

Listen – strange women lying in ponds distributing swords is no basis for a system of government. Supreme executive power derives from a mandate from the masses, not from some farcical aquatic ceremony. (*Monty Python and the Holy Grail*)

I love how Scottish legends like this have become entwined with Arthurian myth. Whether it's a sword in a lochan or stuck in a stone, these are powerful narratives that entranced me as a boy. During those formative years when my mother took me to the Lyceum Theatre in Edinburgh, *Merlin* became my favourite production. With so many intricate allegiances between Arthur, Guinevere and Lancelot, there are big emotions at play. I loved it so much. As a young actor in the early nineties, it meant I was particularly fired up on being asked to audition for *Camelot*, the King Arthur TV show. After auditioning several times, I was called back for the final round. Ruth assured me, 'Darling, they love you, just go in and be you, it's your part.' Fatal words. I walked into the audition room and there, sitting on a wooden chair as if it was the throne of England, was a beautiful-looking boy, adorned with chains and jewellery and looking way cooler than I ever could. This was Jamie Campbell Bower, who was later cast as Arthur, King of the Britons. In my eyes, he literally looked like a knight who had time-travelled his way to a TV studio.

Arthur is such an iconic role. I still want to play him one day. I love the film *Excalibur*, with its stellar cast: Patrick Stewart, Helen Mirren, Ciarán Hinds, Gabriel Byrne and even Charley Boorman, Ewan McGregor's motorcycle-loving partner in crime. I'd be keen to do a remake. I once enquired about the rights to the Merlin play I had seen as a youngster. Somehow, wires got badly crossed along the way, and I found myself presented with the option to take on a children's show called *Merlin the Magnificent*. Maybe old Arthur is destined to evade me, much like Robert's fabled sword in the lochan I now leave behind. If I'm not going to become the undisputed King of Scotland, I should head into Tyndrum and retire to my hotel for the night. Compared to a night under canvas at this time of year, I imagine it will feel like a palace.

THE HARD ROAD

Holding down cash-in-hand jobs in London, while hoping a casting director might look favourably upon me, I slipped into dire straits. I was in no doubt that I wanted to be an actor. I just found myself dependent on other people, as well as an element of luck, to make it a success.

It meant when an offer came my way, from promotions to commercials and low-key parts, I would take it without much question. I needed the money, as well as the experience. I wasn't in a position to choose from multiple offers. That kind of thing just didn't happen to me. So, in 2005 when I landed a role in a Scottish soap opera called *River City*, I saw it as a chance to earn a regular income for a while doing something that I loved. I would miss my good friends, but it was just something I had to do. It also meant moving back to Glasgow once again, and the start of my itinerant existence living out of a suitcase.

In *River City*, I played a football ace called Andrew Murray. I'll be frank here: I am terrible with a ball. I was the kind of kid at school who'd be picked last for a team, and suddenly there I was playing the role of the Scottish Premier League's golden boy. I saw it as a challenge I was willing to embrace, and it proved to be the first of many in my bid to become an established actor.

Filming on the set of a soap opera is very different from being on stage. I still felt new to television. Without an audience, I had a lot to learn about where to direct my performance. In a content-hungry show like *River City*, with a fast production turnover, we would shoot more than 20 pages a day, from 4 different episodes. What's more, rather than stopping to reposition the camera, each scene would be filmed consecutively from several angles. From an acting perspective, with cameras in front of me and over my shoulder, it gave me a lot to consider. The part of my brain that didn't submit to the moment had to work overtime. It was tough and demanding, and a steep learning curve. I enjoyed the ride. Financially, the wolves retreated from my door. It wasn't huge riches, but it meant I could pay the rent and put food on my table, and that felt priceless in terms of peace of mind.

After a year, despite the regular income from *River City*, and the opportunity to continue, I decided that it was time to move on. I needed to get back to my roots, seek inspiration elsewhere and play new, challenging characters. I found myself following the work, and landed the role of Dickie Greenleaf in a daring production of *The Talented Mr Ripley* directed by Raz Shaw. I loved the creativity and physicality of the play, which we performed in Northampton.

I also took on small roles in TV shows, including *Midsomer Murders* and *Rebus*, before gravitating slowly south back to London.

I learned to live out of a suitcase, staying in hotels for a few days or weeks, or even occupying the spare rooms and sofas of generous friends, before moving on once more. Even if I had wanted to set down roots, it would've been impossible. How do you create foundations when you're constantly moving on? As an actor, it didn't feel like a sacrifice. It was just part of the profession. Thanks to my time on a soap opera, having previously struggled to get credit due to my debts, I finally qualified for a credit card with a £100 limit. I was over the moon. It wasn't about finances but the fact that I was making progress as an actor. So rather than build a home, I found myself focusing on what came next.

Over a couple of years, that quickly became a way of life. I was always on the move; forever searching for the next peak to conquer. I also learned to love it. Every time I arrived in a new town or city, or even on location for a shoot, I would feel like an explorer. I avoided buying things that might otherwise tie me down. I needed to be able to transport everything I owned, much like a circus performer. I wasn't alone in living like this. I made great friends with other actors and theatre crew staff, and continued to keep my eyes on the horizon. One rucksack and a bicycle. That was all I needed.

In 2009, I travelled to Birmingham to work on a daytime TV drama called *Doctors*. I played Scott Neilson, a love interest for one of the nurses. On the surface he's a nice guy, only to be leading a secret life as a drug dealer. It was fun to be someone with an immoral side.

Sophie, my co-star, was a total pro. Extremely fun and easy to work with. We had a chemistry and I enjoyed working on set with her and the whole cast. When poor Scott finally died of a heroin overdose, I left the show hoping I would be recognized as an actor who was comfortable portraying dark, conflicted characters.

* * *

At the end of the third day, I was looking forward to checking into a bustling hotel where I could become just another guest. There are times when all of us would prefer to go unnoticed. On finishing this third long day on my feet, I just wanted to rest and relax without feeling the need to speak or socialize. It can be a performance in some ways, and I had set out on the West Highland Way as a break from exactly that.

Tyndrum is a small rural village on the southern fringe of Rannoch Moor, but the Muthu Ben Doran Hotel is massive. It's a reflection of just how popular the surrounding wilderness has become. I can understand the draw. Being in the heart of the glens is a liberating experience. It's a chance to think and breathe and remind ourselves that the natural world is a precious commodity. Checking into the hotel, I was mindful that like so many beautiful parts of the world, the Highlands could become a victim of its own success as a tourist attraction.

Shortly afterwards, as I settled into an all but empty dining room for supper, it occurred to me that the more challenging Scottish seasons should serve to keep the numbers in check.

I only had to look around to register this for myself. There were enough tables in this pleasant and luxurious space to cater for over a hundred guests. I had no doubt that it would be fully booked during the summer, and clearly capable of navigating such contrasting seasons. On a chilly night in early November, however, just two other guests were present.

'I'm on business at the gold mine,' one of the other diners told me when we struck up conversation.

'Gold? In these hills?' I asked. 'I had no idea.'

'What was that?' my dining partner asked, cupping his hand to his ear, numerous gold rings on each finger.

'You said THERE'S GOLD? HERE?' I replied, hoping I wasn't about to start a rush to equal the American one.

Neither of us left our seat to talk. We just addressed each other from opposite sides of the room. It was unusual, but as the prospector offered me a brief history of Highlands mining, I noted that both the third guest and the guy behind the bar were listening with interest. According to our new friend, a seam runs through the rocks from here to Ireland. It was fascinating, and I went to bed after an amazing Thai curry having enjoyed good company from the solitude of our respective tables. In these times, however, it doesn't seem so odd. In fact, it's become quite normal to communicate from a distance.

* * *

In any profession that relies on opportunity, it's easy to let self-doubt creep in. Several years had passed since I'd left drama school, and though my acting CV was growing, I sometimes felt like my big break had eluded me. I was grateful for the parts I had played, and had learned so much from the experience. As time ticked by, however, and I continued living hand to mouth in London, juggling casual work with audition calls, I began to wonder if I was letting myself down in some way. Part-time work was fun at times, but unrewarding. My peers were slowly peeling off, finding other professions or getting married and settling down. But I stayed resilient. Or perhaps stubborn and single-minded.

For any actor, appearance is an important part of the profile. You might be a natural in front of the camera, but that doesn't count for much if you look wrong for the role. For every audition I attended, I was increasingly aware that my looks could be an influential factor. I was a twenty-something male with a physical presence. As a result, I aimed to make sure that I hit the right marks in terms of expectation.

I started taking my running more seriously, and found that I enjoyed it. It kept me in good shape and I liked how it left me feeling. I only had to lace up my trainers and hit the pavements and parks for 10 miles to return with a revitalized sense of well-being. I also started to work out with some borrowed weights. I even worked as a lifeguard, though I was completely unqualified. I was essentially required to fold towels and check the pH level of the jacuzzi, but I still felt nervous each day and quickly handed in my notice, despite the free gym access that went with the job. I've always been an active kind of person, even if I'm not one for playing team sports. I like to push myself, and can be highly competitive, but it has to be on my own terms. I don't like feeling as if

I might let people down, and by extension I'm reluctant to put my heart and soul into something and then find myself disappointed by others. Running carried no such risk. I was accountable only to myself. It also kept me looking lean. I was careful with my diet, but now began to understand the necessity to eat more to allow my body to thrive. I paid attention to calorie intake, and considered every meal in terms of what it might mean for my chances of getting work.

In hindsight, when I consider that time in my life, I recognize that I was living for a while with a low-level eating disorder. The requirement for an actor to look a certain way has driven me too far at times. I love training, but in my early years that led to a bad relationship with food. I rationed what I ate, often consuming just salad and pickles knowing they were low in calories. I certainly wasn't taking on enough fuel for all the running I was doing, let alone for a long day on set.

We often talk about the pressure on women to conform. I certainly felt that expectation upon me, which is why I responded by maintaining a disciplined eating and exercise regime. It was a form of control as I tried to make my way in an industry in which actors are pretty much powerless when it comes to securing work. I just felt like I had to do everything I could in order to make myself selectable for a role. The right clothes, hair colour, accent, etc. They were all things I tried to adapt or change, as the audition required. It wasn't healthy. Nor did it make me particularly happy. It just seemed like one more sacrifice I had to make in pursuit of my dream.

It was only when I set out to become more muscular that I began to think of food in terms of nutrition. It forced me to start researching health and fitness, and that's when I recognized that the body needs a healthy, balanced diet to survive and grow. It was a vital lesson, and even now I sometimes have to remind myself that there can be no compromise.

I still run today, mostly because it does wonders for my head. My work means I've been lucky enough to explore some wonderful parts of the world, from the Hollywood Hills to trails in South America, Hawaii, New Zealand and South Africa. It was indeed a jog with a crew member during a break in filming *Outlander* that led to this walk. Without doubt, it's one of those pursuits that will stay with me for life. When I'm running, I become invisible. Nobody pays me any attention, or at least if I hear someone shout my name then I pretend not to hear them. It's my time and space. Above all, each run is a journey.

In life, it seems to me, I am most at home when I'm on the move.

* * *

At first light the next morning . . . well, I would like to say that I am on the path, ready to explore the next stage of my journey. In truth, I'm still in bed. It's just so comfortable, and with my new, laid-back schedule I have loads of time. Also, after three days of hiking, even at a sedate pace, my body is aching. Normally I'm driven by a work schedule. If I'm not filming, I might be involved in pre- or post-production, or trying to squeeze in a workout between promotional commitments. My diary is full for months at a time, and I love it. Having experienced times of great uncertainty, I've never once taken it for granted. But now that I have a rare week to myself, I'm surprised at just how content I am to go with the flow. 'Another slice of toast? Sure!'

When I finally check out, I have a port of call in mind that's no more than a mile down the road. Yes, I plan to pop into a service station, but this is no drab roadside franchise. It's a delight for weary travellers that shines out like a beacon. The Green Welly Stop at Tyndrum has been in existence for more than 50 years. It's the pride and joy of the village, and popular with bikers. I love to ride, and have headed out this way when filming *Outlander* 30 miles up the road on location around Glencoe. Astride my Harley Davidson, making a racket thanks to the Vance and Hines pipes, I'm the hellraiser who disturbs the hillwalkers as I cruise into the car park. On this occasion, I've transformed into the character who makes a low-key entrance and smiles politely at the lady in the apron who welcomes me. There's no need for me to grab a bite and go today. I'm in no rush to be somewhere.

The Green Welly isn't just a stop-off for travellers to freshen up or pick up snacks for the road. After what can only be an epic, long and winding drive from either direction, the staff and atmosphere in the shop and restaurant make it hard for anyone to leave in a hurry. It's just a really nice place to take a break from a journey, with home-cooked meals on offer and shelves stocked with quality products from food and drink to outdoor clothing. I'm a particular fan of their whisky collection, though I focus on choosing provisions for a decent packed lunch.

Just before I take all the goodies I plan to eat to the till, I can't resist an impulse buy. In no mood to be in any discomfort on my walk, I add a pair of hiking socks to my basket and also throw in a pair of boxer shorts. These are hardly essential, but they're made by my favourite Scottish-based underwear company, Bawbags, and I like the pattern; a Scottish football design. I decide to wear them on the last leg of the journey, Ben Nevis, if I ever get there.

Having settled up for the sandwiches, crisps, socks and pants, and exchanged a pleasant conversation about the clement weather, I prepare to properly begin my day. There are no bikers here at this hour, and very few camper vans, which often pitch in the car park overnight. This is without doubt a quiet time of year, and perfect for my needs.

I have just 9 miles to cover today. I'm in no hurry! I cross the road and rely on my sense of direction to rejoin the West Highland Way. I want this to be a relaxed day, because I've come to really enjoy the new-found pace of my journey. The last time I passed through here, I didn't even have time to stop. I was rushing back from a shoot as I had a plane to catch later that day. From here, it took me 90 minutes at full throttle to get home. It makes me realize that over the last three days, I haven't just walked a long way. Travelling some 60 miles on foot has also opened my eyes to my surroundings. Yes, there is a time and a place to focus on the tarmac and the speedometer on my handlebars. It's just not as rewarding for the soul, as I come to appreciate over the next half an hour as I follow a path around woodland and look out for signs for the West Highland Way. I really do like this new outlook, even when the path drops away over rough ground to reveal the back of a roadside building that looks strangely familiar.

'Ah crap,' I say to myself, halting in my tracks as it dawns on me that somehow I've come full circle to find myself facing The Green Welly once more. Normally I'd curse myself for wasting time. Today, though, I realize where I've gone wrong and quickly make it right. 'Ach well, don't suppose it matters. I've got plenty of time.'

* * *

'How do you feel about riding horses?'

The question came in the closing moments of the audition. I had just performed for a casting panel. I felt it had gone well. I was pleased with my delivery, and if I could read faces correctly, it looked like I was in with a good chance. I was trying out for the leading role in a movie that felt like it might be the break I had been waiting for. Now I found myself drawn back to the spotlight by a question I hadn't expected.

'I *love* riding horses,' I lied. 'I grew up on a farm, in fact. Practically born in the saddle.'

Part of my response was true, in that some of the land around the stable conversion was arable. As for my equine passion, I felt sure I could fall in love with it under the right circumstances. My only notable experience at the time had not been a pleasant one. A few years earlier, I'd had a small role in a TV miniseries about Billy the Kid, playing John Tunstall (and sporting my very first self-grown tash). I was OK clipping around on horseback, but in one scene I had to gallop off while a posse gave chase and then lose them down a ravine path. This was fine by me when I read the script. It was just nobody warned me that my horse wasn't used to gunshots. So when the cameras rolled and the posse fired blanks into the air, she bolted hard. I was pretty much just a passenger in the uncontrolled descent that followed, and simply clung on for dear life. I was shaking when the horse finally came to a halt, only for the director to say: 'Thanks, Sam, could we do it again, but maybe faster?' as he hadn't quite got the shot he'd wanted. I was close to refusing, but my need to please was stronger than my sense of self-preservation, and we went for it one more time.

In the same way, when it seemed that an audition for a big role in a movie might come down to my ability on horseback, I told the casting panel the answer they wanted to hear.

Young Alexander the Great was one of the first movies I'd make. It was a bit of a car-crash in production and I'm thankful it never made it to the big screen. Or any screen. Despite the challenges, of which there were many – wearing a thong while horse riding bareback (painful), the intense heat; the cast and crew suffering from a constant stomach bug (I lost so much weight); language barriers… – we had a terrific time on set and made firm friends with the cast and crew. It was just one of those films with big ambitions and great intentions, a shoestring budget and compromises that were hard to cover up.

My claim that I was competent with horses didn't help matters. We shot the film in Egypt, in and around the capital, Cairo. It was an incredible experience, with hundreds of extras in key scenes. I just hadn't banked on the fact that in playing young Alexander himself, I would be expected to ride not just any old dobbin, but an enormous, powerful stallion. This thing was a beast. There was no way I could admit that I wasn't as capable with the reins as I had made out. I just climbed into the saddle and hoped for the best. In one scene, my character leads a charge into the sunset. I dug in my heels, which was about the extent of my horsemanship, and the stallion duly broke into an epic gallop. It looked great for the camera. It was just that I had no clue how to stop the damn thing once I'd ridden out of shot. Quite literally, that stallion took off across the desert in a cloud of sand.

'Cut!' yelled the director, but it made no difference. My horse was on a mission, and when it finally slowed and turned around, I just had to pretend that I hadn't heard.

As the shoot progressed, I came to realize that the casting director had asked me the wrong question. Apart from a few key scenes riding a stallion with a mind of its own, I spent more time in a saddle rigged to the roof of a local taxi. While it might have saved money, and made close-ups easier to shoot, I felt utterly ridiculous. I was meant to be on a camel, but that was hard to summon in my mind when my ride was belching exhaust fumes. I'd stare meaningfully into the distance, and with a shake of the reins the driver would take his cue to shift into gear. Even if I had been able to ride convincingly, all my powers of acting could not distract from the fact that I was strapped to the top of a clapped-out cab.

Regardless of the finished movie, my memories of that production never fail to make me smile. I look back on it and recognize that every milestone is important in life. The rewards might be unexpected, while the experience can only make us wiser and better prepared. On my return home from Egypt, I vowed that the time had come for me to learn how to ride a horse properly. My big break hadn't materialized as I had hoped, but if I was ever asked to climb into the saddle for the camera again, I intended to be prepared.

* * *

The signpost for the West Highland Way appears to me like a patient and loyal guide. I have lost count of how many I have passed on my walk, but it's always reassuring to see them. I am on my way to Bridge of Orchy, following the train line to the left. The large Munro Beinn Dòrain stands proud in the valley, its steep cliffs sloping down to Loch Tulla in the distance. A small cloud catches its top, but the day is clear and crisp, the sky blue. It will come as no surprise to any visitor to learn that this small Highlands village is named after the river crossing. The bridge was built by the British army in the 1700s after the Battle of Culloden. Having defeated Charles Stuart's Jacobites, and his bid to regain the throne for his father, the army attempted to bring order to the country by building transport networks across what was considered challenging and often impassable terrain.

I have no such difficulties this morning. The path leads me away from the road and then into forest. Here, the breeze snatches lichen and throws it into the air. Catching the sunlight, it reminds me of tumbling snowflakes. It's colder under tree cover, which reminds me that just because it's clear and bright we're in November now. I can see my breath and wonder if a baseball cap, long sleeved base layer and windcheater is going to keep me warm. As Tyndrum becomes one more memory on my journey, it feels like I've walked through the wardrobe and entered a different land. Once again, massing among the beds of fallen pine needles, I find mushrooms scoping me out. This time, I feel no sense of hostility in their stance. Perhaps they are coming to accept my presence in their kingdom, I think to myself, as the path breaks from the forest onto open ground. We might be learning to trust each other, but clearly there is still some work to be done until we rise up as one.

* * *

Following the release of *Young Alexander the Great* in 2010, I began auditioning for roles in bigger television and film productions. Things seemed promising on paper, and yet the years that followed were filled with rejections. To make things harder to handle, sometimes I would find myself recalled. This is the acting equivalent of a second interview. I would try not to get excited, but that could be challenging when some of the projects had the potential to be career-making. As well as chasing casting calls around London, I started flying out to Los Angeles, or more accurately – and to my great excitement – they started flying me.

My first visit to LA was to test for a big-budget television show in the making. Naturally I was excited. It felt significant, as if perhaps I might be going places at last. My last visit to the USA had been while travelling before drama school. Back then, I'd toured the country on a shoestring. Now, the cost of my flight had been covered by the TV company. If I was being honest with myself, however, this was hardly the definition of success. I was still working dead-end jobs because I'd yet to get the work I really wanted to pursue. I had enjoyed the journey so far, but time was ticking. I was in my early thirties and serving drinks from behind a bar. So, having arrived in the City of Angels, I was determined to make the most of my short stay.

With a few hours spare before the audition, I rode the subway to Hollywood Boulevard. People in LA don't realize what a terrific line it is. It might not go far, but if you're going to a game at the Staples Center, you can have a drink and then jump on the fast and efficient tube back up to Hollywood. Hollywood!? It was one of those iconic places in cinema history that I really wanted to visit. I took the escalator up to street level with the kind of excitement and trepidation an astronaut might feel preparing for the spaceship hatch to open on another planet. I was really looking forward to seeing the Walk of Fame and spotting names among the stars dedicated to actors I idolized. As the escalator delivered me into the Californian sun, the sound of my Nokia mobile phone ringing dragged me from my daydreams.

'Sam, you're late.' The sound of glasses chinking and a low hubbub of laughter broke through the noise of Californian traffic. It took a moment to register that the voice belonged to my boss back at the bar in London. 'Your shift started 20 minutes ago. How long are you going to be, mate?'

'Ah . . . what?' I stopped in my tracks and winced. In all the excitement of being called out here, I had completely forgotten to book time off work. 'I'm so sorry. It completely slipped my mind.'

'How quickly can you get here?' asked my boss.

'I could be a while,' I said, and then hesitated. 'I'm in Hollywood.'

The phone went silent. Spiderman approached me from outside the Chinese Theatre: 'Five dollars for a photo with Spidey, bro!?'

* * *

Where the ground is soft underfoot, it's imprinted with tread marks from mountain bikes and walking boots. I swear I can identify the prints left by my companion from the second day of my journey. Graeme always walked on the left-hand side of the path, and the trail I'm following doesn't deviate from that line. There he goes! It has to be him; marching towards Bridge of Orchy with such purpose. Having been reluctant to fall in with anyone, I still feel like he's with me when I spot those boot prints. They look fresh. He's close, I'm sure of it.

The waterway crossing that gives its name to Bridge of Orchy also forms part of the West Highland Way. It's a low stone-walled construction that spans a broad but shallow and fast-moving river. Without any historical context, it's just an old bridge. Knowing it represents a pivotal moment in Scottish history persuades me to just stop and reflect on a feat of engineering we take for granted nowadays.

I have come further than planned today. When I set out this morning, I intended to stop in the village for the night. I have a hotel room booked and paid for, but I'm going to press on. I'm not feeling driven to smash through the miles. I'm just really enjoying being on my feet. It's early afternoon, and while I regret my late start now, I've decided I can combine two days into one. I am mildly confident I'll reach my next destination before I have to break out my head torch. I am still rebuilding my relationship with my rucksack. We're on speaking terms again, at least. I also have food and water to see me through. As long as I don't find the path blocked by dandy mushroom highwaymen, I feel I can extend my day from 9 to 19 miles. Fuelled by a solid breakfast and a lucky pair of pants in my rucksack, nothing can stop me. 'Let's go!'

* * *

With a big-time audition that had taken me out of my bedsit and across the Atlantic, it was impossible not to get my hopes up. Even though I knew the competition to play an iconic superhero like Aquaman would be intense, I was disappointed to head home having missed out on the role. The audition had been very strange. Three other blonde, buff kids sat in the waiting room. We each took turns to throw down some push-ups, then one by one were picked off and paraded in front of a large audience of suits. It felt like everyone from the network was there: casting, execs, lawyers, maybe even the kitchen staff. The press-ups were intended to get us looking pumped. More immediately, they left me sweaty. I just can't handle the heat. Literally. California has seen me soak through many a shirt, awaiting an audition. That's why I settle for black in most situations: hides a multitude of sins. I began to pick up further calls that brought me back to LA over the months and years that followed. While I learned to be realistic about my chances of success among so many actors in my situation, I never gave up on the dream.

Everyone knows that image is everything in Hollywood. As I spent more time auditioning stateside, I came to realize that I had to play the game according to LA rules. In the UK, I relied on the tireless work of my agent. Ruth's faith in me was incredible, and gave me such strength. In America, I realized that actors also had managers. Their role was slightly different, I learned on teaming up with one. While an agent got an actor in front of a casting director, a manager focused on their public profile with a view to earning attention from all the right people. Once I recognized that this was a means of making the most of my time in LA, I found myself being advised on what to wear, and where to eat and be seen around town. It was completely new to me, and kind of weird, but I considered it to be part of the process. Having come this far, and with so little to lose, I could afford no half-measures in terms of the image I projected. I soon looked like I was going places, but secretly I did so by public transport. With what little money I had from my bar work in London, any time I spent in LA would see me travelling around by bus or Metro. It was all I could afford, but not something I could share with the movers and shakers. That upper echelon of the Hollywood industry isn't for me. I just can't buy into the indulgence, but I do love the healthy lifestyle and the sunshine.

'I'm here for the casting,' I once said at the reception desk for Paramount studios (my favourite to visit – good air con and lavatories to change in), where I was due to audition. I was wearing a crisp white

T-shirt (fatal mistake), which I had just slipped on in an alleyway, having learned from experience that riding the bus quickly turned me into a sweaty mess.

'Mr Heughan?' the receptionist said to confirm. 'Would you like me to validate your ticket for the car park?'

'Oh, I'm good,' I said in my best British accent (the Americans love it). 'Thanks all the same. Cheers. I caught the bus.' The receptionist looked shocked and slightly confused. 'You did WHAT?!'

At a time when I was shuttling between friends' sofas and short-term rentals in London, I received an invitation to audition for the movie *Tron: Legacy*, with a blockbuster budget. The initial audition in London went surprisingly well. As a result, the studio wanted to fly me out. They laid on first-class flights and a stay in the kind of hotel I could never have afforded from my own pocket, up near Universal studios. It was exciting, but I had been quite ill with flu in the week preceding the trip. I didn't feel like a million dollars as I packed my suitcase. I felt like crap, in fact. When the purr of an engine pulling up in the street outside my bedsit drew me to the window, I looked out to see a top-end Mercedes. I was living in a rough part of north London. Even the drug dealers next door were probably hanging out of their window, checking out my sweet ride. Or they would have been if it wasn't so darn early! In a way, it felt like Hollywood had come all the way out to this dump to collect me. All I could do was jump in and hope a restorative sleep on the plane would help me to live up to expectations.

It didn't.

Anyone at the tail end of a flu bout looks absolutely terrible. Whenever I caught a glimpse of myself in the darkened windows of the car that picked me up at LAX, I saw a dishevelled, unshaven stranger looking back. It didn't help that I was stressing out about the fact that I might have to tip the driver. I had a couple of dollars in my pocket, and that was it. I guess my guy was experienced in reading the minds of his passengers just by glancing in the rear-view mirror, because he accepted my pitiful offering with good grace, and wished me luck.

Inside the studio, the auditions were in full swing. They had the Tron light cycle, the fluorescent suits, a mock-up of Sam Flynn's apartment. Sam. *Sam*?! We had the same name! A sign? Several crew members registered my arrival. By the looks on their faces, I think they assumed I was just some guy who had wandered in off the street.

'Come this way,' said a nice assistant director, who promptly steered me through the studio lots to the hair and make-up trucks.

Some time later, I emerged from the wardrobe department looking transformed in every way. I'd been given a shave and a smart haircut. I was wearing clothes that didn't belong to me (a pair of Dolce & Gabbana jeans, a tight T-shirt and a slick leather jacket) and that looked incredible, while a sheen of professional make-up suggested I was practically glowing with good health. It was all a front, of course, but for a brief moment I felt like I belonged. It was the first time in this strange city that I'd believed I had a right to be there. It meant I could stand before the casting director and be proud of my performance.

Ahead of the first scene, with a full crew, I was confused. Only one camera? I was used to multiple cameras from my soap opera days. 'You mean I have freedom to do what I want?' I asked.

'Yeah, go where you feel inclined, whatever your instincts tell you,' replied Bruce Boxleitner, an old pro and original cast member.

The space and freedom to do what I wanted threw me momentarily, and I forgot my lines. Then, to regain control, I did some press-ups, breathed deeply and relaxed. It was fun. I kicked the door closed and jumped over the sofa. It was Sam's house, after all!

On my return home, back to reality, I heard from my agent that ultimately casting for the film had gone in a different direction. I wasn't surprised. I was a nobody, though I did look a little like Garrett Hedlund, who did such a great job with the role. I told myself that it was only a matter of time. I couldn't blame myself for not getting the part. Acting was a competitive industry, with factors beyond my control, but this time I knew that I had been a truly serious contender. Even if so much of it came down to luck, I was doing the right thing by following this path in life.

I had to believe, because frankly, I had come so far there could be no turning back.

* * *

Having committed to going the extra mile or ten, I discover that my Achilles tendon isn't going to deliver me to my destination without complaint. I stop to retie my walking boots, loosening up a little space at the back of the ankle. I hope I'm not going to regret my decision to press on from Bridge of Orchy. All I know is that it's relatively flat from here. The path takes me around the base of Loch Tulla and then across the heart of Rannoch Moor. In bad weather, I imagine this stretch must be wind-blown and arduous. It's completely exposed, but today that's limited to views of backlit clouds as they drift over the mountain ranges. At times, the sun breaks through. Beams of light fan across the moor, as if restoring colour to the gorse and bracken. It's a nice distraction from my ankle, which is really beginning to bother me. I've already taped it up in anticipation, but The Green Welly didn't have any spare tape on sale, and I'm running low.

Looking back, I think it was the weight of my rucksack that inflicted the damage before I lightened the load. Now, thanks to my aching Achilles, every other footstep sounds a minor alarm bell in my mind. It isn't a big deal at the moment, but out here on the glen, I have an unbroken and somewhat forbidding view of the path. It disappears at the crest, and then snakes over rises all the way to the horizon.

All I can do, I remind myself, is forget about whether my ankle will hold together to deliver me to my destination, and just take one step at a time.

* * *

Every year, I would save up so that I could spend time in LA for pilot season. Traditionally, this three-month period in the television calendar was when production companies developed new ideas in the hope of transforming them into long-running hit series. Many would flop in development. Some might make it to a single pilot show, while every now and then a nugget of gold would gleam in that pan of grit. Actors flocked to the city, despite the odds of finding success, and I was among the number who also tried to find the cheapest accommodation possible. On my first visit, I picked a hotel that was affordable and also close to where my manager lived. We got on very well. He believed in me, which counted for so much, and took me under his wing during my stay. Later seasons, I'd stay at a producer friend's apartment in Eagle Rock, then an unknown outskirt of LA, now a trendy area for creative types.

On the morning before my first audition, I stopped off for breakfast at a diner. In true Californian style, I had eggs and avocado toast with hot sauce (and ketchup, of course). The food was delicious, and I washed it down with American coffee. (Ugh! That drip-made coffee is the worst). It also cost me $20, and that was before the tip. As I slipped on my sunglasses and headed outside, I realized that even eating out on a basic level during my stay would be a luxury I couldn't afford. I would have to pick up food from supermarkets to eat in my room, and rely on the goodwill of my manager. To his credit, he was deeply generous and also a really good laugh. After each long day of auditions and test shoots, he would invite me to head up to his house.

It was only a short walk in the Hollywood Hills, near the Kodak Theatre, but a steep climb that got my lungs and heart pumping. I was always desperate to keep my clothes as fresh as possible, as I had such a limited wardrobe. Under the West Coast sun, however, it proved all but impossible to stay cool. Over time, the heat had cracked, melted and boiled the sidewalk. I had to cross fissures in places, as if even the ground beneath my feet was conspiring to make life difficult for me.

My manager's house was an oasis, and a welcome respite from the heat of the day. We would sit under tree shade on the deck in his large walled garden. He kept a few chickens. They would sail across the lawn and poke about in the grass and flowers. With a cold beer in hand, I loved watching them. And his two Highland terriers. A reminder of home. The dogs were a calming presence, and as my manager reviewed how things were going, I felt sure that in time it would all work out.

As my stay wore on, and the auditions and meetings began to merge into one faintly dispiriting blur, he would take me to a bar or restaurant, on occasion the Four Seasons Hotel. It felt like such a treat. There, we drank lychee martinis to wash away the sour taste that had come from being told by some well-meaning executive that I was destined to make popcorn movies.

'I love popcorn movies. Everyone does,' the suit had declared, like that made it better. 'Nobody cares if they're any good!'

As the days and weeks passed, I found myself changing in subtle, unexpected ways. I was used to living out of a suitcase, with no roots in the form of family or routine to keep me grounded. I had travelled all over the UK for work, and grown comfortable with clinging to hope, seeing it slip away and then grasping for the next opportunity. I had plenty of friends, most of whom were following the same path as me, but in Los Angeles, I couldn't relax. Either I was an alien in this city, or the population was alien to me. Even though I had no place that I could call home, apart from a run-down, miserable London bedsit, I felt a long way from something.

One evening, at the front of a queue for a downtown food truck, I asked for a burger in what sounded like a faintly American, mid-Atlantic accent.

'Coming right up, my friend,' said the guy at the hatch, like he'd been serving me on this street for years.

On a subconscious level, I just wanted to fit in. If I could feel like I belonged out here then perhaps the breaks in my career would open up to me. Slowly but steadily, my new-found accent bedded in. On occasion, if someone picked up on it and asked where I was from, I'd give some vague answer about living in the UK for a while. It was kind of an understatement, but I hoped it carried the faintest suggestion that I had started out on this side of the Atlantic.

As my accent enriched (at times I pretended to be Canadian, with no idea what that actually sounded like), what money I possessed began to run out. Through my eyes, so too did the goodwill of my long-suffering manager. The feedback from so many of my auditions was less than promising, and I just couldn't help feeling I had let him down. He'd shown me such kindness and generosity, and yet any potential I'd promised him refused to be unlocked. At the same time, my need to be embraced by this city of dreams had taken a desperate turn. Having arrived looking like a low-budget Londoner, I had taken to wearing cowboy boots and jeans, a vest and open shirt and . . . yes, a Stetson. It wasn't big or clever. Well, it was big, and somehow I had convinced myself that it would take me one step closer to a sense of belonging. In America, a big personality earned attention. If I could create that impression through my appearance, so I thought, perhaps I would be recognized as a contender.

Despite looking like I was in an Elvis movie, it was a last-ditch attempt to fit in. In reality, I'd tried to be someone else and lost myself for all the wrong reasons.

When the money – and with it my stay – came to an end, I left my manager's house for the final time. The sun was setting, releasing the city from a prison of heat, and I just walked. I had no desire to go back to my hotel just then. All I needed to do was throw my stuff into my suitcase at dawn and take the bus to the airport. Despondently I crossed Hollywood on foot. As a pedestrian, with my dreams all but gone, the streets revealed themselves as dusty and rather dirty.

I drifted along the Walk of Fame, where almost three thousand cement stars in the pavement commemorate past and present entertainers in the world of stage, screen and music: *Patrick Swayze. Robert Wagner. Douglas Fairbanks. Kiefer Sutherland. David Bowie. Paul Newman.* Tourists stopped and took photos of famous names, but I just focused on the fact that other lesser-known or forgotten celebrities were simply disregarded or trampled over.

Dropping down onto Sunset Boulevard, I passed landmarks like the Pink Taco and Chateau Marmont, but everything felt off limits to me now. Only a cowboy-themed restaurant, the Saddle Ranch, seemed like the kind of place that might have me, and that was because I looked ridiculous in my Stetson. I caught sight of my reflection in the window. The tourists at the tables on the other side must have wondered if I'd arrived for my shift bussing tables. All I wanted to do was toss the damn hat into the bin.

LA was laughing at me.

By now, my feet were hurting. I had walked a long way in a pair of stupid boots, with no destination in mind. I was just counting the coins in my pocket, hoping I had enough for a Metro ticket back to my hotel, when my mobile phone beeped. I opened my messages, hoping perhaps that one of my last auditions might have resulted in the break I needed so desperately. Instead, I found an alert from my bank. On learning that my account had gone into the red, I just wanted to disappear. I had zero money and no way home. I was lost in LA and I couldn't stop crying. I was a failure. Hollywood had spat me out.

* * *

As a hiker, I feel like I have really found my feet today. I am standing tall, and looking both up and around. When I set out on this journey, I was reluctant to make eye contact with anyone in case they recognized Jamie from *Outlander* and stopped me for a chat. I was tense, carrying stress on my shoulders from a long filming schedule along with half the inventory from an outdoor store. Now, after nearly four days on foot, I appear to have shed that baggage, and not just physically. I've fallen in love with the landscape and the lifestyle, and right now there's nowhere else I'd rather be.

What's more, on the rare occasion that I do run into fellow travellers, I am first to converse.

'Afternoon, ladies!' I say as two silver-haired women in anoraks approach me from the opposite direction. 'Are you going far?'

'Bridge of Orchy,' one says. 'Before the midges descend.'

I walk on with a spring in my step, despite the sore foot. I still have my walking poles with me. They're strapped to the outside of my rucksack. Even though they saved me on that fateful second day, I've no plans to use them. Nor have I any intention of ditching them. Now that I've slowed down the pace, the poles serve the same purpose as a comfort blanket. It's just good to know they're within easy reach.

Later that afternoon, when I come across a herd of Highland cows, I wonder if I might need the sticks for protection. Once again, it's the horns that rattle me. When some of the beasts give me the side-eye, that doesn't help my nerves one bit. These guys are just grazing, but I don't trust them. They're on the path in places, and I really don't feel comfortable just weaving between them. I tramp all the way down to the river and through thick bog to circle past them, only to spot a couple of elderly walkers just breezing past the hairy beasts without a second look. I scramble and squelch through the bog to rejoin the path. Who would have thought it? Jamie Fraser 0–Ginger heifers 2.

I spy a boulder that looks like a comfortable place to sit, and take a break for a few minutes. I swig down some water and then decide to strap up my ankle. I have some physio tape in my bag, which I apply like an amateur, but it makes me feel better. When I walk on, I do so with a limp. I'm still moving, however, and figure it just adds a layer of authenticity to my new character.

It's a long way to Tipperary,
It's a long way to go.
It's a long way to Tipperary,
To the sweetest girl I know!

Today, I have felt well-fuelled from the outset. I have the hotel waiter to thank for that. He was a nice guy. His Romanian accent reminded of the time I filmed a movie on location in his homeland in Transylvania. In *A Princess for Christmas*, Sir Roger Moore (of the Bond variety) played my aristocratic, castle-dwelling father. He was in his eighties at the time, and such a gentleman. Towards the end of one long day, he was required to shoot a key scene with me and Katie McGrath, who played my love interest. Roger and I had a couple of brief lines, and then Katie had a lot of dialogue to cover, which the director was keen to catch in one take. She's a brilliant actress, but I could tell she was feeling the pressure. I've been in that situation, where you muddle through a moment in a scene and just know you could've done better. It's really common, and in this case Katie pushed on feeling that perhaps it wasn't her place to delay things by asking to reshoot. Sir Roger must have picked up on it as well, because all of a sudden he started coughing furiously, which forced the director to cut.

'Ahem, oh I do apologize,' he said. 'I guess we'll just have to start the scene again.'

I had to force myself not to smile. Sir Roger had just sabotaged filming to give Katie another chance. He was such a pro! I loved him as much as I love a Christmas movie. *Bad Santa* is one of my favourites ('You wanna see some magic? Here, let's watch you disappear'), but I don't think you can beat Bill Murray in *Scrooged*. I switched on the TV as I was preparing to check out of my room this morning. They were talking about Christmas, and frankly it's too soon. We've only just had Halloween. It's also lovely and sunny, which is practically unheard of for this time of year in Scotland! We should enjoy it. I know I'm a late adopter of the concept, but what's the rush?

* * *

In my years striving to build my career as an actor, searching for that tailor-made role, I lost count of the number of auditions I attended. Shuttling between London and LA, funded by what money I could earn, I tried out for all kinds of parts in both film and television. Yet anxiety always crept in at the corners. Sometimes I managed to overcome it, but there would always be occasions when I felt that I had let myself down.

My agent assured me that nerves were only natural. I knew she was right. Without a little self-doubt to keep us on our toes, we'd just sleepwalk into any challenge expecting to be successful. Even so, it wasn't something I thrived on. To make things tougher, in America if I made it through the first audition and into the recalls, often it would be time to negotiate a contract. Even though I hadn't secured the part, my agent would be expected to strike a deal with the studio that could be signed if it all worked out. The system is designed to promote confidence and efficiency for the production. In reality, for a broke actor like me, it meant I knew the value of a role – and sometimes it had the potential to be life-changing. I'd calculate what debt I could pay off, perhaps where I would move to, and start to dream big! It did little for my nerves, of course. Whenever I found myself in this position, I couldn't help but think that if fate looked kindly upon me, everything would be all right. I never saw it as a chance to make money; it was more about the possibilities that would open up for me.

There were times when I came within touching distance of a dream opportunity. Once, I landed a co-starring role alongside Jim Carrey and Ben Stiller. Pure comedy. The script for the movie was so funny, I could barely believe my luck. My agent sent me hampers of food and wine to celebrate. I was over the moon. Then, as so often happens, the project fell apart before filming had even begun. There are all kinds of reasons why a potentially great movie fails to get made. Film and television productions rely on countless moving parts, from finance to location management and scheduling. All it takes is for one of those parts to break down and the whole venture can grind to a halt. When my future rested upon everything running smoothly, I found it hard not to be gutted when the Carrey movie died.

I was also in the running for the Superman reboot, having been taken under the wing of the original film's producer, Ilya Salkind. Inevitably, I placed all my hopes on landing the role. Back in LA, I was lent a house to stay in, along with a personal trainer to help me fill out such an iconic superhero costume. I was prepared to do anything for the part, and that included introducing meat back into my diet to help build muscle.

I had been quite happy living life as a vegetarian. Then my trainer suggested that protein from sources like chicken and steak was an effective way to help build muscle, and that was something I couldn't ignore. Tasting that first piece of chicken in an LA diner was an experience. It was slightly dry, tasteless and rubbery, and yet after eating it, I was full! That came as such a revelation.

While that Superman project ultimately took off without me, I sought comfort in the fact that working on my physical presence could well help me to stand out for future roles. If that meant maintaining my new diet, it was just one more commitment I was prepared to make. Ever since then, I have always thought of myself as a vegetarian inhabiting the body of a carnivore. One day I might well return to those roots.

You have great powers, only some of which you have as yet discovered. (*Superman*, 1978).

* * *

The views are panoramic. That's the word I've been searching for as I cross the moor. If I turn full circle, the horizon is defined by forested hills and the copper haze of distant mountain ranges. The muscular pyramidic peaks of Buachaille Etive Mòr are the most brooding and romantic. The path will take me around the foothills towards Glencoe, and so I use this commanding landmark as a reference for my progress. I'm also mindful that I've been carrying a book in my rucksack that I threw in partly for work reasons. It's all about the mountaineer George Ingle Finch. In the 1920s, pioneering the use of breathing apparatus on Everest, this maverick Australian became the first person to climb to over 8,000 metres. His life achievements are incredible, and I'm looking forward to reading all about his rivalry with another iconic mountaineer, George Mallory. I also have a personal interest, as I'm due to play Finch in a movie set to go into production shortly, alongside another Scottish actor and motorbike enthusiast, Ewan McGregor.

All the way here, this character has been waiting in the wings of my thoughts. Now that I find myself studying the Buachaille's buttresses and crags, he's taken centre stage.

Naturally, everyone wants to know how I'm getting on with the Aussie accent. Fair dinkum. With summits all around me, I just want to understand what it takes to set eyes on some of the more formidable climbs, with no limitations, and conquer them.

* * *

Getting close to landing roles but never lighting that cigar, it was technology that came to my rescue, in the form of the home video camera. In the world of casting auditions, it sparked a revolution. Casting directors no longer needed to spend days watching a string of unsuitable actors trying out for a part. Nor did actors have to trek to a cramped studio and sweat through their freshly ironed shirts. Instead, applicants could film themselves delivering lines to the camera and directors could then view the results at their leisure. It worked both ways, because this seemed infinitely more appealing to me too. I could just keep retaking until I relaxed into the role, with no sense that anyone was watching me while wondering what time they would break for lunch.

Recording audition tapes in private and with no pressure did wonders for my confidence. Over in Los Angeles, I quickly found it opened doors. I was invited across for more auditions or called in to talk about roles in detail, which made me feel like I was inching ever closer to the role that would lead me out of the acting wilderness.

By accident rather than design, my new-found passion for self-taping turned into a sideline business. At the time, I was sharing a London flat with friends in Crouch End: a close buddy from my Steiner School years, Fergus, who worked as a sound engineer for the National Theatre and other large-scale productions, and Nic 'Cashmere' Karimi, who had appeared with me in *Knives in Hens*. I was still striving to earn a living from acting, but mostly making money from cash-in-hand jobs at catering events. My shifts tended to take up the evenings, which gave me plenty of time during the day to keep chasing my dream. Once I realized that recording my own auditions had potential, I spent what little cash I had on a half-decent video recorder and a couple of lamps. Then I cleared a space in the house, put up some bedsheets (I promise they were clean) and created a DIY studio.

I worked hard on creating the right environment; sometimes switching white sheets for blue because it helped to make my eyes pop.

I left nothing to chance, and that was when my other actor friends began to pay attention. I started shooting tests for them, and they also got involved behind the camera. As well as filming auditions, we edited them on our computers to get them into the best possible shape for submission.

Our house became known as 'the Factory'. Every day we would be working on two or three auditions for ourselves or other aspiring actors. It was a happy time, full of hope and promise, and that fed into my outlook. Each audition call began to feel more like it had the potential to take me places. In turn, that helped me to relax when required to perform in person, and ultimately led me to a role that I simply could not refuse.

* * *

I pause at a stream to wash my hands and face. The water is cool and clear, just one more little thing that helps me feel connected to this landscape. Without this grounding, I think my seemingly endless slog might play tricks on my mind. Ninety-six miles is such a long trek that my progress has seemed insignificant. With every minute and every mile, I am still just a dot in a vast wilderness. What's more, the terrain across the moor has been bobbing and dipping imperceptibly, like waves across an ocean. It means I've been focusing on reaching one ridge only to get there and find myself facing another. To keep myself sane, I've been reciting a little *Romeo and Juliet*. It's been imprinted on my mind since staging it as a youth, and I'm free to deliver my lines with gusto into this great emptiness.

Two of the fairest stars in all the heaven,
Having some business, do entreat her eyes
To twinkle in their spheres till they return.
What if her eyes were there, they in her head?
The brightness of her cheek would shame those stars,
As daylight doth a lamp; her eye in heaven
Would through the airy region stream so bright
That birds would sing and think it were not night.
See, how she leans her cheek upon her hand!
O, that I were a glove upon that hand,
That I might touch that cheek!
(*Romeo and Juliet*, William Shakespeare)

It was the sight of the stream, winding across the moorland, that put an end to my performance. I'm tempted to take off my boots and refresh my feet, but think I might become living bait for midges. Those blighters love me. On *Outlander* location shoots, they always find a way into my wig and then munch away on me. Instead, as I continue on my way, I find a little packet of fruit and nuts in my pocket. Some of the nuts have sprouted, I discover. I eat them anyway. I'm sure that means they're better for me. I don't want to die from damp cashews.

Finally, the endless path I've been following banks out of view behind a hillside. I press on, feeling like I have really found a rhythm here. My Achilles has calmed down considerably, and frankly that's a weight off my mind. I just want to lose myself on this journey without worrying that my body might let me down. Where the path rounds the slope and becomes a little technical, I focus on my boots to be sure of my footing. It's only when I hear movement in the scree just ahead that I look up and find myself face to face with the Highlands' famous red deer.

Had it been a stag, with those intimidating great antlers, I would have backtracked. The females compensate with a penetrating stare. The breed have become so accustomed to tourists that they don't shy away at all. Just feet away from where I'm standing, this one appears to be assessing me.

What have ya' got, pal? Gie us some o' ya' protein bars.

Whether or not she's aware of my cowardly form with the cows, I simply can't be bothered to scramble down the slope to circle around her. I'm too far gone in every way. So I just walk on, and she skitters away empty-handed. I do hope the mushrooms are watching, because this pretender to the throne just proved himself to be fearless!

A few minutes later, I sense that I am being watched from an elevated point on the hillside, and glance up to see an actual stag watching over me. Those antlers look extra large to me, which persuades me to pick up my pace. I feel like perhaps I've messed with his missus. I just hope he can see that I'm on my way and will let the matter go. Even when I catch my boot on a rock and somehow smash my toe, I don't stop to see what I've done to it. I need to get to cover, I think – and then remind myself that deer aren't known to hold grudges.

'Sam,' I say out loud. 'Maybe you've had enough alone time.'

* * *

Everyone knows and loves Batman. The caped crusader has become an iconic figure, not just in comics but in film and television too. The idea that the concept might translate to a stage show was something I couldn't ignore. On that basis alone, I went to the audition simply to find out how on earth they planned to pull it off.

Batman Live called upon ambitious physical elements of theatre and acrobatics, high-octane pyrotechnics and stage illusion. It was bonkers, spectacular on every level, and totally magical. When I arrived for the audition, the whole place was humming with activity. Cast members were literally soaring into the rafters on wires or battling one another in choreographed punch-ups. It felt like the kind of experimental theatrical production I had missed out on at drama school. As I was there to try out for the lead role, it was also something I really wanted.

I can stand my ground as a fighter. On stage, at any rate. Don't ask me to throw a real punch. I'd probably look to miss. Having learned judo as a boy, I had gone on to pick up some martial arts moves from various roles. I'd also tried a little boxing and had some sword experience. I had even earned myself a fencing certificate during my time at drama school. It was just one more skill that I believed might help me as an actor. As I tried out for the part of the Caped Crusader, my efforts contributed to an outcome I had been chasing for years.

At last, a major role was mine, albeit dressed as a bat.

To be precise, the role of Batman in this live extravaganza was shared between myself and another actor. It was such a punishing undertaking that the producers decided two alternating superheroes would be better than one. The show debuted at the Manchester Arena. With a cast of 50 acrobats and actors, and a moving mechanized stage that took on a life of its own under the spotlights, it was a truly grand-scale event.

With the show proving to be a hit with audiences and critics, we took *Batman Live* on an arena tour of the UK. Like any theatre production, cast and crew became like family. I hung out with the acrobats, trained alongside them and enjoyed a kind of circus lifestyle. These guys were all ex-professionals, some competing for the UK in the Olympics or having featured in other Cirque-du-Soleil-style shows. Together with a strong group of actors, it was a truly unique experience. Sharing the main role, I always made the effort to be first to rehearsal. I wanted to be seen to be ready, prepared and approachable, and would make an effort to talk to everyone and lead by example. Having been waiting in the wings for so long, I wasn't prepared to take this moment in the spotlight for granted.

I knew that our success depended on everyone pulling together. Whatever it took, I was ready and willing, and this was a commitment that put me to the test during a preview show one evening. It was the turn of the other Batman, to be on stage. Rather than take time out, I had found a seat among the audience. I wanted to watch from their perspective and make notes that I could use to improve my performance. My fellow Batman and I got on really well, but naturally there was some competition between us. I wanted to be a fitter and more dynamic Dark Knight. I always felt I had the upper hand in terms of physicality. We were just different in our delivery.

The show was reaching its climactic battle, in which Batman takes on foes from all sides. Everything from the acrobatics to the special effects lifted it to another level. It was a dizzying and deliberately disorientating scene, and so when Batman hit the floor and didn't get up again, it took me a moment to realize we had departed from the script.

An uneasy silence unfolded over the arena. Batman had clearly injured himself. As members of the cast rushed to his assistance, I noticed the show's producer and director hurrying in my direction. When I made eye contact with the producer, he gestured for me to leave my seat and make my way down to meet them.

'Come with us,' he said in a low voice, grasping me by the elbow as if we were about to descend to the Batcave.

By the time I arrived backstage, my co-superhero was there looking very sorry for himself. Mask off, the poor guy was clutching his knee in disbelief.

'Can you go on?' the director asked me, and there could be only one answer.

Having stood in for Injured Batman, I was glad to see him hobble back on stage as the show closed, joining us to take a bow. He'd escaped serious injury but had suffered a nasty knock, which required him to rest and ease back into the role. As a result, I covered for him as the tour continued, and would do so for quite some time.

With the UK dates successfully complete, *Batman Live* hit stages around the world. We took the show to Europe and the USA, and then down through South America. Slowly and steadily the show's profile rose, and with it the names of the leading players. By the time we reached Argentina, I felt like all the years I had spent pursuing my dream had begun to pay off. Above all, rather than considering myself to be a barman with ambitions, I had the confidence to call myself an actor.

I had a blast. Batman really is a brilliantly dark character. Losing his parents at the beginning of the show scars him mentally; the guy literally dresses up as a bat to seek revenge on criminals. He's filled with rage and anger as the Bat, but as Bruce Wayne, he's controlled, kind and hyper-intelligent. He takes Dick Grayson under his wing (ahem) and ultimately helps him create his own alter ego, Robin. Thus the dynamic duo are born.

During a performance in Buenos Aires, I earned a reputation as having a true superpower of my own. This manifested itself one evening on stage following a hearty steak supper with cast and crew. We were in the home of quality beef, after all, and I had wolfed down my meal along with a glass of red wine. It was still sitting heavily in my stomach as the show opened, and the fact that I was required to be so physical didn't help my digestion. At one point, as a whole bunch of the Joker's henchmen surrounded me, I couldn't help but break wind. Just a little. A bat-sized squeak. Zipped up into my Batsuit, complete with padded muscles in all the right places, I felt sure it would go unheard. What I hadn't banked on, however, was the fact that my potent fart would seek an escape route through the neck of my suit as I threw one stage punch after another. Let's just say that I didn't have to put much effort into repelling my attackers in that performance. They pretty much wheeled away before my fist had swung past their faces.

Over drinks after the show, nobody let me forget my surprise move, but by then the tour had become a memorable experience for all the right reasons. I'd spent a year and half in a spectacular physical and theatrical production. After so long on the sidelines, dealing with rejection, I didn't take one moment for granted. I'd joined the production having set myself high standards, and sought constantly to improve. Working closely with a cast and crew that went on to become a travelling family – Christmas in Paris, opening night at the Staples Center in LA, wine-tasting in Santiago, exploring the Giant's Causeway in Northern Ireland, playing in a poker tournament each night in Vegas – I had so many incredible experiences. I'd found my feet in a starring role while recognising that I was also just one cog in a huge machine.

By the time I hung up my mask and cape, with that level of experience in a lead part under my belt, I was ready to fly (that's enough Bat jokes).

* * *

As the sun sinks towards the horizon, the West Highland Way presents a new challenge. Apart from the occasional scramble or river ford, the track that snakes over Rannoch Moor has been hard-packed underfoot. Now I find that it's defined by a stony surface. It feels like rudimentary cobbles, with boulders on each side every now and then. It takes me a while before I register that these have been placed with purpose, and serve to define the old military road.

As with the Bridge of Orchy, the British army made a lasting mark across the Highlands landscape in the 18th century. With garrison stronholds at strategic points, the roads enabled the redcoats to travel freely and impose order on the people. At the same time, their construction was pitched to the population as a means of improving transport and promoting trade. The Highlanders, who already knew how to move around their homeland, regarded the military roads with disdain.

As the stones underfoot make my progress heavy going, I have my own grievances. The toe I bashed on a rock is really making life miserable for me now, while my Achilles decides that it's not done complaining after all. Above all, however, it's the hard, uneven surface that seriously puts my patience to the test. I'm sure the engineering that went into it is impressive, but right now, I hate it. It feels to me like barrowloads of builders' rubble were dumped in one long strip before a drunk on a steamroller rampaged across it to finish the job. If I was a Highlander trying to navigate this stretch by horse and cart, I'd be complaining to the council. 'Och sir, now then, yon cobbled military road is playing havoc with my bunions.' The military roads must have wrecked wheels and axles, and yet somehow both soldiers and civilians travelled for miles along them. I opt for the grassy verge, and by the looks of it, so have many before me, a path worn into the heather.

In the weakening light, as the sun hovers behind Buachaille Etive Mòr, I am thankful that my hotel for the night must be close by. I underestimated the sheer scale of this moorland. It's incredible to walk through the heart of it, but I am weary now. Tonight I'm staying at the Kingshouse Hotel in the valley of Glencoe. Having consulted the online map when I booked the room, I know that all I need to do is follow the path around the mountain and it will deliver me to the door.

Just over 200 years ago, travellers would have had to make camp for the night in the wild and keep an eye open for wolves. One good thing about modern Scotland is that there are no more predators. Unless you count adders (never seen one). And ticks. Oh, and midges. I'm not so worried about disturbing a snake, even when I take a break from the road to walk on the grass verge, but I am concerned about those wee spider-like creatures whose bites carry a risk of Lyme disease. It's enough to make me take my chances back on the stones once more. I really don't like the surface, but hopefully the ticks feel the same way.

I'm growing hungry now. Having set out on a surprise full Scottish, I'm finishing the day thinking it wasn't quite enough to get me over the line. I am aware that my West Coast taste in breakfast wouldn't have got me far, but I'm over fry-ups for the rest of this walk. From tomorrow morning onwards, I decide, as the road begins to skirt the Buachaille, it's porridge every step of the way. I daydream about the hotel, its warm fire, hearty food and soft sheets.

A twinkle of lights draws my attention to the ski resort at the mountain's foot. The building houses restaurants and the departure point for the chair lift during ski season. The rugged slopes and walls of rock above look absolutely stunning. The last time I went up there was with my friend and co-star Graham McTavish, shooting our pilot material for *Men in Kilts*. Graham hates heights, and even the chair lift proved to be a challenge for him. It was rather rickety and old, and we went up to the highest point of the ski resort and looked down to the valley below. It's actually the first place I ever skied on snow, after years tearing myself up on the wire-mesh dry slope outside Edinburgh. Falling in snow was comparatively comfortable and much less scary. Though one time I did go over a small cliff in a whiteout, only noticing the *Danger: Cliff* sign moments too late. I guess I survived to tell the story. With the sun behind the ridge, and dusk settling all around, this epic Scottish landmark practically glows. It looks heavenly. If there are gods at the summit, I believe I know how they start their day. After a well-earned night's sleep, I will follow their example.

For now, I have at least another 30 minutes of walking ahead of me. In what could be described as barren, desolate land, which has, however, been a paradise for me today, the distant hotel lights draw me onwards. I wonder if I can finish without my head torch, and then promptly stop to put it on when a car swoops across the main road between me and my destination with its beams on full. It's darker than I thought, I realize, which persuades me to pick up the pace as I cross the road. Like in the closing stage of a marathon, all I want to do after such an epic undertaking is to finish and be still.

DAY FIVE

FUN GUYS

I've always wanted to be known as an approachable and good person. It's only human nature, I think, and when that comes from the heart, we should feel like we're being the best version of ourselves.

As an actor, however, being nice isn't always a quality that opens doors. Even though I am quite capable of playing anti-heroes, or characters with a dark or troubled core, people often fail to see beyond my natural character. During my wilderness years before *Batman Live*, when I was basically shuttling between fruitless auditions in LA and London, I was called in by the makers of James Bond to try out for the leading part. The whole thing was cloaked in so much secrecy I even felt like a real-life agent. It was so hush-hush that nobody ever confirmed that I was being considered for the main role, but I knew. Of course, it blew my mind to think I might even be in the frame for such an iconic figure. I loved Timothy Dalton in *The Living Daylights*; he was darker than the other actors. But the real icon was another Scot, Sir Sean Connery, who had it all: charm, ruthlessness, physical presence and the accent to match. 'The namesh Bond, Jamesh Bond.' I had to remind myself to relax and let them see what I could do with the character.

So I went along to the Bond HQ and tried out for the casting director. Afterwards, I was invited to head up to the next floor, where producer Barbara Broccoli was waiting for me, like M, sitting in a leather chair across a large table. A replica gold revolver served as a centrepiece in front of her. The director of *Casino Royale*, Martin Campbell, was also there. We spoke a little about Scotland and about Bond, read the scene once, then I left. It was all so quick, the sweat beneath my leather jacket just starting to form. It was all just so cool and crowned by the fact that Barbara was charming and delightful. When I left, I half wondered whether I was about to be tested with a car chase home.

I knew there would be stiff competition, of course, and ultimately Daniel Craig made Bond his own. When I learned the role had gone elsewhere, however, the feedback I received boiled down to the fact that I wasn't edgy enough by nature. I'm always keen to take on criticism so I can improve as an actor, but the suggestion seemed to be that I lacked this quality in my real character. I could not see what bearing that would have on playing the role, but it was out of my hands, and meant to be. Following that experience, I learned to appear naturally on that level when required. Even though I was essentially acting outside of the actual audition, it became just one more thing I was prepared to do in order to land a part. I considered it to be a challenge in some ways; a performance I could pretend was really me that I could switch on and off at will. It wasn't a question of becoming a bad boy. I realized that the edge the Bond team sought could be achieved through self-confidence, which to be fair I was certainly lacking at the time.

Even today, it can be frustrating to be assessed by who I am rather than what I can become in a role. I'm sure any actor will feel the same way. I currently play Jamie Fraser, the unofficial 'King of Men', and although it's true that I use my own personality to imbue Jamie with some of his traits, I'm not actually that guy at heart. Ultimately, I don't believe I need to be wild or unpredictable in the real world in order to bring such qualities alive on stage or screen. Having faced years of rejection, which can be a bleak place, I have a wealth of emotion to draw upon. That experience forced me to raise my game, and since then, I've always set high standards for myself. It means I'm prone to punishing myself if I fail to achieve what I set out to accomplish. I also won't stop until I get what I want. Perhaps that stubbornness and determination is also down to the Taurean in me. I don't get angry very often, but if someone tries to take advantage of me, or my loyalty is abused, then the red mist can descend. It's just not something people expect from that nice guy. You know? The people pleaser . . .

It had been a blast to play Batman, and though he's a brooding soul, I wanted to move on to more complex characters who also wore their pants on the inside (I mean, that's Superman, but you get my meaning). I was aware that coming straight from a spectacular show, and having worked at building my physique to fill the costume, I could well find myself funnelled into similar roles at a time when I was ready for new challenges. In truth, I still considered myself to be a theatre actor at heart. On stage, there's always more freedom to move between very different roles, and yet I still hadn't arrived at a point in my film and television career where I could pick and choose.

So rather than wait for the right roles to come to me, which could have meant spending yet more time in life's waiting room, I built on my new-found confidence from 18 months in a large-scale production. Instead of heading back to London and sleeping on sofas once again, I placed all my chips on finding success on the other side of the Atlantic. With my earnings from the tour, and high hopes that my rising profile might open doors at last, I took a gamble and moved to America.

It was an exciting time. I'd spent many years travelling to and from Los Angeles, but this time I brought a sense of resolve with me. Having been conditioned to expect rejection, which no doubt had helped me to grow a very thick skin, I settled into my new life believing I had something to offer. Sleeping on a mattress on the floor, north of north Hollywood, I was driving the cheapest car I could find and keeping my head down. At weekends, me and my good friend Kirk, also from the Batman show – he played multiple parts, understudying many of the lead roles – would treat ourselves to an all-American BBQ and perhaps a few beers at an Irish bar on Hollywood Boulevard. It's so odd now to pass those same streets we would frequent, our dreams of being successful keeping us fuelled. We were on the far fringes of the industry but were doing all we could to land ourselves that elusive game-changing part. That outlook, I think, is so valuable to an actor. It's not arrogance or self-importance. It's determination and conviction that it *will* happen. Like that edge I learned to summon out of character, it's a deep-seated belief that you've acquired the experience and ability to deliver on stage or screen.

With a temporary visa that allowed me to work stateside, I found a place to live next door to Denny's, a drive-through fast-food joint. I'd regularly wake early, around 4 or 5 am, to watch the Six Nations rugby tournament back in the UK. The drive-through was already busy with the breakfast rush, or perhaps late-night munchies. 'Welcome to Denny's, can I take your order?' It wasn't much, but as a base it was perfect, though it did have a family of possums living under the deck – weirdly ugly creatures that clearly hadn't opted for a replacement Hollywood smile and facelift.

I also knew how to create the right impression in terms of what I wore and where I hung out. This time, however, I didn't attempt to go undercover as a local. Older and wiser than my last attempt to break America, I felt I had something to offer as me. Lean and muscular, with my hair now brunette, I definitely saw the parts become more interesting. Now I was being considered for bad guys or troubled characters, anti-heros rather than good-looking jocks. *Batman Live* certainly brought me a level of attention in LA that I hadn't experienced before, and I did not shy away from it. I filled my diary with auditions and meetings, and arrived at each one (despite the LA traffic and a series of parking tickets) truly believing that this would be my next big break. When rejection came, I was so battle-hardened by disappointment that I just brushed it off and pressed on.

Five months into my new life in LA, I was looking at a matter of weeks before my visa expired. I would have stayed until the last day, chasing opportunities and clinging to unqualified promises that a role would be mine if I just jumped through a few more hoops. Instead, for the second time in my attempt to break America, my money all but ran out on me. This time, I didn't set out for a long, desolate walk of broken dreams along Hollywood Boulevard and Sunset Strip. Instead, I took comfort in the knowledge that I had put my heart and soul into making this new life shine. I also had a small but good group of friends, all of us chasing the dream and supporting each other in our failures and minor successes.

I'd screen-tested on a few shows, the last being *Agents of S.H.I.E.L.D.* When I turned up for the test, they gave me perhaps three scenes to learn, all on the spot. The talented, beautiful girl I was paired with seemed to suck it up in a second, but it took me a lot longer to get it into my head. Then, despite being told to prepare in my own accent (English? Scottish? What am I?), the execs said to do the next take sounding American. This might have thrown me in the past, but now, thanks to my Batty experience, I felt confident, and deftly switched into an American accent, whatever that may be!

Agents of S.H.I.E.L.D. didn't go my way, but I felt I did a good test and it came down to me not being what they were looking for. I could feel my experience and growth cushioning the blow; my armour was now strong. I packed my bags, and with what money I had left booked a flight back to London. I had given LA my best shot, but now I had to face the facts. Just then, there seemed little reason for me to think I could strike lucky on a third attempt at breaking America. The time had come where I had to think about a future in which perhaps I should do something else. But what? Should I leave acting behind?

It was good to see my London friends again, the eclectic mix of actors and bartenders, and they welcomed me back with offers of a sofa to sleep on while I found a room to rent. However, I couldn't help noticing a change in my social circle since I had last lived in the capital. Most of my mates had been chasing the same dream as me. We had always been actors trapped in the casual roles of coffee baristas, bike couriers and waiting staff. Now it struck me that many of them had embraced their casual jobs to make ends meet as full-time professions, while others had got married or were planning families. I couldn't blame them. I had reached my early thirties. This was a time to be settling down, starting a family and living a responsible life. A normal life? I'd never chased that, but I wasn't getting any younger and I began to question whether I could continue in this nomadic fashion. What was more, several people I knew seemed to be making a great success of moving into a more conventional way of living. One friend, Tim Robinson, had started up a catering company serving high-end cocktails at social events. It had been intended as a means of funding an acting career, but as the business took off, it took up all his time. He was even employing people I'd once believed were destined for the stage, and frankly it looked like they were having a ball. They had an income and security, and that was something I couldn't ignore.

Shortly after my return, with no immediate means of earning a living, I signed on for unemployment benefit.

My time on the dole lasted a week, maybe less. The whole process was just so miserable and dispiriting. I attended the required assessment interview and outlined my experience as an actor. The woman interviewing me looked less than impressed.

'You should probably go and find a real job,' she said eventually, which made me feel completely worthless.

As a condition for receiving benefit, I was expected to apply for a number of jobs. I am not workshy by any means. I'd worked in so many different casual roles that I couldn't remember them all when recounting my employment history in the interview. Despite the fact that I was beginning to think about what else I could do with my life, I still had more than the embers of a dream smouldering inside me. I had a fire. I had worked so hard to make it as an actor. I had been patient in the face of rejection and seized every opportunity available to me. That ambition had guided me through my twenties. Now that I'd reached my thirties, it appeared to have no place. Get a job, people seemed to be saying. Get a life. Get real. Give up.

It was the first time since I had set out to become an actor that I'd questioned what I was doing. I could look back over the years and confidently say that I had made every effort. It just hadn't been enough. While I didn't have the courage to extinguish that last ember altogether, in that moment I knew I needed to focus on surviving. So rather than accept a state handout, which felt utterly depressing, I came off the dole after a week and found work behind a bar with my friend Tim's company. I knew what I was doing. I felt comfortable in the role. Just perhaps, I thought to myself, this was how my life was meant to be. 'Another glass of champagne, sir? Yes, of course.'

* * *

The Devil's Staircase does not sound like a pleasant climb. It marks the start of the fifth day of my journey, which will take me to the highest point on the West Highland Way. This section is in fact part of the military road. It's no surprise to learn that the soldiers tasked with constructing it came up with the name. Their hearts must have sunk when they reached the foot of this rise.

I start my ascent as the early sun reaches across Glencoe. Swathes of bronze and golden heather define the landscape. The ascent switches one way and then the other, and in a couple of places I use my hands to negotiate steep rocky steps. Near the summit, at 550 metres above sea level, the breeze stiffens considerably, but it feels refreshing as I huff and puff my way to the top. I stop for a breather when the path finally levels out, and a chance to admire the view. Throughout the previous day, this section was looming on the horizon of my thoughts. The name hardly helps, but mostly I was wary after the trials and tribulations of the second day of the walk. That ordeal had been a humbling experience, and I was preparing myself to be thrown back into that mindset.

As it turns out, climbing the Devil's Staircase isn't as challenging as I feared. If anything, I arrive at the top feeling ready for the next stage of the walk. Why? Well, for once since I set out on this journey, I have fuelled up on Scotland's breakfast of champions: a proper bowl of porridge. Secondly, I'm now feeling 'walking fit'; the last days have really prepped my legs and my body has adapted. Walking for more than seven hours a day feels like the new norm, a natural way of life. I'm eager for each step. Plus, if I dared to mutter or moan on this early ascent, I would be taken to task by the hairy figure following in my footsteps.

* * *

Pursuing a dream is like chasing a star. Or desiring the oldest whisky in the bar – on the top shelf. In any walk of life, it always seems like it's just out of reach. Often we question if it's even possible to catch it (or afford it). Some of us fall away, and that's fine. We only have one life, after all, and I had reached a point where I had to question what I was doing with mine.

Despite a great deal of thought and contemplation after flying home from LA, I just couldn't abandon my ambitions altogether. At the same time, on my return I needed to come back down to earth safely. That meant making sure I had an income to put food on the table and keep a roof over my head. Working behind the bar, I had a chance to catch up with friends and enjoy their company once again. If I settled back in London feeling somewhat downcast, I soon picked myself up in their company and the social life south of the Thames. Working for Tim's catering business, I found that pretty much everyone in his employment had some connection to acting. We were all 'between jobs'. Whether they'd stopped chasing the dream or still held out some hope, it felt good to be among people who shared that passion and experience. Some staged amateur productions or made their own independent features. We went to the theatre, discussed auditions and shared the night bus home.

For some time, I mixed and served drinks with my out-of-work actor friends at posh parties and corporate events. It was fun. Actors tend to be outgoing and gregarious, and that meant it could even be a blast at times. I remember a high-end fashion event at the V&A museum. I'd been tasked with holding a tray of the guests' drinks while they nipped outside for a puff, and was gossiping with a colleague when I looked up and saw Richard Madden – of *Game of Thrones* popularity – walking over to place his gin and tonic on my tray. 'Hi, Richard!' I exclaimed, but the words caught in my throat. He hadn't recognized me, even though we had met a few times (my ex-girlfriend had lived in his Glasgow apartment). It wasn't Richard's fault (he's the loveliest fellow and we've met since), but the fact that he was my peer and I wanted to be on the other side of the serving tray hurt. Richard went outside, smoked a cigarette then came back and collected his drink. The whole time I just gripped tightly to the tray, my knuckles turning white, hoping the ground would swallow me up. He never noticed me and, once he'd left, I made a feeble excuse and made for the closest exit. I felt ashamed and embarrassed, but it also perhaps made me more resolved. I just couldn't settle into hospitality as a way of life. In my heart, it wasn't what I wanted to do. As an actor,

I wanted success like the King of the North. You know nothing, John Snow.

My agent, Ruth, still believed in me, bless her heart, and continued to line me up for auditions and casting calls. I had become almost immune to rejection. Rather than place my hopes on landing a part, I would give it my best shot but expect to be turned down. I had heard every reason in the book why I wasn't quite right for a particular role. Then there were times when I would come close to touching that star, only for it elude me for reasons beyond my control.

I should have set up a fallback plan long before. When I first set out to become an actor, the smart move would have been to establish a map so I didn't end up at a dead end. Some 15 years after graduating from drama school, while mixing drinks behind a bar, I couldn't help but wonder if I had run out of road. I was struggling to find the money to cover my rent – £500 a month for a small box room – but I also knew not to wallow in hindsight. I didn't regret my journey to becoming an actor. It had led to some incredible experiences, even if the magical break I sought had eluded me. So instead of wishing I had done things differently, I looked ahead and set myself an ultimatum: if I still hadn't truly made it by the time I turned 40, then I would bring the curtain down on my dreams.

When you play the game of thrones, you win or you die. There is no middle ground. (Cersei Lannister, *Game of Thrones*)

By accident rather than design, throughout my years trying to establish my career as an actor, I had become a pretty good cocktail bartender. I knew how to mix drinks on request. I also enjoyed the creative showmanship that went into blending ingredients in a glass. In many ways it was like being a chef. I wasn't ready to give up on becoming a professional actor, but if that failed to happen before I hit my next milestone birthday, then maybe my destiny lay behind the bar. I was OK with the idea. I liked working with good food and drink, after all. I had a little time left to keep chasing that dream, but if it slipped away, I knew I would be fine.

That took away any sense of panic for me. I could remain committed to auditioning for a few years yet, while knowing that everything would be OK. In short, I could just be myself in front of casting directors, with a confidence that came from years of experience. Actors my age who had known nothing but wall-to-wall work and then found the opportunities harder to find seemed to carry the weight of the world on their shoulders. It was as if they faced each audition as if their future depended on it, and then forgot to blink. In some ways, that put me at an advantage.

* * *

At the tail-end of my previous day on the West Highland Way, darkness had fallen by the time I arrived at the Kingshouse Hotel. It made my arrival feel all the more comforting. Just as the temperature was beginning to bite, I pushed through the doors into a warm and welcoming lobby. There, a cheerful receptionist told me she had once completed the whole walk from Milngavie to Fort William in three days. Three days?! I was only just finishing my fourth, with another full day to go. I picked up my room key with a smile and hoped she didn't register how inferior I was suddenly feeling. I had to remind myself that this wasn't a competition. I had come this far having shed all sense of urgency, and was loving every step of the way. Just because the end was within reach, I wasn't going to be tempted into a late surge. As I shrugged off my rucksack and flopped onto the bed to rest before supper, I even felt the first pang of melancholy. For this journey would soon come to an end, and though there would be others, the West Highland Way had been a chance to both recharge and reflect at a time when I needed it most.

The dining room was a welcome sight, and not just because I was ravenously hungry after a long day on my feet. It was the sight of the Viking at the table across the room raising his hand in greeting that told me I would be in good company.

'Sam!' declared my erstwhile walking companion. 'Join us!'

Rising to his feet to greet me, my pal with the long beard and tribal hair introduced me to his wife, Tracy. She had taken over from his father in meeting him at the end of each day, which sounded like a lovely, supportive way for him to enjoy the walk. As I sat at their table and caught up with his news, however, I learned that he had been struggling with shin splits. It also sounded like he had been negotiating with his wife as to whether he should carry on. I ordered haggis, neeps and tatties as a starter, followed by fish and chips for my main meal, along with beers and a fine aged whisky for the table, as if that might help the couple reach an agreement.

* * *

'Hey, Sam, it's Ruth. I'm calling with good news, lovely. They really liked you, and want you to come back in.'

I believe an element of luck plays a hand in life. It sometimes seems as if fate looks kindly upon some more than others. At the same time, I am in no doubt that persistence pays off. If you can keep going, remaining committed to the dream, then luck plays less of a decisive role. As an unemployed actor by day and a bartender by night, I was still attending every audition arranged for me. Afterwards, if we heard anything at all, I expected to learn that the role had gone elsewhere. On this occasion, as I played the voicemail on my mobile after a long shift behind the bar in Victoria, my agent sounded unusually upbeat. My hand stuck to the phone, and not because of the sticky Cointreau cocktails.

A few days earlier, I had auditioned for a role in a drama that was described to me as a kind of time-travelling Scottish romance adventure. It was called *Outlander*, based on a series of historical fantasy novels by the American author Diana Gabaldon. I hadn't read them, but when I mentioned to a friend that I was going for the part of a central character in the stories called Jamie Fraser, she became terrifically excited. I mean *really* excited. According to my friend, Gabaldon's books had a huge, devoted following, and if I landed the role, all eyes would be upon me.

It sounded exciting, but then I had learned to set that feeling to one side. High hopes could cause anxiety, and that always got in the way of bringing a character alive. I was also very used to these things coming to nothing. So I had gone along to the casting with no expectation or indeed appreciation that this project was potentially a very big deal.

Ahead of the audition, I'd received an extract from the script. This was quite normal, and gave me a chance to prepare. It was the amount of it that was unusual. I had about 12 pages, which was a lot. Not only that, but it was also dialogue-heavy. I had a great deal to learn, but I also found it revealed a lot to me about the character. Jamie Fraser was fiercely loyal, intelligent and stubborn. He was also strong, grounded, stoic. All number of things. He could also be playful and physical, and loved from the heart.

I know this guy, I thought to myself as I ran through my lines. I know *exactly* who he is.

A few days after the audition, when my agent called to confirm that I had been recalled, my friend could barely contain her excitement. Despite this, I still refused to get my hopes up. It was only when I returned to see the casting agent, Suzanne Smith, that I began to sense that this time things might be different. I had known her for a long time, and she was formidable at her job. She had a huge amount of responsibility on her shoulders, and often managed that by simply being efficient in her search for the right actor for a part. So on previous try-outs in front of her, I had often gone away with a clear sense that I wasn't what she was looking for: 'Again, Sam. Faster. And what IS that accent?' Suzanne had cast *Band of Brothers*, one of my favourite shows at drama school, when my flatmates and I had watched it on repeat, re-enacting every scene in the living room, throwing fake grenades over the battered leather sofa.

This time, however, she seemed to give me more time and attention than ever before. I felt strong and in charge. She worked with me on a scene and challenged me to deliver my best work. Even if she was showing the same enthusiasm to every hopeful actor under consideration, it was a glimmer in the ember that I couldn't ignore, and so I just got into character and let go. Jamie felt like the culmination of all the parts I'd played until now: the power of Pony William, the romance of Romeo, all the skills I'd learned, and the auditions I'd attempted and failed came into play in the scenes. I could do this. With my eyes closed! (Though Jamie can't wink, so perhaps not.)

There was something about that recall that left me feeling like I might be the cog that fitted into a bigger machine. Even so, I refused to let myself get carried away. What was the point? I knew not to court disappointment. Even if the interest in me was genuine, the path to landing a role like this could give way under my feet at any moment. As I had a shift behind the bar awaiting me, with a guaranteed outcome of cash-in-hand to pay my rent, I simply returned to my reality.

A few days later, while pushing a trolley along the fresh fruit aisle of my local supermarket in Muswell Hill, my mobile began to ring. On seeing Ruth's name, I took the call.

'Congratulations, Sam,' she said. 'You've got the part.'

'For what?' I was frankly stunned at what I'd just heard, though she could mean only one role. 'Not *Outlander*?'

'You're Jamie Fraser,' she said, and it was a moment in my life that will stay with me forever.

Whatever she said next was lost to me. I remember answering yes to everything before she finished the call. Then, oblivious to the shoppers all around me, I tipped my head back and roared with elation.

Abandoning a trolley I had yet to fill, I headed straight for the pub next door to tell my gathered friends. We partied hard that night, and for the next few weeks I was on cloud nine. This was a turning point that had been years in the making for me. There had never been any certainty that it would happen. All I could do was keep faith in myself and learn to stay strong when fate seemed to keep twisting and turning against me. At last, I had a big role in a production of substance. It was exciting, challenging and intriguing.

Having been invited to join the *Outlander* production, things happened very quickly. Within days, I was back in Los Angeles to assist in the search for the Sassenach. Suddenly I was being driven through the Sony studio gates in a large SUV, free water and mints in the back, passing the familiar bus stop a few blocks back. The story revolves around a Second World War nurse, Claire Randall, who is swept back in time to the 18th century. There, in a world of wild adventure and romance, her fate entwines with the Highlander Jamie Fraser. The chemistry between the two characters had to be key, and so the production wanted me on hand to see whether my prospective co-star and I connected. Tough job, but someone's gotta do it.

Even though Jamie doesn't travel through time as Claire does, as the actor tasked with bringing his character alive, I felt like I had arrived in a different world. The last time I had been in LA, I was skint. It felt like every door had shut on me, which left me no option but to return to my life of bedsits and casual employment. This time, I found myself being invited into production meetings and involved in conversations about the creative process. It was exciting, but the reality hadn't really sunk in. I still thought of myself as the guy from behind the bar who had temporarily struck lucky. At lunch with exec producers and drinks with casting directors, the mystic and inaccessible nature of these powerful figures disappeared. They were just normal people, and I was invited to the table. Though I wasn't quite ready to let go of my old life in case I had to return to it.

Then I found myself sitting on the other side of an audition panel, and it struck me that I wouldn't be going home for a while. Instead, I watched a long string of talented actresses inhabit the role of Claire. This also involved stepping up as Jamie and acting a scene with them. Some were visibly nervous, and I really empathised with them. Having been in their position so many times, I was quite prepared to give them the time and space they needed to relax and show what they could do with the role. One of the most memorable was Laura Donnelly. We had been at drama school together, though she was some years below, and would later appear on screen with me in other ventures. She read for Claire and then ultimately was cast as Jenny, Jamie's sister.

Another actor who made it into the show was Mr McTavish, my sly uncle and now firm friend and travel companion. I really should have tried to sabotage his audition, though the set wouldn't have been quite as much fun without him!

Outlander is an epic, sprawling story, and yet everything coalesces around Claire and Jamie. The chemistry had to be just right between them. Even though we were pressed for time, as the shoot was looming, everyone involved was determined to create the perfect partnership.

When the dark-haired model with the beautiful blue eyes (not whisky-coloured like Claire's, but nobody's perfect) introduced herself to the casting panel, I paid attention. In the first instance, this was down to the fact that the character of Claire speaks in the Queen's English, while Caitríona Balfe has a lovely soft Irish accent. This proved to be no obstacle for her as she tried out for the part, and I could sense that I wasn't alone in seeing a spark. It was the casting director who asked me to perform a specific scene with her – the famous riverside scene: 'You're tearing my guts out, Claire.' Despite their enduring love, the two characters can be quite antagonistic in their relationship. In the heat of that moment, born from love and frustration, we literally began tearing at each other until the director called time on us. It was intense, physically and emotionally. It left us breathless. She was wrapped in my arms, and I think we both know that Jamie and Claire had just come into existence together. I did feel sorry for her, though, as I was sweating profusely, the LA sunshine still a challenge to my Scottish skin.

Caitríona was new to acting. It was a big leap for her, and I felt that I needed to be protective towards her; as supportive as Jamie is with Claire. In some ways, it seemed as if that dynamic developed between us as actors, and we then went on to amplify and explore it in front of the cameras. She was overwhelmed by work and the pressures of being thrust into the feature role of the show, but she tackled it head-on. I just made sure I had her back.

Before filming commenced, and consumed our lives, we were invited to attend a two-week *Outlander* boot camp in Scotland. With the cast assembled, we basically learned to become Highlanders. I set aside my experience riding the rooftop of an Egyptian taxi and took the reins of a proper horse – Sleepy, my trusty Friesian. I'd picked up a fair bit of experience over the years, and taken some lessons for just this eventuality. Even so, it was great to benefit from the guidance of a proper riding instructor, who could take us to the next level. Over the course of that fortnight, locked away in our own little world, we got to grips with 18th-century weapons, learned to speak Gaelic, and piled into Diana Gabaldon's series of wonderful books so we could appreciate the bigger picture beyond the scripts.

I also talked to Diana at length, via email and private message. 'Gabs' is a wonderful, fascinating woman who has always revealed so much to me about character subtleties and motivations. When the first season went into production, she had written eight novels in a planned series of ten. With the narrative mapped out in her head, she even told me what would happen in the closing pages of the final book. It's been our secret ever since, with only perhaps Maril Davis, the show's executive producer, also knowing. And I can reveal right here that the ending is . . . REDACTED . . .

Also, when the producers send Diana the scripts for feedback, she replies, blind-copying me. It's fun to see what she likes and where she feels things can be improved. She doesn't hold back, but her contribution is always appreciated and taken on board. She's even written several episodes, and really understands how a script should stand up when played out for the cameras. I adore Diana, and that trust she placed in me simply strengthened my commitment to bringing Jamie Fraser alive as she imagined him.

I have always loved the kilt, and now there I was wearing one for work purposes. I would daily pleat my own kilt, then lie on the floor as I wrapped it around my waist; challenging in a small trailer. I suspect Caitríona wondered what I was doing, my feet kicking the walls and the trailer rocking from side to side. Jamie is also a fiery redhead, so I was required to dye my hair. We tried so many times to get it right. It was dyed and bleached 7 times in the first 2 weeks, then had to be rested every 2–3 weeks. Eventually, my hair rebelled during the beginning of Season 2 and refused to take any more abuse. It literally turned purple and started to fall out. It has never been the same since. So, production quickly had some wigs made (some more successful than others!). Season 1, however, was a wonderful time of bonding and banter. As actors, we immersed ourselves in an era of Scots history that has fascinated me since I was a child. Boys with toys, we were kitted out at the armoury and felt like children playing make-believe, McTavish always trying to get the best weapons for himself. I felt passionate about my role as Jamie Fraser. He spoke to me on different levels, and I really believed I understood him. I could not wait for the first day of filming.

Such immersive and intensive preparation meant that by the time we arrived on set, it didn't seem like an acting job. We'd had a chance to develop our characters and their relationships with each other, so everything felt completely natural.

It meant that when the cameras started rolling, we had become like family, and continue to be some eight years later.

Much of *Outlander* is filmed at Wardpark Film & Television Studios, and on location in the Highlands. Initially the studio was a dusty, empty electronic factory with zero creature comforts. It has now grown to a huge facility with many soundstages and workshops. We're cut off from the wider world, surrounded by a wild, dramatic landscape while creating a narrative that largely takes place over 270 years ago. In filming that first season, the sense of isolation was as intense as the shooting schedule. It gave us very little time to catch up with what was going on beyond our creative little community. Both cast and crew were committed to bringing the story alive. As momentum built, so did a sense that what we were making here was something really special.

After two months of filming, we had completed the first four episodes. In that time, the *Outlander* gang had forged bonds and created firm friendships. The entire cast got along well, in fact, and so when Caitríona and I were asked to attend a fan event in America for Diana's books and a sneak peek at the show, it felt like a side quest we could undertake together.

Just before we flew out for the event, a short teaser trailer for the show was released online, which attracted a lot of views. It wasn't until we arrived in New York, however, that we realized what a big deal the show had become. Over two thousand fans attended the event, which had sold out in no time at all. People were queueing around the block to get in. It was something neither Caitríona nor I had ever experienced before. When we travelled on to another event in San Diego, and were met with the same frenzy, it became clear that we were part of something bigger than we had imagined. Jet-lagged and delirious, I looked down from my sky-high hotel room to where thousands of fans circled the hotel's exit, waiting for a glimpse of whichever actor might appear through the reception. I had a stylist and groomer; everything was supplied and paid for. I could even help myself to the minibar! We'd been in a bubble, and in that time an air of anticipation and excitement had approached fever pitch.

The first books in Diana's series had been published in 1991. Over the years, the titles had attracted a huge fan base. There had been talk of a film or TV adaptation for a long time. Now a story beloved by so many was set to hit the screen, and with that came responsibility. Naturally I worried that people would be wedded to an idea of Jamie based on how they imagined him, but right from the start I was shown nothing but enthusiasm and acceptance, despite being an inch shorter than the book version. I was proud of what we were doing, and excited to be part of something people really wanted to see. I just needed to get to grips with finding myself the focus of so much attention.

* * *

I was up early the next morning. With the Devil's Staircase awaiting me, I didn't want to waste time. Having showered, I dried my feet and made full use of what physio tape I had left. I had no idea what I was doing, but as my ankle felt tender, it seemed like a good idea to strap it up. After dressing for the day, I went through my rucksack in search of anything else I could jettison. There was no way I could say goodbye to my walking sticks. By now, the thought of leaving them behind seemed inconceivable. Instead, out went a pair of used socks and a shirt. On this last leg, feeling tired but happy, any reduction in weight was the most valuable thing to me. I even emptied my flask of whisky down the sink; what a waste, but every gram counted. This was it, the last push for the summit.

At breakfast, I stopped the waiter as he began to run through my options. I had no time for a full English or full Scottish. There was only one thing I needed to see me through the day.

'Porridge, please,' I said, handing back the menu. 'That will be all, thank you.'

He caught my eye, looking as if I hadn't really thought this through. 'Coffee?'

'That too,' I said, as if I had assumed it was part of the package, and was delighted when a large mug of espresso-based rocket fuel appeared. Devil's Staircase? Pah!

With breakfast in front of me, I was just spooning in the Scottish honey that had materialized alongside my bowl when Graeme joined me at the table. He had chosen to stay here overnight with his wife, which sounded like a more relaxing option than yet another drive home. While Tracy was enjoying a lie-in and would check out later on, Graeme had convinced her that he was fit to complete the last 14 or so miles of the West Highland Way.

'Aye, it's gotta be done,' he said, though when I asked about his shin splints, he looked at me as if they were holding him hostage.

* * *

Having got a taste of the wild reception that *Outlander* could expect when the show finally dropped, it came as a relief to return to filming the rest of the series. The schedule was intense, often requiring 12-day blocks of shooting every fortnight. It was hard work, but everyone involved shared the same commitment to adapting the novels to the screen in the most compelling way possible. As a result, we didn't have much time to concern ourselves with the rising tide of expectation that closed in all around us. Every now and then, we'd be reminded of it. Online and in the media, a hum of excitement seemed to rise over the following weeks and months. When I joined social media, my follower count exploded overnight. I was no longer Sam from behind the bar, it seemed. I was the actor bringing Jamie Fraser to the screen. I enjoyed the interaction with fans and teased as much as I could about what we were shooting.

In America, Caitríona and I had been dazzled by the glare of the spotlights. It was lovely to meet the fans. We attended other events, rubbed shoulders with successful actors and drank cocktails

'O ye'll tak' the high road, and I'll tak' the low road, and I'll be in…' Balmaha… before nightfall?

Left: At the start of the West Highland Way. Just under 100 miles to walk, then climb the highest mountain in the UK. Sure. No problem. Right?!

Hamish. Glad he's behind a fence.

Day 2. Side of Loch Lomond. Hasn't stopped raining for the last 12 hours. Be drier (and quicker) swimming.

Drovers Inn. Scotch broth, Black Isle blonde beer, Islay dram and crusty bread. Just the starter…

Left: First morning breakfast. Managed to make peanut butter and cinnamon porridge and a mug of good coffee. Also managed to get an ice burn from the canister of propane.

Halloween eve trick-or-treat stash! My dessert, consumed in bed.

Day 3. Tyndrum. Luxury! Underpants drying on the radiator. Nap before dinner.

Lochan of the Lost Sword. Didn't find Robert the Bruce's sword and haven't been named King of Scotland, yet…

The slopes of Beinn Dorain, heading towards Bridge of Orchy and Glencoe beyond…

Right: Sharing a reflective moment in the forest with one of my many mycelia friends.

My Viking pal Graeme with Buachaille Etive Mòr behind. I don't know who/which looks more imposing.

The military road. Desolate and beautiful. My feet did not like the 200-year-old surface.

Above the Devil's Staircase, adding a rock to the summit cairn.

A troop of mushrooms. At ease, lads!

Final day. On the slopes of Ben Nevis.
Looking back to the Bronze Age fort
Dun Deardail.

Deep into my solitary madness. The fungus selfie I was caught taking by Lucy.

Looking down from before the snow line of Ben Nevis, towards Loch Linnhe.

What a great spot for a home! The most photographed abandoned house in Scotland, I imagine. Just beware falling stones.

At the snow/ice line. Looking down towards Fort William. It was a warm, balmy day at the base. Minus 12 degrees Celsius on the summit.

One of the many cairns on Ben Nevis that line the route to the summit and guide climbers in bad conditions. It's important to keep to the path, as the north side has extremely steep cliffs and many people have lost their lives there. I came close to Gardyloo Gully in the fog.

I made it! The summit of Ben Nevis. My hands and face froze so quickly, I only removed my covering for this brief moment.

Part of the old observatory, built in 1883 and used for 20 years to record mountain weather. Hard to believe the scientists lived and worked up here year round. Harsh conditions!

The original end of the West Highland Way. Still about a mile from the town centre, pizza and a beer (or three). A statue of a weary Highland walker marks the new finish line in the town square. He is occasionally decorated with a traffic cone by local youths, as is the Scottish way.

at the Chateau Marmont, directly above Sunset Boulevard, where I'd had my quiet breakdown a couple of years before. The fans' passion was so heartfelt. I just wasn't used to the intensity. In the space of a few crazy months, I had become someone people believed they knew based on the character I was playing. I understood that that was how it worked. I just needed time to adjust. All my life, I'd been quite comfortable out of the spotlight. It was where I could be myself. On stage and in front of the camera, I was free to come alive in character. I loved both sides of my life. Now it seemed as if that spotlight was beginning to swing into the wings, and I wasn't sure how to respond. I didn't want to be someone who turned his back on the attention. I simply needed time to work out how to give people what they wanted while retaining the freedom to be just some guy in the crowd when it suited me.

Going for a drink or attending an event, there would occasionally be photographers and paparazzi. It was a whole new world; my life being documented, each moment shared with the greater public.

I'm often asked how much of my own character is in Jamie. Honestly? A great deal. At the same time, there is a freedom to go further, and also a therapy in that. I can explore my deepest, sometimes darkest emotions without consequences because it's all for the camera. While I felt like I knew him from the first page of the script, Jamie has evolved and does constantly surprise me. I'd never bought into the idea that a character can only behave within set parameters, because in life we can all be surprising and unpredictable. I just felt I needed to let Jamie take over and see where he ventured. As the end of the first season's shoot approached, I knew that would lead to a dark, bleak and challenging place.

Outlander has never turned away from sexual violence. As a reflection of the era, the story can be unflinching, and with that comes a sense of responsibility. A case in point is Jamie's brutal rape at the hands of his nemesis, Jack Randall, played superbly by Tobias Menzies. The focus, of course, is on the consequences, but at the time we felt it was also important not to shy away from the act itself. It had to be difficult to watch, and that made it all the more challenging to shoot.

A clause in my contract required me to film nude scenes. Even so, this wasn't a moment where I felt that being naked would add to the horror of what Jamie undergoes in that castle dungeon as a form of punishment, subjugation and humiliation. I pushed back, reasoning that nudity sexualised a horrific experience for my character, and it sparked quite a debate. Creative conversations are a feature of all productions. Good art is made by questioning the truth, and we all wanted to get it right. Eventually we agreed that Jamie should only be seen naked in the aftermath; sprawled on the dungeon stones in a state of absolute defeat. Those closing scenes were incredibly challenging to film, even though, thankfully, the nude shots ended on the cutting-room floor. It was a harrowing, exhausting experience. I spent hours in a state of undress, covered in fake blood, for the scene in which Jack drives a nail through Jamie's hand to pin him to the table, and then Jamie's eventual rape and acceptance of his fate. If we were to shoot that chapter today, I think it would be handled differently. Times have changed. The cock shot was unnecessary and did betray my trust in the creative team a bit. We don't need to see the horror to imagine what the characters go through. Imagination is way more powerful.

Afterwards, I went back to my trailer and tried to process how I felt about it. Caitríona and I had started out just finding our own way through the intimate scenes between Claire and Jamie. We were constantly looking out for each other, but elsewhere in the industry I know that doesn't necessarily happen. As a result, I've always been keen to find ways in which we can support and protect actors required to place themselves in positions of great vulnerability. A few years ago, I met a fantastic woman who works as an intimacy adviser on film and television sets. I was so impressed by Vanessa Coffey that I introduced her to the *Outlander* producers. Ever since, she's been a central part of our crew. Good drama should never shy away from any subject, but those portraying it should always feel protected.

* * *

I am in no doubt that the porridge powered me to the top of the Devil's Staircase. It also helped that Graeme wasn't short of good conversation. We talked about all manner of things as we picked our way up the hillside, from our shared love of motorbikes to the fact that he too had noted along the way that the mushrooms seem somewhat sentient. 'Buggers were definitely watching me, pal!' I sensed that he hadn't advanced to speaking to them as I did, and decided to keep that detail to myself.

At the summit, we spend a minute in silence just absorbing the view, then place a rock on a small cairn to signify our achievement. The glens never fail to impress me, their grandeur and tranquillity combining to create something truly unique. Graeme and I might be walking companions, but in that moment each of us is lost in contemplation. My pal is first to come back to the present, where he curses his shins.

'Is it bad?' I ask.

He nods, his lips pressed together stoically, before setting off to lead the way. It's all downhill now, to Kinlochleven and his pickup point. I suggest we run down some sections, and Graeme gamely follows, two mountain goats scrambling and picking our way down the well-trodden path.

Having made it to the top of the Devil's Staircase, our next waypoint on the journey sits just a couple of miles to the north. With a gentle descent all the way, we can see the village of Kinlochleven. It sits at the easternmost point of Loch Leven, which is a finger of silvered water against a backdrop of rolling hills and mountain ridges. The walking is easy here, though Graeme is quite clearly starting to struggle. He's developed a limp, I notice, which seems to be from a reluctance to place too much weight on the leg that's troubling him. I don't want to ask, but when I catch his eye, I see a hint of resignation there.

'Ahm gonna call Tracy,' he tells me a short while later. He sounds choked.

'You can do this,' I insist. '*We* can do this.'

I only have to meet his gaze to see that he is serious. For a moment, I feel like I can't let my friend's journey end in this way. I offer to carry him, which makes us both laugh.

'It's been good while it lasted,' he adds, nodding to himself. 'Aye, it's been good.'

'It's been great!' I correct him.

'Ah just have to do the smart thing,' he says, glaring at the shin that has undermined his adventure. 'Time ah called it a day.'

He's come so close to completing this journey. I reckon we've covered well over 80 miles, so I understand how crushed he must be feeling. But I am determined to crack on. This is the final leg, and I'm happy to take it on alone.

Before we say our goodbyes in Kinlochleven, I leave my despondent companion to call his wife once more with his exact location, and pop into a small grocery store. With a long final stretch to go, I need provisions. I pick out a tuna and sweetcorn sandwich (my new favourite), along with a pot of raisins, but for some reason they don't have any bottles of water on sale. When I ask, the storekeeper rummages around in the back of the shop and gives me one for free. I'm touched by his generosity. There was no reason for him to be so kind, after all. I'm just another customer, but also one who had asked how his day was going. In cities like Glasgow, London, New York and LA, where everyone is rushing to be somewhere, I wouldn't normally feel I have time for this sort of thing. Having thanked the storekeeper once again and agreed that it's shaping up to be a pleasant day, I leave thinking I like this version of me.

I find Graeme sitting on a low wall with his rucksack at his side. He looks glum, in stark contrast to the cheery fellow I have known for the last few days. He rises to his feet as I join him, and without a word, we hug. I'm tempted to try and persuade him to keep going, but Tracy won't thank me. Instead, we promise to catch up over a drink at the Scotch Malt Whisky Society, of which we're both members. I have no doubt that I'll see him again.

'I'll be back,' he says, and I sincerely hope he means it, because without him I might have given up before this adventure had truly begun. 'This isn't finished for me yet.'

* * *

Shortly after we wrapped filming the first season of *Outlander*, I landed another role. This one was in a crazy independent film that took me inside the Arctic Circle. *Heart of Lightness* is about a group of actors who travel to Norway's furthest reaches to stage an Ibsen play at a time of year when the sun doesn't set for a month. The perpetual days transported the cast as much as their characters from their everyday lives. I couldn't have been more removed from both *Outlander* and the outside world. In some ways, it served as a chance for me to take a breath. On my return, with season one set to premiere in America, I knew life would be different. I just had no idea how transformed it would become.

Early reviews of film and television productions can give an indication of how they might go down, but nothing beats the public response. When episode one of *Outlander* premiered, it felt like a celebration. I only had to look at the chatter and conversations online to switch from being nervous to joyous. Like everyone else involved, I was proud of what we had created. The critical and commercial reception just meant that we were fired up to build on the success. With production of each season happening in close succession, and growing in both scope and ambition, *Outlander* quickly became a central part of my life. Now, looking back on six seasons over seven years, and as we prepare to begin filming the next, I can appreciate how it's shaped me as both an actor and an individual.

In Jamie Frasier, I had found a role I could call my own. The charismatic Highlander is a complex, compelling character who is thrown into an epic journey. He starts out as a kind of puckish, youthful spirit before we take him into really dark places, and I just went for it. By season three, it felt like I was channelling Macbeth and Theseus rolled into one. In each episode, Jamie assumes a new character – Jamie MacTavish, the Dunbonnet, Red Jamie/Seumas Ruadh, Mac Dubh, Alex MacKenzie, Alexander Malcolm, Bear Killer and Big Red, to name a few. So much backstory has to be portrayed. To explore a role so deeply, in a show with global appeal, has been nothing but a privilege. Jamie has been the making of me as an actor.

Away from the production, I'm still the same person as I was before I took that call in the supermarket and startled the shoppers with my euphoric cry. What changed – and I had sensed it coming before the first season aired – was the way in which people related to me off screen.

Unquestionably, it's a privilege to meet fans and feel like I am part of a story that has brought joy into their lives. I only have to attend conventions and events to appreciate that we have made something people genuinely love. I don't take this for granted. After years of knocking on the door of opportunity, I am always mindful of the path that led me to this place. All I have ever wanted to do was act, and to find myself starring in a show of this reach has been a dream come true. *Outlander* changed my professional life, but inevitably it has also had an impact on my existence when the cameras stop rolling.

It's an odd thing to be recognized in the street. At first it was a novelty, but as it persisted, it began to feel like something beyond my control. As I could be approached when I least expected it, I found it hard to switch off in public. At six foot three, I'm a big presence. It's hard to miss me, and yet throughout my life I could still melt into a crowd. We all have that ability by simply tuning out from the world around us. In the wake of *Outlander*'s success, that cloak of invisibility began to wane. I found myself becoming more self-aware whenever I was out and about, and by extension less like me.

Sometimes I wondered how I would have handled this change in my life had it occurred earlier in my career. Finding fame as a younger man, I might have struggled. Back then, if I thought anyone might look twice at me and then approach like an old friend, I would've just hidden away! With maturity on my side, and an inner confidence, I taught myself to respond to the attention in a way that gave people what they wanted but also allowed me to live my life. I could be on the street or in a restaurant, killing time in an airport departure lounge or hanging out at a hotel bar. If I dodged every advance and scuttled away, there would be no point in me leaving the house. I don't want to go on the defensive or create disappointment. That's not how I want to be. Instead, if someone asks me for a selfie, then of course I'll oblige, along with a brief exchange, and then we can all be on our way. At the same time, I needed to learn not to let my entire life be consumed by a role that has put me in the public eye. It's a balancing act, and a work in progress that continues to this day.

Inevitably, as the years pass, I've also discovered a dark side to fame. It's the one part of my job that unsettles me. I like people enjoying my work, but when they invest in my private life, it takes away something that all of us value. The vast majority of fans who get into a series like *Outlander* recognize it as entertainment. For a small minority, however, the line between entertainment and reality can become blurred. On one level, it can mean that people confuse the character with the actor. There are times when I have found myself held accountable for actions taken by Jamie, which is ludicrous. Or they have created false narratives around relationships I've had (or not even had). In particular, this can focus on Jamie's relationship with Claire. Off screen, Caitríona and I enjoy each other's company. We've worked with each other for long enough to relax and be ourselves, and we know each other extremely well, perhaps like brother and sister; we have been through a lot together. We've learned to take it in our stride, but I sometimes resent having to address the made-up stories about us. By doing so, I just give it substance.

Social media is an amazing platform that enables fandoms to flourish. The *Outlander* community is incredible and supportive, and I value and respect that so much. Like in any walk of life, however, I am mindful that what takes hold on the fringes can cross a dangerous line. When it comes to the portrayal of people in the public eye, the press must also take responsibility. Recently my home address was published in a prominent Scottish newspaper. I had only just moved in, and the place is special to me for all sorts of reasons. First and foremost, it's where I feel I might finally set down roots, after years living an itinerant life. I came back to Glasgow, a city I love. There I could close the door on whatever was going on in my public life. For the sake of my well-being, that sense of privacy was precious. It's also quite fragile, as I came to appreciate when it was taken away from me.

Despite the challenges to my personal life, I appreciate that I am part of a complicated package. I work in a profession that demands attention, but I can't then totally shut it down when I step away from the spotlight. Becoming an actor in a high-profile series has opened so many gateways in my life, and not just on stage and screen. If I want to continue to do something I love, I must live with the attention that comes with it in a positive way. I'm still learning on this journey, and my week in the wilderness has been a case in point. Whenever I'm recognized while going about my everyday life, the people pleaser in me takes over. Even so, there are times when I put on a mask in the form of a hoodie and dark glasses, and then keep my head down. It can bring the anonymity I crave, but at a price.

I only have to think about my first day on this walk. I set out in a state of alert; wary that I might be recognized. Even though people are generally nice – and I had enjoyed a very pleasant exchange with a fan of the show before taking my first step on the path – my half-hearted disguise put me on guard by default. It was only later that morning, when I stopped hiding behind my snood, that I relaxed and began to breathe.

What persuaded me to drop the act? After so many years of playing other people, I have a deep-seated need to just be my true self.

* * *

Without Graeme at my side, I walk on through the village. There is very little sign of life. I pass a cheerful woman in leggings, flats and a Playboy T-shirt, which seems somewhat out of keeping with the brisk weather but is clearly in season around here. Maybe she and the shopkeeper are the only two people who live here, I think to myself as the path leads me up into the hills. I'm just contemplating how my queen and I would dress if we presided over an empty kingdom when I spot my first mushroom cluster. Ah, my wee pals.

'Hey, it's the fungi,' I declare. 'The fun guys, right?'

The mushrooms do not respond. Either they've heard the same quip from a string of wise-guy travellers, or they're under orders to continue assessing whether I possess the qualities to become their leader. With this in mind, I salute them respectfully and press on for the hills.

Before Graeme retired from the walk, he was concerned that the climb out of Kinlochleven would be challenging. He's not wrong. The path follows the contours, and proves quite steep in places, but if anything it comes as a relief from yesterday's long-distance hike across the moor. It feels like a workout. In the gym, I often focus on my quads. They're certainly put to the test here as I dig in one foot after the other. I build up quite a sweat, but knowing the end is within reach drives me onwards. I reckon it'll take me the best part of the day to reach Fort William. As ever, I just want to be sure that I complete the walk before darkness falls. Over the course of this week, I have learned that progress on foot takes a lot longer than anticipated. At least it does now that I've found my stride, which is more relaxed than the power march I came to hate on the second day, but perhaps just as fast. I'm moving easily and with joy and sheer pleasure, no longer out of necessity.

It feels so good to be walking again. Nothing but the sound of my own footsteps for company, the regular rhythm and sway of the road, the scenery slowly changing. With just a few miles ahead of me, I find myself reflecting on how far I've come. In this short time, I've changed in so many ways. Now, when I come across a couple out for a morning walk, I make no attempt to keep my head down. In fact, I've become the guy who breaks the ice with a cheery wave, asks how they're doing and hopes the good weather will hold a while longer. If this carries on, people will take one look at me approaching and keep *their* heads down. I feel like a completely different character. I am, I think, an annoyingly cheerful hillwalker – the man I want to be.

The climb out of Kinlochleven is spectacular. As I gain elevation, the mountains and even the sea reveal themselves in the distance. From the hills, I look back at the village on the shore of the loch and realize just how picturesque it is. There is some moisture in the air, but

I wouldn't call it rain. Pressing on, I feel proud of the fact that I have walked all this way from Glasgow.

As the path opens up, I note several walkers in the distance. As soon as I realize they're heading in the same direction as me, the competitive urge kicks in to beat them all to Fort William. Then I note that the hills on the far side of the valley are shrouded in cloud. Why would I want to hurry into that?

I'm thoroughly enjoying this new pace of life. Since I chose to take my time to complete the walk, even the rain has decided to move on. The weather still looks changeable, but I'm content with sunshine or showers.

At the same time, I can't ignore the fact that I am gaining ground on the walker ahead. It's a woman, I realize, which makes me feel a little awkward as I get closer. The last thing I want to do is make *her* feel uncomfortable. She has a large pack on her back and is occupying the centre of the track, meaning that the margin on each side for me to get by is uncomfortably slim. Anxious not to seem like I'm sneaking up on her, I cough pointedly a couple of times. She seems not to hear. So in a bid to do the right thing, I decide to power on past her. She's not slow by any means. It's just I am a fraction quicker.

As I move into the fast lane, she glances over her shoulder and I see that she's on her phone. I smile and nod, and then all but break into a trot to get by. The woman seems unimpressed by my efforts. Without breaking off from her conversation, she moves to the inside to give me more space. I mimic my thanks, like I'm a mime artist all of a sudden, and then cringe my way into creating some distance from her. At the same time, I wonder how anyone can maintain that speed while holding down a call.

The track is largely stone here, and skirts the edge of the valley. I can see drizzle falling in the middle distance. Sunshine has also broken through in places, fanning the landscape with light. It's constantly changing and truly spectacular. Capturing it by phone camera just doesn't do it justice. Only a painting could reflect the scope, depth and vibrancy of colour. It reminds me of those early-19th-century works by Scots artists such as John Knox and Horatio McCulloch. As a boy, my mum used to take me around galleries in Edinburgh. Those were the paintings I could lose myself in. They definitely left an impression on me.

Once I feel that I have created enough distance from the walker behind me, I slow back down, just to enjoy the moment. I can tell that rain has fallen here, because there is a fresh smell of earth in the air. Petrichor, I believe it's called by some (pishy rain by others). It's like the essence of nature. They should bottle it.

When I get home, I have a lot to do. Preparations are under way for the Everest movie, along with a whole host of filming and promotional commitments. I'm looking forward to it, but right now I don't want to think that far ahead. It's just so blissful here. I pause for a moment at one of the many streams that cross this landscape. My feet are aching somewhat, but then I remind myself that in recent days they've transported me across nearly 100 miles of countryside. Of course they're going to be sore! Now that I've stopped, I notice just how many great boulders are scattered all around this valley. In centuries gone by, they would have rolled down from the ridges and then fallen still in time. In our fast-moving world, there's something so grounding about being out here.

I take a deep breath. 'It's all good.'

* * *

Without doubt, *Outlander* proved to be a turning point in my career. It's given me confidence, experience and, of course, the invaluable thing I'd chased since leaving drama school – opportunity. Starring in a huge series like this can be all-consuming at times, but I have always strived to retain my sense of independence. As an actor, I've pursued other projects that provide me with fresh challenges. I am drawn to roles that take me far from what people might expect. It would have been easy for me to play characters that call upon Jamie's identity – as the show found success, those opportunities arose – but I've always been committed to exploring new paths.

In the breaks in filming six seasons of *Outlander*, with a seventh slated for my return from this journey, I've appeared in action comedies like *The Spy Who Dumped Me* – which stars Kate McKinnon and Mila Kunis and was a lot of fun to make – and played the villain opposite Vin Diesel in the superhero movie *Bloodshot*. It was a thrill to be the bad guy, Jimmy Dalton, and explore what that really means, why he is filled with anger and resentment; and I thoroughly enjoyed the action scenes. There's so much scope to test what motivates a character who believes he's doing the right thing for all the wrong reasons. Even playing special forces veteran Tom Buckingham in the thriller *SAS:*

Red Notice allowed me to push a good guy to extremes. Who doesn't want to play a 'good' psychopath? We shot the movie in Budapest, Mallorca and London, and prep for it was so fun: tactical movement with Andy McNab, weapons training, and even a drugs bust with the local constabulary. With *Everest*, I have a chance to take a pioneering mountaineer to the limit in a vertical sense. Working with director Doug Liman will be a superb opportunity and challenge. On stage or in front of the camera, I just love to explore what makes us human.

* * *

Today, I make a point of stopping to eat my lunch, a soggy sandwich, before I start feeling hungry. This walk has really encouraged me to think about food in terms of fuel. I didn't eat enough in the first couple of days, and paid a price. So another mile on, I decide to stop beside one of the boulders and keep it company for a few minutes. I've no idea what kind of rock I'm leaning against. It's an opaque pink and orange colour. It could almost be precious, but the fact that it's everywhere tells me otherwise.

My tuna and sweetcorn sandwich is nothing special. Then again, I'm only really interested in the carbs at this point. I just want to get through the remainder of the day without feeling like I'm running on fumes. I love food in all its forms, but sometimes I play roles that require me to put on muscle, like in *Outlander*, or more recently a T V crime thriller called *Suspect* starring James Nesbitt. Then my diet has to support a workout regime, and that can be tough.

Often it's photo shoots that demand a very specific preparation.

The camera wants to see definition, after all. There was a time when I achieved this by regulating how much water I took on in the hours beforehand. Purposely dehydrating yourself is hardly best practice, as I learned to my cost one time. I was scheduled to shoot a topless scene for *Bloodshot* in South Africa, but first I had to fly to and from New York for another work commitment. I thought it would be easy. I could drink 4 litres on the flight out, and then slowly cut down my fluid intake over the next day before drinking next to nothing on the flight home. That way, I would look drawn for the camera.

Back in Cape Town, I was thirsty as hell but ready for the shoot, only for it to be delayed by a few hours. Then it got pushed into the afternoon. When they cancelled it completely, I was on my knees with thirst. As well as being dehydrated, I was really hungry and also very jet-lagged. So I had a blowout meal with plenty of water, and then fell into bed.

First thing the next morning, I dragged myself out of bed and assessed myself in front of the mirror. I looked terrible. My face was puffy, my stomach bloated, and my eyes reflected the fact that my body clock was all over the place. We still shot the scene, where make-up, lighting and glittering angles worked miracles, but I'd put work before my health. Now I have age and experience on my side, but it's been an interesting journey as a man in the camera's gaze. I have a great deal of empathy for female actresses and models. The pressure to look a particular way continues to be hard to manage. I think men also have a huge amount of body issues, and are expected to just perform on demand, without any support. Perhaps it's less invasive than it is for women, but men are still expected to have washboard abs and great pecs. I would certainly like to be more involved with men's mental health and their support network.

However, this lunch will do nothing for my abs; it's all about calories right now. And it does taste pretty damn good, despite the soggy texture.

With my lunch settling in my stomach, and a renewed sense of purpose, I follow the path out of one glen and amble into another. I can see the track stretching out before me into the far distance. A steady breeze stirs the heather. Sheep from a scattered flock pretend not to notice me. This feels like a very secluded stretch. The only other sign of life is a ruined cottage. It's literally in the middle of nowhere. In the last century or the one before, someone considered this to be the perfect place to make a home. Naturally, I must investigate. 'Ah, the perfect break spot,' I think, 'and I won't have to share it with anyone. Not even the sheep.'

Silhouetted against the russet hills, all that's left of the dwelling are the remains of brick walls and chimney stacks, and some corrugated-iron sheets. The roof is long gone. The masonry has darkened with age. It's practically camouflaged amongst the terrain, as if being reclaimed by the mountains. *Dangerous building! Keep out.* Naturally I went in.

Inside the old bones of the place, I find an open hearth and a window frame with a peculiar view of the hillside rather than the full range of the valley. I wonder if the owner positioned it this way so he or she didn't feel overwhelmed by the vast open space. Then again, maybe they just wanted a heads-up in case the enemy staged a surprise attack and came marauding down the slope.

I drop my rucksack from my shoulders, pick out some loose raisins from my pocket and just stare through the frame for a while. Curiously, as I gaze outside, I feel a pang of homesickness. I haven't lived in my new place for long, but it's dawning on me how much I love it there. This week, following a path for miles on end, I feel a renewed appreciation for just being still. I know things will be hectic when I return, but in due course I look forward to putting down roots for the first time in my adult life.

As the wind picks up and the sweat under my windcheater starts to cool, I shiver and pull at the zip. It's time to get going, I think to myself, and feel a surge of excitement. I am in love with this way of life. I don't look at my phone to check the time, for example. I can gauge it vaguely from the position of the sun when it emerges from behind the clouds, or the length and direction of the shadows. I feel a renewed burst of excitement. I love this. Nothing to do, no responsibility but to keep going, and who knows what sights I'll see next.

The path takes me down to a river, and then follows dutifully alongside the clear running water. Far ahead, beyond the hills, I see the ghostly traces of mountain ranges. My thoughts turn to the one peak I intend to conquer to complete this journey. Ben Nevis stands just to the east of the West Highland Way, but if I can reach the path's end in Fort William today, I intend to devote tomorrow morning to climbing to what is the highest point in the land.

It's the first time in days, I realize, that I've let my thoughts venture ahead. All I've really done is make a rough plan, but when my attention returns to my surroundings, it strikes me that that means my journey is almost over. It comes as a jolt. I don't want it to end, but nor do I want it to weigh heavily on my shoulders. So given that I am completely alone, I throw my arms wide in celebration.

'Scotland!' I yell, simply because I want to hear my own voice across this great glen.

I walk on, sensing that my woolly friends are hoping I won't hang around if they continue to ignore me. I even wonder if my outburst might have moved one of them to call security, only to stop in my tracks at a familiar sight at the side of the path.

'Well hello there,' I say, addressing the cluster of what look like tiny military helmets on long, spindly stems. 'How you doing, little fellas?'

The mushrooms don't respond. Not outside my imagination, at any rate. In my head, they're reporting for duty at last. I have been nothing but respectful towards the landscape. I've upheld the countryside code every step of the way, and I can only think that has persuaded them to adopt me as their leader. Keen to present myself as a firm, fair but friendly figurehead, I crouch to engage with them.

'Troops,' I say, 'Fort William could be ours by sundown. Who is with me?'

In a bid to forge a closer bond, I wonder if they'll allow me to take a picture in their company. Having walked among mushrooms for almost 100 miles now, it's only right that I go home with a memento.

'Stay right there,' I tell them, manoeuvring myself so I'm lying on my side and at their level. Fishing my phone from my pocket, I wriggle into position. 'Ready, guys? Say cheese! OK, maybe not cheese. We're not making an omelette here. Just smile for the camera...'

The flash on my phone goes off multiple times. Determined to capture the perfect shot, I adopt several poses, including one with my arm outstretched around them like we're buddies who go back years.

'Um, hello.' The voice comes out of nowhere, but at horribly close range. 'Is everything OK?'

With a gasp, I twist around to see the hiker who was on her phone when I passed her. She looks concerned.

'All fine.' I blink, and then realize her attention has turned to the screen of the phone in my hand. Presented with the evidence of a snap of my grinning face, I can't deny that I have just been attempting a mushroom selfie.

'They're pretty special,' she says, as if to make me feel less awkward, while also taking a precautionary step away from me. 'I've taken loads of photos.'

Sheepishly I rise to my feet. The woman is in her twenties, I think. She's rocking a knotted yellow headband and an expression of quiet amusement that suggests that if I wasn't a total stranger, she'd be ripping the piss out of me.

'I'm Sam,' I say.

'Lucy.'

'Pleased to meet you, Lucy.' I gesture at the path ahead. 'Are you going my way?'

Understandably, given that I look like I might have a weird thing for fungi, Lucy seems to weigh up her response. I don't blame her, and so I suggest I'll be getting on, to give her some breathing space.

'I'll walk with you,' she says as I turn, and the pair of us seem to exhale at the same time. 'So long as your mushroom mates don't mind?'

I glance at the fungi beside the path.

'They're cool,' I say. 'They must like you.'

'I hope they do,' she says, and we fall into step, the mushrooms waving us bon voyage.

Nature alone is antique, and the oldest art a mushroom.
(Thomas Carlyle)

* * *

I don't believe in restricting myself to just being an actor. After many years in the wilderness, I found opportunity and success. It's been everything I imagined, but if I did nothing else with my life, I'd still feel like something was missing. I'm always looking for the next challenge on the horizon. This has given rise to several projects far from film and television, including one dear to my heart that allows me to give something back.

My Peak Challenge started out as a way for me to raise money for charity. In preparing to film *Outlander*, the producers paired me with a personal trainer, John Valbonesi, and sent us to London to train for a few weeks. There, in breaks between punishing sessions, John and I started talking about the benefits of personal objectives and goals. We all need a focus in life, and by introducing targets we can begin to take steps towards achieving goals that might at first appear unreachable.

It was John who challenged me to take on not one marathon but two in the space of a month. It was a daunting proposition. John himself is not a runner by any stretch of the imagination, though he'd happily bench press all day. Every day. And I'd never run that distance before. Still, I couldn't dismiss it. Under his guidance, I focused on the process of training rather than the outcome. So rather than worry about the finish line, I set my sights on being in the right mental and physical shape to put one foot in front of the other. By breaking down the challenge into manageable steps, I completed the marathons and raised over £30,000 for cancer charities. The support I received was incredible, and I was struck by the sense of unity and camaraderie as people got behind the cause. It was rewarding on so many levels, and inspired us to create My Peak Challenge (MPC). Alex Norouzi, my good friend and business partner, the creativity to my grind (though he always does the hard work), started working with me, and helped to turn a crazy idea into reality.

What started out as a 60-day training and nutrition programme, designed to help members develop the foundation to meet their challenges, swiftly grew to offer a full 12 months of workouts and meal plans. At our first MPC gala in Scotland, thousands of 'Peakers' from the global community came together to celebrate at the Kelvingrove Art Gallery and Museum with activities from hiking to dining and dancing. We had a blast, and it's become an enduring venture that gives me great pride. More recently, we have held the annual event at the International Conference Centre in Edinburgh, with tree planting, workouts, yoga and mindfulness, just some of the activities. The Scottish government and our charity partners were all in attendance. It's a really rewarding evening and a great way to thank our 'Peakers' for their support. MPC is my baby and a lifelong commitment. We're based in LA with a hard-working and dedicated team of seven, and the community continues to grow by the day. We are a small not-for-profit organization, so it does have its challenges, but to date we've raised more than $6 million for our charity partners. Lives have been changed and friendships forged. Plus we have sweated a lot and do burpees for breakfast.

* * *

It doesn't take me long to fall into step with my new walking companion, or at least I try to – she's fast! With a yellow polka-dot headband, chunky walking boots, bright eyes and a wide smile, she's a fun character and talks as quickly as she walks. She tells me she's from England, and was drawn to walk the West Highland Way for the very same reasons as me. The only difference between us is that she's set to smash it in just four days.

Four!? I scream internally, then remind myself again that it's not a competition. I try to move faster and she matches my pace.

'This is my fifth,' I say, hoping to sound like that was my plan all along.

'Oh dear. What happened?' Lucy looks across at me. I smile despite myself.

'Just . . . everything,' I say by way of explanation.

We follow the path through the glen. As shadows from clouds skate down the hillsides and across this wild open space, we talk about our experience on the walk so far. Lucy asks if it's acceptable to talk to yourself, and I can hardly argue otherwise. Crying is also permissible, we agree. In fact it sounds like she's experienced every emotion, and I share the heart of darkness I found on my second day. Lucy tells me her feet have been causing her problems, which makes my aches and pains easier to bear. She's welcome company, an efficient hiker, and we pass several miles in easy conversation.

Towards mid-afternoon, and with perhaps just a couple of hours left to trek, I decide to stop and rest. If I'm honest, I feel my journey is near its end, and I want to relish these last few miles. I need to feel I achieved this journey on my own, a personal victory, and walking with a companion almost feels like cheating. On this breezy but beautiful day in the glen, I feel happy and at peace with the world. I'm also mindful that, like me, Lucy is content in her own company. I don't want her to feel obliged to complete this walk with some random Scottish mushroom revolutionary, and so I make it easy for her to press on alone. She's been a delight, and I hope the fungi watch out for her across these last miles as they do for me.

After a short but much-needed rest, I soon return to the realm of false summits again. It seems to me that one ridge just conceals another on this stretch, but I'm happy to go with the flow. What really commands my attention is the roof of a mountain taking shape beyond the forested slopes beyond. It's quite far away, judging by the fact that it's just the trace of a shape against the blue sky, and somehow it reminds me of the visible tip of an iceberg. It has to be Ben Nevis, I decide. The ultimate destination on my journey.

At the top of the next hill, arriving at a bend in the path with a clear line of sight between the trees, I stop and stand in awe. As if to prepare for my first unrestricted view of Ben Nevis, the clouds have cleared from the glen. All the mountains around it are impressive, but this one stands out like a ghost giant. It's massive. A behemoth. A kingdom in its own right. I can't be sure if it's snow or sunlight that blankets the slopes of the south-west face. I'm so in awe it's difficult to process the sheer enormity of this great throne of rock. Nor can I wait for tomorrow, when I will attempt to reach the top. I'm excited and intimidated, and move on with my heart thumping. As the path chips down the hillside, I think about how a climber like George Ingle Finch would have responded when he first set eyes on Everest. It must have been humbling and exciting in equal measure.

I'm elated, filled with excitement to be so close to the end of my journey and also by the prospect of an even greater adventure. I start to run. I want to share this moment with someone, the sheer joy of seeing that mountain. 'Lucy?! Wait up!' I call, but she's long gone. I press on, enjoying the change of pace and the exhilaration of the prize ahead.

Traversing another valley, I cross the floor of the valley at pace and then storm up the switchbacks in the path on the other side. I can sense it now. As the light begins to turn golden and then wane, I am confident that I will reach Fort William before nightfall. According to my map, I don't have far to go. Since I first set eyes on the mighty mountain peak, Ben Nevis strikes me as being at the very heart of this Highland wilderness. Even though Fort William lies just a few miles north of here, on the shore of Loch Eil, I can't stop looking across at the immense knuckles that dominate the skyline. Shadows might be lengthening across my path, but that summit will remain bathed in light until the sun sinks behind the horizon.

I'm so looking forward to setting out tomorrow for the roof of this world. While I prepare to reach the end of a walk I have come to love, it's comforting to know that a new chapter awaits me at first light. For me, this journey has removed the noise and demands of everyday life to remind me that we're all just passing from one waypoint to the next. What matters is that we can look back at each stage knowing we made the most of it.

Pleasingly, once I've climbed out of the valley, I find that the track begins to wind downhill in a way that feels like a home run. It's a long, gentle descent through the forest. I haven't stopped running (well, more of a shuffle jog, my rucksack bouncing along, practically empty and light-headed), but even after nearly 96 miles, my energy is limitless. I'm not in bad shape after such a long journey, but I really shouldn't be running. It makes the prospect of a big climb tomorrow somewhat daunting. For now, however, I just want to enjoy the late sun slanting through the trees and let gravity help me on my way. 'Run, Forrest, ruuuuuun!'

I have to stop for one last selfie with the mushrooms. A tight cluster catches my attention. With their overlapping caps, they look like centurions holding their shields in battle formation. This time I peer around a bend in the path ahead, then check that nobody is approaching from behind. Confident that I'm alone, I grab a photograph with these silent guardians of the West Highland Way.

'At ease,' I say, pocketing my phone. 'Until next time, eh, lads?'

Fort William is so close now. This downhill section feels like the last stage of a roller-coaster ride before it comes to rest. I start to feel quite emotional that my trek is almost over. The West Highland Way has been a constant companion to me since I set off from Milngavie. I have cursed it in places, and hold it fully responsible for my aching Achilles. Even so, it's kept me on track and now promises to deliver me safely to Fort William.

Soon I catch my first glimpse of the town. It's just a loose network of rooftops and roads on the crescent shore of the loch, but I'm excited to see it and double my pace. Somewhere down there, I think to myself, a bar stool is waiting for me. No sooner have I started imagining the beer with a whisky chaser than my attention turns to a sight that will add at least another hour to my journey. It's some kind of ancient lookout post, high up on a slope and peeping out from the tops of the pines. I stop in my tracks, knowing that I have to investigate. Once upon a time, I imagine soldiers were stationed there on account of the extraordinary views it commanded. If enemies appeared on the horizon, they would be the first to know about it. While it's little more than another grassy hilltop, in such dramatic late light I can't think of a better place from which to appreciate this wonderful world within a world.

I find a path that zigzags towards my destination, all uphill. It's so steep I'm on my hands and knees at times. I can hear water tumbling from nearby, and estimate I'm about to add at least 100 metres of elevation to my trek. The effort just makes me all the more determined to get there, and when I finally make it, I do so at a crawl. At the top, I stop on all fours for a moment to get my breath back. Then I rise and turn to the light.

'This is it,' I say to myself in wonder at the rough-hewn tapestry of glens, lochs and mountains. The only movement I can see is in the subtle wash of light through the clouds and the graceful twists in the mist gathered at the seat of Ben Nevis. '*This* is why I'm here.' I'm silenced. My breathing slows. I'm welcomed into the landscape. The mountain consumes me.

* * *

I'm serious about my Scottish whisky. I can nerd out on tastings and talk about malts and distilleries with whoever will listen. Over time, I've invested in quite a collection. I'll try anything. It's just something I really enjoy. It can also bring people together, of course: 'the water of life'. So when I discovered that Alex was visiting Scotland for the first time and had never tasted a dram, I made it my mission to enlighten him.

Alex Norouzi is American, of Persian and German origin. He was, in effect, a blank canvas when it came to my favourite spirit – the original 'visky wirgin' in his Germanic accent – and it was such a blast to enlighten him. He loved it, and as our sampling session extended into the night, he made a suggestion I couldn't ignore.

'Sam, we have to make our own. Vat do you sink?'

It sounded crazy, but I know Alex well and he has always dreamed big. Having laughed as if he'd just cracked a joke, I found myself discussing how we could make it work. As I had a public profile by this time, we recognized that the easiest way would be to lend my name to a white-label brand. I could team up with a drinks company and they could slap stickers on some mass-market product. It's worked successfully for other actors, but it just didn't sit well with us.

If we were going to launch a whisky business, it would need to be on our terms. Most importantly of all, and this was non-negotiable, the spirit would have to come from the heart.

So the next logical step in our quest was to take two weeks out of our work schedules and tour the finest distilleries Scotland had to offer. Our road trip took us across the Highlands and the whisky isles, meeting family-run distillers whose ancestors had been producing malt for hundreds of years. We sampled different blends throughout, and gradually began to refine the taste we had in mind. It was a wonderful, fun and enriching experience. By the time we returned home, having met a master blender who shared our vision, we had discovered what we were seeking. We paired a careful selection of single malts, aged between 9 and 12 years, with a 19-year-old organic single grain Scotch whisky. The blend just reminded me of everything I love about Scotland, with a unique sweet finish. It reflected the Asian blends, balanced and approachable but with a distinct malt content. Spirit of home, a reflection of Scotland in a good Scotch whisky.

Our whisky had to be called the Sassenach. There could be no other name, we agreed, before turning our attention over the following months to everything from the bottle design to the logo, marketing and distribution. We worked closely with agencies and experts in the field, and finally brought the Sassenach to market. In the summer of 2020, our blended whisky launched in the USA, followed by the UK later that year. Since then, it has picked up a host of awards, including two double gold medals at the San Francisco World Spirits Competition.

It's been a sell-out hit based on its quality, and I could not be more delighted. Alex and I have worked so hard to basically start a drink brand from scratch and then grow the business ourselves. We attended endless meetings, forged relationships with retailers, and even went around New York bars and restaurants inviting owners to try a dram. When we found a distributor, I made it very clear that our drink shouldn't be classified as a celebrity brand. In some ways, that would have been the easy option. Instead we forged our own path, believing in the quality of the drinking experience we had created, and that just made the journey so much more rewarding. What's more, seeing our whisky on the shelves proved to be another waypoint on a bigger adventure for us both.

The Sassenach Select El Tequileño tequila has recently joined the collection. Scotland is my homeland, but I love Mexico and its culture. Alex and I spent time over several years visiting the country, meeting producers and refining blends until we found the taste we had been searching for. Tony Salles, a third-generation master distiller, collaborated on our new double-wood reposado. We all love good spirits and bonded over our similar cultures, love of the terroir and quality ingredients. Despite the time, energy and commitment, creating a tequila to stand alongside our whisky has never felt like work. I just love it. This is no side hustle for me. It's about sharing a passion with my friend, and then with the wider world. Like My Peak Challenge, I truly believe in the Sassenach. If people share my passion for each venture, and then discover I'm behind them, that's even more rewarding for me.

* * *

My descent from the watchtower is mostly done on my arse, using my hands and heels as a brake. Once I'm back on the path, I brush myself down and break into a jog again. The going continues to be gentle and easy underfoot, though dusk is most certainly beginning to settle. With less than a mile to go, judging by the glimpses of Fort William through the trees, I am quite sure I will make it without having to stop and search for my head torch.

Usually I run with one eye on my sports watch. I like to know my pace, but it's not about that right now. In the closing stages of a marathon, I cannot wait to cross the line. This time, even though I've learned to travel light, I am carrying so many memories from my trip. They are weightless, of course, and I am glad that I slowed down to collect them on the way. Right now, I am just running for the love of it, and that feels like a fitting way to complete an adventure that will stay with me for a lifetime.

I only drop back to walking pace on joining the road that takes me the last few hundred metres to the end of the West Highland Way. It's the old finish, according to a box of text on the last panel of my map. Apparently there's a statue in town that makes more of an occasion for those pilgrims who have come all the way from Glasgow, but this one is good enough for me. For there on a bench beside the sign, I find a familiar figure grinning at me as I approach.

'Heard you coming, Scottish elephant. Glad you made it,' says Lucy. 'What took you so long?'

I chuckle and reach out with the palm of one hand to touch the sign.

'I'm the Mushroom King,' I say, as if to remind her. 'My subjects needed me.'

Having set out on this journey alone, it feels right to complete it in company. Along the way, I've overcome obstacles in the landscape and demons of my own making. I've reflected on how I've arrived at this point in life and made friends I hope to see again. Now that my walk along the West Highland Way is over, all I want to do is eat and drink in good company. So before she departs, I'm delighted when Lucy agrees to join me on a search for pizza, beer, and a wee dram to toast our achievement.

DAY SIX

WAYPOINTS

Just before the first season of *Outlander* went into production, I learned that my father was dying.

The call came from a stranger. At least she was a stranger to me at the time. With a strong German accent, she introduced herself as a friend of my dad. She told me he had been living in Canada for many years and was now facing the end of a battle with cancer. As time was running out, she wanted to know if my brother and I would like to fly out and visit him. It was a lot for me to take in during one call, and so it barely registered when the woman added that she was in fact his ex-wife.

Not only had my father remarried, but he had also started a new life across the Atlantic. Given that time was running out for him, I didn't give much thought as to how I felt about reuniting. He had been absent from my life for so long that I didn't even consider him as someone who was missing from it. My brother agreed when we spoke that answering this call seemed like the right thing to do.

And so, at a time when I was preparing to play a character that would transform my career, I found myself hurriedly packing a bag for a part that had been denied to me since I was a little boy. Cirdan and I had lived our lives without a father. Thanks to the love, commitment and grounding our mother had provided, we had grown into independent adults. So, in rushing to catch a flight to reunite with someone who should have meant so much to us, I couldn't help feeling like I needed to find myself in this role.

* * *

I sleep like a king. It helps that I lucked out on checking into my hotel in Fort William. Spoiled for choice when it came to rooms – a surprise benefit of doing this walk out of season – I found myself with a four-poster bed for the night (perhaps like Jamie's in Lallybroch) and a majestic view across the rooftops to the hills beyond. Before setting out from home, I would have been appalled at myself for not camping under the stars from start to finish. On unlocking the door to my room, with the reality of almost 100 miles under my belt, I found a new appreciation for comfort that I would have previously taken for granted.

This morning, I have a mountain to climb. The highest. Literally. With the West Highland Way behind me, and lasting memories of every step of the way, I intend to complete my week away by trekking to the summit of the great Ben Nevis. To mark the occasion, the sun presides across the sky. Those clouds in attendance are just courtiers. It's all about the dazzle today.

Fired up by a breakfast of porridge and coffee, I head out with a view to stopping at the mountain's visitor centre. My feet won't let me forget that I plan to take them over the 100-mile mark today, and I've run out of tape. I feel sure I'll find some there. With a climb of 1,345 metres, into thinner air and with temperatures that can drop significantly, I very much doubt they'll just sell commemorative teddy bears and key rings. I've no plans to panic-buy more equipment. I'm dressed for the climb in suitable boots, several layers under a windproof jacket, and, of course, my snood. I also have my walking poles strapped to my pack. I couldn't possibly leave them behind now. I imagine if I dared to climb a mountain without my good-luck charms, I'd probably return this afternoon by rescue helicopter.

I make my way through largely empty streets. A dust cart is doing the rounds, and a shopkeeper folds open a chalk board on the pavement. I've never particularly liked Fort William, but right now it looks like a charming and sleepy little town. It's early, and I intend to seize the day. Just between us, I could've happily enjoyed a lie-in. Physically, I'm tired, but I can wait to catch up on sleep. Before the sun goes down, I plan to catch a train directly back to Milngavie, where my adventure began; hopefully my car is still there. I'm looking forward to dozing as the landscape I have trekked across rewinds through the window.

The air is cool, crisp and clear as I complete the short walk out of town. It helps clear my head after the craft beer and numerous whiskies of the night before. But I don't regret the carb-loading, ahem; that was my excuse for consuming mine *and* Lucy's pizzas. Ahead, Ben Nevis sits like a great knuckled fist, with the upper reaches lost in that cloud veil drawn to summits known as clag. The sun might be weaker at this time of year, but I hope it's enough to burn off any moisture in the air. For a moment, I worry that I might get all the way up there to find I can't see anything. Then I reconsider and decide that it really doesn't matter. I just want to make the most of every moment of this climb from the bottom to the top.

This trek has been transformative. I set out to walk the West Highland Way on the spur of the moment. Purely in a bid to fill a gap in my schedule, I set my sights on racing across Scotland's great outdoors in record time.

Now, having reached the end of one adventure and about to embark on another, I feel like a different person. This time in the wild has opened my eyes to so many things, from where it all started for me in life to the direction and pace in which I intend to continue. The most immediate revelation is that I have learned to truly appreciate the moment. Throughout my career, and as reflected by the opening stages of this walk, I have focused on targets. It's always been about the destination, but now I realize I've been in such a hurry to get there that I've missed out on the pleasure of the journey.

Isn't it funny how day by day nothing changes, but when you look back, everything is different? (*The Chronicles of Narnia: Prince Caspian,* C. S. Lewis)

It went against my nature to slow things down. When I packed up my tent after that first and last night of wild camping, and then set off on what would become a day that nearly destroyed me, I didn't feel good about myself. Looking back now, I realize I had undermined what could have been a magical day by setting myself a goal. Intent on marching through the miles, I had no time to stop and rest. If I'd just halved the distance that day, and progressed at a leisurely pace, I know now that I would've come to tune in to the sound of the rain falling all around me rather than resenting it. Little things like this, I realize, I have always dismissed in my bid to be somewhere. Only when I removed the blinkers that focused my attention on the way ahead did I come to appreciate how much a moment in time could mean to me.

I have encountered my first setback of the day. The visitor centre is closed! My poor feet will just have to manage without the aid of tape. Right now, my sore ankle and battered toes don't feel too bad. From experience, there's likely to be some aching by lunchtime. If all goes well, however, I'll be on my way back down by then.

The distance from the visitor centre to the summit is approximately 5 miles. It might not sound like much, but although the incline is gentle to begin with, I can see that it will soon become quite steep. My view is restricted by clag, which seems far higher up now that I'm at the foot of the mountain. It feels as if this is nature's way of reminding me not to think too far ahead, and rightly so.

Very quickly I start to lock into the rhythm of my footsteps. They might be measured, but I'm enjoying the simplicity of the task. Normally, with the day ahead of me, I am thinking about all the duties and tasks I need to perform. Since I set foot on the West Highland Way, I haven't even checked my emails. My mobile has become a camera, video recorder and carrier of messages to and from friends, and nothing more. When things looked bleak after my second day, I reached out to my mates. Their responses encouraged me not to give up, even if one or two of them disguised it in savage banter. Since then, I've been keeping them posted about my progress. It's been nice to feel I can share the experience on my own terms.

I have dressed with great respect for the mountain. In my research for the Everest film, I have learned that conditions can change without warning. I don't want to be one of those tourists who heads off in sandals and a T-shirt, never to be seen again. Within half an hour, however, I have stopped to remove a layer, and continue with my coat unzipped. It might be November, but I am *sweating*. I couldn't ask for more glorious sunshine. It really is a treat.

Yes, I know I have been talking up the virtues of taking my time, but sometimes you come across people in life who move painfully slowly. I approach a small group ahead, and find myself politely squeezing by at the first opportunity. I smile and nod and thank them as I pass. One of them gives me a second glance. I see that look of recognition, but rather than bracing myself for the inevitable question as to whether it's really me from the television, I'm the first to strike up an exchange about what lovely weather we're having. On this path, I'm not the actor they think they know. I'm a hiker just like everyone else; a little gregarious perhaps, but I'm here for the star of the show.

'What a day to be climbing a mountain,' I say. 'Have fun! What a magnificent day!'

'Er, yeah, thanks,' they all agree, bemused by the over-the-top greeting by this apparent American on a day trip. I'm wearing a sports top with a small university team logo on the front: the Trojans.

Sing to me of the man, Muse, the man of twists and turns, driven time and again off course, once he had plundered the hallowed heights of Troy. (*The Odyssey,* Homer)

Eventually I reach a height where I can't stop looking at the world around me. The glens are revealed in full, and in such beautiful, vibrant colours. The temperature has dropped a little with so much elevation, but I'm still hot from the effort of the climb. I assumed by now that my head would be in the clouds. Either the summit clag is rising, burning off from the bottom up, or I just failed to take in the sheer enormity of this spectacular mountain. The track is demanding but well defined, while the steep scree slopes demand a great deal of respect. My Achilles is beginning to grumble, and yet I have no intention of turning around. I'll keep plugging away, pausing when I feel like it to look out across the Highlands and feel blessed to be here.

After this, my first mountain ascent, I had made up my mind to see the world: to see it from above, from the tops of the mountains. (*The Making of a Mountaineer*, G. I. Finch)

A breeze drops in to greet me as I ascend into the morning. It strengthens on occasion, which just serves to make me all the more aware of my footing. The path steepens in places, and my hike becomes a clamber and a scramble, but I push on. I think I must have reached a low-lying halo of cloud, because a thin, swirling mist forms for a few minutes. I zip up my jacket, and then a short while later stop to add a layer underneath. The temperature starts to drop quite noticeably, and so I pull up my snood from around my neck to cover my mouth and nose. I keep thinking about my mountaineer friend, Mr Finch, and how this experience might inform the role. It's a big challenge for me, as it is for most people, and I ponder whether the feelings of excitement, wonder and trepidation are the same for experienced climbers when faced with something like Everest. We're all human, after all, and there's nothing like nature to humble us.

As I reflect on the journey I have taken to get here, I realize how quiet it is for a popular tourist trail. It's still early, and yet I'm glad I made the effort to get up and go, because the rising sun brings out the best in such a rugged landscape. I pass a mountain runner on his way down. We nod a greeting as he deftly places one foot in front of the other on what is a testing descent, and I can't help but admire his dedication – he must have set off for the summit before daybreak. Perhaps he was seeking solitude up there; that's something I can appreciate.

I have always been content in my own company, and yet naturally I look for love and companionship. When I am seen out on dates or with a woman in public the press are quick to conjure up stories, but the fact is, I have invested in several meaningful relationships in my life. In the past, when I met someone on my wavelength, I used to go in with 100 per cent commitment. I didn't hold back. I adore the romance, and making that person feel good. It's an amazing, heartfelt feeling when two people connect and create a genuine bond.

Then, just as everything feels so perfect, I find myself looking ahead. Instead of being in the moment, wrapped in that sense of happiness and bliss, I wonder if I can sustain it in two, five or ten years' time. Then I factor in my work, which makes it so hard for me to settle down, and question if it's right to be establishing foundations for the relationship. The last thing I want to do is encourage someone to commit themselves to me, only to find I can't return it, and that's when I move on. I'm more guarded and unsure. I hope for the simplicity once again. Being able to see the whole landscape below, no clouds obscuring the view. I will continue to seek it, even if I have to work harder and keep climbing.

In this time to myself, once I'd learned to enjoy the walk with no pressure to see what was over the next hill, I have come to find a new appreciation of the world around me. It doesn't take much for me to realize that perhaps I should apply the same approach to relationships. I'm also mindful that I am the son of a man who disappeared.

Having committed to setting down roots and starting a family, my dad chose to leave us, and the last thing I want to do is follow in his footsteps.

Now, I know I am not my father's son. For sure, there is a genetic bond between us, but he played no part in shaping my formative years. I have walked my own path in life, and intend for that to continue. Even so, deep down there must be a small part of me that fears I might find myself in his situation. Having lived with the consequences – and no doubt his absence has shaped my outlook – I just do not wish to repeat it. He created a family and then removed himself from it, and left us with no choice but to find our own way. As a result, I find myself bailing from relationships because things look *too* good. It's a protective mechanism because I don't want to cause hurt to myself or anyone else.

By looking ahead like this and fearing the worst, I'm well aware that I could be undermining my chances of sharing my life with someone special. We are all masters of our own destiny, of course. So perhaps this journey has taught me that the next time I fall in love, I should simply enjoy the moment rather than worrying about where it might take me. I had to learn to let go as an actor, after all, and not think about the next line in the script. I also know from experience that you can't run a marathon by focusing on reaching the finish line from the moment you start the race. It's about taking one step at a time in a kind of mindfulness on the move, and letting the process dictate the outcome. Having adopted the same outlook on this walk, and learned to be myself as a result, perhaps I can complete the picture by just being present in my personal life.

If I can lose myself in the here and now, I realize, the future will take care of itself.

When I first came across my hiking friend Graeme, he had submitted to exactly that moment. I might have been privately annoyed that he had claimed a lookout spot I had in mind for myself, but we soon fell into step with one another. Later, when he introduced me to his wife, Tracy, I really admired their relationship. She had joined him at the end of a long day on the trail, and was there to pick him up when his journey came to a premature end. In my eyes, they embodied values that help us to live our best lives: love and friendship, encouragement, faith, trust, support and respect. Graeme had set off alone on the West Highland Way, but ultimately Tracy was with him all the way. Looking at it like this, they shared the experience. That's my kind of adventure, and I hope that one day I'll find a travelling companion who has that same outlook.

The path begins to wind and switch now. Every step requires some effort, and I'm thankful that I have food and drink. The rock here has a grey complexion. It's formidable and somewhat scary. I can certainly sense my heart rate quicken as I look up through the fog and see what I believe to be the outline of a peak.

I have been hiking for hours. It feels like I am midway between the earth and the heavens, as if I've dared to come this far for an audience with the gods. It's amazing what flights of fancy have passed through my mind throughout my week in the wilderness. There have been times when I've given voice to my thoughts, as if I've created my own travelling companion. I could've walked in silence, but over such a long distance, it was good to talk to myself. So much of what I've come out with has been nonsense, and yet in among it have been moments of clarity that can stop me in my tracks. In future, even when my work is at its most demanding, I need to make more time to let my thoughts out to play. From experience, however – and I'm still cringing at having been caught consorting with mushrooms – I should make sure that I really am quite alone.

For the first time in an age, I come across another hiker. She's on her way back down the mountain, and we exchange a cheery hello. As she skips on by, I can't help wondering what time she set out this morning. I have at least another hour to go, and another to get back to this point. I can only think she left in darkness, and for that she has my full respect.

Soon after I pass the early bird on her return to earth, the climb levels out onto a broad ridge. It's surprisingly flat, and feels about as challenging as a garden path. The giant flank before me that rises into the clag, however, is hard to ignore. I can see the path cutting diagonally across it like a scar. It looks like quite a trek, and something a mountaineer like George Ingle Finch would have taken in his stride. He was such an experienced, positive and energetic guy, who refused to be held back by convention. In his heyday, some hundred years ago, the established way to reach a summit involved a team throwing people and equipment at the mountain. They'd effectively lay siege to the summit by going up and establishing camps at different levels. Finch used to climb with his brother. They'd take the bare necessities to keep them safe and then just go. What a guy!

From the ridge, I think I can make out a split in the path on that great flank that would take me on a more direct route to the top. While Finch might've instinctively taken that option, I'm not in that kind of hurry. I'm happy to follow the tourist route, even if it can feel like a kind of rocky StairMaster.

I wonder if there is a record for the number of bad selfies a hiker has taken on the climb to the summit of Ben Nevis. I reckon I would be a contender. I'm just so mesmerized by how far I've climbed. I am now quite clearly higher than the surrounding peaks. If I peer down, I can see hikers so far below they could be ants, while the great rivers flowing through the glens look like silk threads. Honestly? The only way I can get some perspective on such a scene is by sticking my face into the foreground.

I realize while zooming in with my camera phone that I can make out the final stages of the West Highland Way. Through the viewfinder, I work back from Fort William, up through the forest trail and then all the way to the pass where Lucy first busted me with my mushroom buddies. I try to trace it further back, but it just turns to a pale and shimmering haze. I take a picture anyway, and then remind myself that I'm not here to dwell on the past, in the same way that I've learned not to focus too far ahead. Given the drop on one side of the path, and the wind now coming round the mountain, I realize it's best if I just concentrate very, very closely on the present.

* * *

My brother and I arrived at Calgary airport feeling jet-lagged and apprehensive about what awaited us. Despite the fact that both of us felt like we had been uprooted from our lives to answer this call for compassion, it was good to travel with Cirdan. We'd both been so busy that we hadn't seen each other recently as much as we'd have liked. On finding ourselves thrown together in this way, it felt like we had each other. It was an opportunity to bond with him too, and I was thankful for the chance, despite the intense and strange circumstances.

When she met us in Arrivals, my Dad's ex-wife turned out to be lovely. In her flowing, free-spirited manner, she struck me as someone who came from the same way of life as our father. With 500 kilometres of driving ahead of us, which would take us through the night, we rented a car and took turns behind the wheel. The Rockies would have been magnificent had we been travelling in daylight. Instead, with just the car's headlamps lighting up the highway, and one frightening encounter with an elk as it crossed our path, Cirdan and I simply did our level best to deliver us to our destination in one piece. Our host was confident with her directions, which was something, but the conversation never quite shifted gear from polite, formal talk. Like us, this was someone who had once been central to David's life, and that was a common thread that felt a little fragile.

After 12 hours on the road, we arrived at my father's cabin, just outside the city of Kelowna in British Columbia. It was a beautiful, serene place to live, surrounded by mountains and deep in pine forests, with views of Lake Okanagan. That first visit was brief; cut short as my father wasn't well enough to see us, but momentous for my brother and me. The moment we stepped inside to find that he had been keeping track of our lives, it brought him alive in some way. Perhaps it was a good thing that we didn't see much of him straight away. It gave us time to gather our thoughts, and also get some much-needed sleep.

We had been invited to stay nearby with a friend of my father's. Everyone was very pleasant and welcoming, but it was hard to relax. Cirdan and I were given a shared room. It had bunk beds, which made us feel like kids again. We laughed a bit, and that served as a balm for the fact that we both felt far from home, but we also retreated internally to process the situation.

A day after our first visit to the cabin, we finally had an audience with our father. I hadn't seen him since he'd appeared out of nowhere to see me in a play all those years ago. It felt like a lifetime had passed. On setting eyes on him in bed, he didn't seem too bad. We spoke for a while, but nothing was as impactful as those first moments at his cabin as I tried to assess who this character was from his environment and trappings: the outdoor kitchen, the worn armchair, the candles on the desk, the model aeroplane, the felt wizard's hat, and the books, photos, DVDs and trinkets on the shelves and ledges. Every object told a story, and represented waypoints on a journey undertaken from his childhood to this moment. In person he was harder to read; his stare unsettled me and reduced me to a child once more.

Our stay lasted a week. In that intense and intimate time, David felt well enough to visit the shore of Lake Okanagan with us. We sat under a tree together and he told us about himself. He was humorous, a talented gardener and champion of biodynamic farming. He revealed that the key to successful agriculture was, well, shit. Bullshit, to be exact. In the view of this man from the fringes of society as much as our lives, the secret to growing great produce was a truckload of steer manure. And maybe a little hocus-pocus.

At one point, as I listened while looking out across the lake, I noticed a wave form out of nowhere. It rose up, gathering pace at the same time, surged across the body of water and then disappeared. My brother saw it too, and when we mentioned it later to our host, we learned that we had seen Ogopogo: the Loch Ness Monster of Lake Okanagan. Whatever we had witnessed – and no doubt there could be many explanations – somehow it felt fitting that folklore from both Canada and Scotland had featured in this precious time with a man who loved a fantasy odyssey.

Dad. David. Pebbles. This was someone who meant different things to me. I forgave him for taking off, despite the pain he had caused, but I still couldn't pin him down. From his time in Germany to his new life in British Columbia, it just struck me that he was someone constantly drawn to see what was over the horizon.

As he had barely registered in my life, and then chosen when to appear in it, I recorded everything he had to say on my phone. It felt like a means of capturing something of him, and I hoped that perhaps when I listened again, it would reveal new layers of meaning to me.

My father passed away shortly after our return home. Cirdan

and I had been expecting the news, but it wasn't just geographical distance that blunted our grief. Despite being his sons, we had hardly known the man. At the time, production of *Outlander* was in full swing. The shooting schedule was so demanding that I had little time for anything but my role. I had no life outside of this family of cast and crew, and simply lived out of a suitcase in a hotel room or set trailer. I would often mislay things in this hectic environment, like a script or my toothbrush, only for them to turn up in due course. So when I couldn't find my phone after filming on location one day, I just assumed it would surface. I knew full well what was on it, which served to intensify my search. I asked around, but nobody had seen it. I couldn't just halt such a huge production, of course, and so as it moved on, I resigned myself to doing the same thing.

My phone had vanished into thin air, and with it the sole recording of my father's account of his life. I didn't have time to think about it, which summed up my existence until this week in the Scottish wilderness. I just had to tell myself that somehow its disappearance was a fitting epitaph.

* * *

I'm into the clag at last! (I hate that word, it sounds sticky and thick, which I guess it is.) From the moment I arrive, the temperature tumbles. I pull my jacket hood up over the crown of my faithful baseball cap and press on. Having not seen a soul for some time, all of a sudden I find that the path ahead is dotted with hikers on their way down. Most strikingly, despite the fog, I can see the summit at last. Everything else is shrouded but for this dome of rock with the sun behind it.

This is it, I think to myself. This is the end as much as a new beginning.

Clambering up into this cloud world, I find my internal voice falling quiet. All the wonderings that carried me this far make way for a sudden well of emotion. For the first time on this journey, I find myself close to tears. I guess I'm just sad it's all over. What I need, I decide, is a hug. Ideally from someone I love, but in their absence, no doubt I'll have a couple of beers in town before catching my train and seek comfort from chat with the bartender. Maybe I'll call my mum on the ride home. We speak on a regular basis, but this time I feel I want to thank her for some things. I'm also aware that I can't hang around up here. As much as I'd like to spend a while at the top of this world, it's clear to me that if I do, I'll freeze to death. The cold really does take me by surprise. Having worked up a sweat on such a long climb, I can literally feel it begin to freeze on the surface of my skin. I'll be fine for a short while, though, so I press on up the path as it winds towards the highest point.

The mountaintop is within sight, but the going is much slower here. It's steep, easy to trip and also slippery. Ice coats the rocks, with crystals in the air, and it feels like it's been quite some time since this hidden realm has felt the warmth of the sun. I begin to feel short of breath, which might be something to do with the thinning air, or the fact that I'm just knackered. The wind comes at me from all directions, as if the mountain gods would like to make it known that only the bravest of hikers should dare to tread this far.

Now I feel like Finch, I tell myself. With the production awaiting me in the coming weeks, it's as if I'm mixing business with pleasure. And really it is a blast to be up here, even though it's bitingly cold and the moisture in my snood is making it hard for me to breathe comfortably. I focus on the skyline, just metres away where the path seemingly vanishes into the blue, and with one final push, I reach the summit.

Here the sun reveals itself to me in full. What's more, for all the people making their way down, I find there's nobody around. I stand at the highest point in the UK, all alone but alive and well, and it's glorious. I'm exhausted, my muscles ache and my bad Achilles is threatening to mutiny, but above all, I'm elated. What a feeling! What a journey! From the lowlands of Scotland to the magic of the Highlands, and now the top of Ben Nevis. It might be one more waypoint, but ultimately this adventure has charted a map to the heart of who I really am.

EPILOGUE

On the road, Scotland

Gunning my motorbike on the lochside pass, I feel like a man reborn. I love heading out on my Harley. It's a weapon, noisy and rather unpolite. Give me any good reason to ride and I'll seize it, and today I have a mission in mind. It's early, and so the road north is largely empty. As a rider, I feel so connected with every twist and turn. It's just me, the tarmac beneath my two wheels and that epic Highlands sky above.

I've only been home for a week, but it feels good to be out here once more.

As soon I arrived back at my house, having descended Ben Nevis to catch a train back to reality, I found my life waiting for me. For the first time in a week, I checked my emails and voicemail. Rather than stay up for hours working through the backlog, I took my time and felt all the better for it. Nothing changed in my world while I was away, but my place in it feels more grounded now. Just being at home feels good, in fact. Before my long walk, I was restless and bored. Even though I had a rare week to myself, I couldn't settle. Quite literally, since my return, I have savoured the stillness. My house also strikes me as a place I could settle in for a long time to come. A family home, perhaps, whatever that might mean.

I'd like to say that I'm ready to throw myself into the role of the character that took shape in my mind as I approached and ascended Ben Nevis. On the train, I finished the last chapters of the book about George Ingle Finch, only to learn that the production has been put on hold indefinitely. At first, I was gutted. I'd been so looking forward to filming. The whole experience of conquering a mountain had fired my enthusiasm to explore what it meant for someone who had taken it to the next level.

Then I reminded myself that disappointments can happen even at this stage in my career. I might have spent decades clinging to hope and living with rejection, and yet the pathway for film and television projects to reach the screen can be as challenging as a long trek. Learning to be resilient is important, and I'd discovered in the last week that we can always dig deeper than we believe. Since this production fell through, I've found myself looking back at my preparation for the role and consider it time well spent. I love that process of working out a character and learning to get under their skin. I was a hiker for 100 miles, but I finished as a mountaineer in spirit, and that proved so rewarding.

As much as I love my bike, I have a new-found passion for travelling by foot. In this world, we're primed to focus on pace, speed and destination, but I feel differently about that now. Yes, it's great to power into the glens like this, and it's taken me no time at all to get here, but it's no substitute for putting one foot in front of the other and losing myself to the moment.

Of course, my week in the wild wasn't one long idyll. The first two days were a lesson in humility for me. I was overambitious and overladen. In the pouring rain, that combination could've crushed my soul had it not been for the kindness and companionship of a fellow traveller. I still feel sad that injury prevented Graeme from completing the West Highland Way, but I know he'll be back. How? Because I messaged him in the week and he's already making plans to walk the last leg. (As it turns out, Graeme went back out on the West Highland Way in March/April 2022 and completed it in 5 glorious, sunshine-filled days. He even sent a photo of him having a dram of Sassenach! I'm looking forward to toasting the completion of his journey when we next see each other.)

I also heard from Lucy, who is safely home in England. Her boyfriend gave her a West Highland Way medal and she persuaded him to join her in hiking up a mountain in Wales. She even sent me lessons from her journey, which made me nod to myself, smile and feel glad that we walked those closing miles together.

1. 96 miles is a long way.
2. Toenails are overrated.
3. It's absolutely OK to cry (but won't get you there any quicker).
4. Talking to yourself is not a sign of madness. Quite the opposite.
5. Scotland is breathtaking.
6. People are kind.

I pull up in a layby that I spotted when I set out on the morning after the storm. Tipping my bike onto the stand, I pop off my helmet and breathe in the fresh air. A breeze stirs the wild grass in the meadowland behind me. A bird of prey circles high overhead. In a heartbeat, I could be back on the path. Sadly, I have work commitments later today, and so I can't spend too long here. That's OK, though. I'm in no rush any more. I can stay a short while enjoying the solitude. To think I had a whole week of this seems incredible to me now, and somewhat poignant seeing that I've returned to the precise point where I lost myself in it.

Here, on the third morning of my journey, I bundled up all the stuff from my pack that was holding me back and stashed it in undergrowth. From that moment on, I found my rhythm, and it's one I intend to maintain. Making my way along the verge, I look out for markers I had noted in my mind before settling on the hiding place. I'm sure I'll find it any time now, because otherwise I'll wonder if my whole journey was just one blissful flight of my imagination.

Usually, the best way to find the yellow brick road of your life is to start out on the dusty, dirt one. And then let yourself become so preoccupied in making the best of it, having fun, and challenging yourself that you actually stop paying attention to the path. (*Notes from the Universe: New Perspectives from an Old Friend*, Mike Dooley)

WILD MUSHROOMS OF SCOTLAND

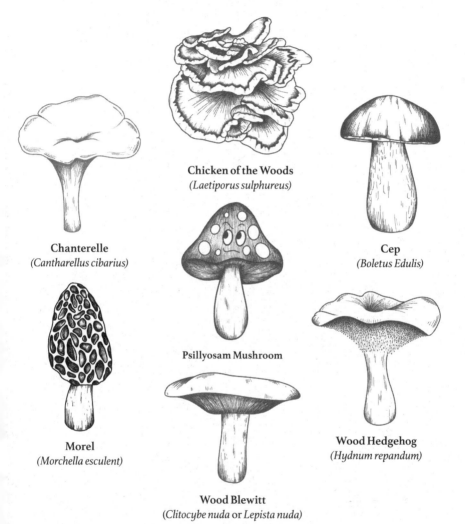

Chicken of the Woods
(Laetiporus sulphureus)

Chanterelle
(Cantharellus cibarius)

Cep
(Boletus Edulis)

Psillyosam Mushroom

Morel
(Morchella esculent)

Wood Hedgehog
(Hydnum repandum)

Wood Blewitt
(Clitocybe nuda or Lepista nuda)

I have to admit, I'm not much of a forager. But I do love wild mushrooms – and Scotland has a rich supply of them! On my walk I encountered all shapes, sizes and colours, and wanted to share a selection of my favourite to spot.

Though foraging in Scotland is a fun and exciting way to get up close to nature and wildlife, please be careful where and what you pick – some species of mushroom and fungi are poisonous and can even be fatal if eaten. Make sure to read up on the various species and guidelines beforehand, as well as ensure your information is reliable and up to date.

REFLECTIONS FROM THE WEST HIGHLAND WAY

Dear Reader,

It would be fair to say that the journey along the West Highland Way that I took in the deep winter of 2021 was a challenge that proved to be more significant than I'd first anticipated, and one that has stayed with me long after completing it.

It's been a little while since I recorded those hundreds of voice notes on the walk in order to write the book that would become *Waypoints*, and I wanted to reflect on how writing about my life and career has changed my outlook and impacted my mental and physical well-being, and the ways in which the whole *Waypoints* journey was liberating yet challenging.

So without further ado, here are a few questions I've put together to give you an idea of what's been happening since the book was published.

Thank you for your continued support, and I hope you enjoy reading these updates as much as I've enjoyed writing them.

Taking on the West Highland Way (especially in the winter!) turned out to be a much bigger challenge than you first anticipated. What advice would you give to someone who is considering embarking on this walk?

My best advice is to try not to rush a walk like this. I had to learn the hard way that the journey is certainly more rewarding than arriving at the destination. On a practical note, the West Highland Way can be broken up into smaller sections. I was doing around 20 miles a day, which was manageable and still gave me time to enjoy the scenery, etc. But with a shorter distance to cover each day (or walking in the summer with more daylight available), you can also explore some of the historical sites along the way. From Rob Roy's Cave to Steall Waterfall (Scotland's second highest), there is so much to enjoy in the dramatic Scottish landscape. If you want to make the journey easier, there are companies that will transport your luggage so you don't have to carry it all on your back (though don't forget the coffee press!). I would like to return sometime and redo the route, wild camping the whole way. Perhaps in the early summer months, avoiding the dreaded midges.

Can you share some of the most significant lessons from your journey that you have since applied to your personal and professional life?

Taking time out for yourself is really important. I already yearn to be back out in the mountains. The solitude and clarity you gain from hiking alone is priceless. Not only is it good for you physically, but allowing yourself time to switch off is essential when you've got a busy schedule. I've promised myself I will start to book a weekend or a couple of days off regularly and escape to the hills. Recently I 'bagged' a few Munros – a terrific ridge walk near Blair Atholl – so I'm making good on that promise to myself.

When looking back over your career and reflecting as you walked, is there any guidance you'd give to someone who is following a passion that might not immediately pay-off that you wish you'd known sooner?

I never thought I would/could be a writer. I also never thought I'd complete the West Highland Way on my own, but I surprised myself by doing both of those things. It's important not to set limitations for yourself. Anything is possible if you put your mind to it. I have always loved to test my limits and hate to fail at a project or task. Perhaps that's why I took great delight in torturing my co-star, Graham McTavish, during the filming of *Men in Kilts*. I certainly enjoy pushing him (and occasionally myself) to the limit. If there's one piece of advice I'd give, it'd be: give it a go, follow your gut and persevere, and you will surprise yourself (and maybe others!).

C an you talk about the impact of your journey on your well-being?

I like trying various sports and disciplines. I train a lot in the gym and run regularly, but walking long distance is a different kind of challenge . . . my poor feet! I think my toes have only just recovered. But it's amazing how your body adapts. After a couple of days I could feel my legs getting accustomed to the distance, and after finishing the hike, I missed the repetitive (almost meditative) daily movement and the benefits it brought – not only physical but also mental. They say walking is the best exercise you can do, and I believe that. Just make sure you take enough snacks, fresh socks, and plenty of physio tape!

Y ou talk candidly in the book about body image. How has that been received? Have others opened up to you about their own struggles?

I spoke in the book about the pressure that is put on actors to look a certain way. I know that men traditionally don't really speak about health concerns, and I think it's important that we are more open about our physical and mental health. For anyone starting out in the industry, it can be especially intimidating. It's for this reason, among others, that I really enjoy working with youth theatre groups and speaking to students at drama school, and I hope I can provide a little insight and alleviate their fears and concerns in that area. That's also one of the reasons why I started My Peak Challenge: not only to support vital charity work, but to provide access to sound information in order to help establish new healthy habits.

*W*aypoints **has been praised for being 'revealing', and readers have responded to you telling your story on your terms. Was writing the book liberating? Did you find it a challenge to share parts of your story?**

I deliberated over the more personal sections of the book. I was wary in particular about revealing too much of my family history, as I didn't want to hurt anyone close to me, but I also realized that I had never really explored my own relationship to my past. It felt good to take ownership of our story, and it has actually helped my family talk more openly about past history/relationships, and perhaps even laid some issues to rest.

The **book begins with you meeting your father after many years at the end of his life, and his absence is a part of your story and the man you became. Has writing about this aspect of your life given you any closure about that relationship?**

I didn't want the book to be primarily about my father, but the lack of his presence certainly did shape who I am today. Writing about it felt cathartic and perhaps put that ghost to rest. The journey along the

West Highland way was not only a physical one; it also gave me time to reflect and the opportunity to let some things go. It's important to take time out of your daily life, and the Scottish Highlands is a great space to process (or just talk/sing to yourself out loud . . .!). I'd recommend it to anyone.

As much as your father's absence was a feature of your young life, your mother's presence helped define it in a positive way. How has she influenced you?

I realize how fortunate an upbringing I had. My mother, Chrissie, brought us up in idyllic surroundings in rural Scotland. Despite the financial challenges, we were very lucky to have the Scottish landscape as our playground. As a child, the ruins of Kenmure Castle, Loch Ken and the deep Scots pine forests were where I let my imagination run wild. My mother provided us with all we needed, even if she had to go without. I feel very fortunate to have grown up there, with creativity at the heart of our upbringing; it's probably partly the reason why I became an actor.

So much of this story – on the West Highland Way and in your career and life – is about perseverance and finding your own path among the difficulties and options that life presents. Do you have any words of advice for other people who are struggling to make it through a challenging time?

Despite seeking to complete the walk as a solitary adventure, I met some really amazing people along the way. Sharing the experience with Graeme and Lucy was very fulfilling, and they were a great support during some of the tougher moments. They both became a part of the story, and I was thrilled when I could invite them along to the live book events to celebrate our achievement together. Both were so generous with their time, and they gave their own insight into walking the West Highland Way alone (and bumping into a hungry hiking actor). We shared a few drams together and it was great to hear about what they have been up to since we met on the rocky trail. I think Graeme has now completed the route twice (he even camped along the way), and Lucy has been walking all over the Welsh hills (she's so fast!). I suppose with this in mind, my advice for anyone facing a challenge seemingly alone is to be open to help and companionship – you never know how another person's perspective could help when you're feeling up against it.

Nature plays a role in your journey, from the nasty weather that nearly drives you off the trail to the fungi who keep you company. How has that experience changed the way you see the world?

I would like to thank my fungi friends for keeping me company. I'm convinced they have an ulterior motive, and would gladly accept the role of mushroom king and ascend the toadstool throne.

What message do you hope readers will take away from the book?

Waypoints was very personal and reflective in parts, yet also cathartic. It felt like the end of the first chapter of my life and the beginning of a second. I'm nearing the end of my time on *Outlander* – eight seasons and ten years' shooting – and the show has really shaped who I am. It has given me great opportunities and valuable experience that I can build on moving forward. I'm excited for the future, but it feels vitally important to acknowledge where I've come from. I wouldn't be where I am today without my past success and (multiple!) failures. As a young man, I dreamed of working in the acting industry and being well respected. It's certainly a dream come true, and now I'm ready for the next challenge. The message I hope readers are left with is that in life and your career there are ups and downs, and both of those are important for shaping your future.

Can you share any plans you have to embark on similar journeys in the future and what you hope to achieve through them?

A dream of mine has been to see the highest mountain in the world, Mount Everest. I wrote in *Waypoints* about the Everest movie project that fell through, and was disappointed that I never made it to Nepal. However, more recently I have been pitching a TV show that follows that dream (and the footsteps of George Mallory) from the UK to the Himalayan plateau and the slopes of Everest. Perhaps, if I'm lucky enough and dream hard enough, I may yet find myself on the slopes of 'Chomolungma', the earth's highest mountain. However, this time I'll be better prepared and ensure I'm not walking alone (and carrying plenty of snacks!).

ACKNOWLEDGEMENTS

This journey was supposed to be a solitary one, but then when I look back it's filled with friends, old and new. A huge thank you to everyone I have met along the way, who have shaped my life. Special thanks to: Philip Howard for giving me that first opportunity and experience; Ruth Young for believing in me; my whole team at United Agents and UTA; Alex Norouzi for being the most creative and brilliant business partner and friend; Valbo for the burpees and great coffee; the Great Glen Company team; Briony Gowlett for her patience and support in creating this book. The Octopus team for getting this book into people's hands. Matt Whyman for being my silent companion on the journey and for helping me gather my life into these pages; my brother, Cirdan, and of course my mother, Chrissie, who gave me every opportunity and inspired me with her creativity.

PICTURE CREDITS
& PUBLISHER
ACKNOWLEDGEMENTS

The author and publisher would like to thank the following copyright-holders to reproduce images in this book:

ITV Shutterstock / Royal Conservatoire of Scotland, Kevin Low / Richard Campbell / Jonathan Keenan. All rights reserved 2022, Bridgeman Images / Douglas Robertson, Traverse Theatre / Royal Conservatoire of Scotland, KK Dundas / Tim Morozzo 2005.

All other images are care of the author's personal collection.

The author and publisher have made all reasonable efforts to contact copyright-holders for permission and apologise for any omissions or errors in the form of credits given. Corrections may be made to future printings.

The publisher would also like to thank the creative team for their work on the cover: Chris Terry, Yasia Williams, Michelle Methven, Wendy Kemp Forbes, Laura Strong and Scott Richmond. And Rachael Shone and Peter Liddiard for additional illustration.

ABOUT THE AUTHOR

Sam Heughan is an award-winning actor, producer, entrepreneur, and philanthropist, best known for his starring role as Jamie Fraser in the hit TV show *Outlander*. His career in theater, television, and film spans almost two decades. He is also the #1 *New York Times* bestselling coauthor of two previous books, *Clanlands* and *The Clanlands Almanac*. For his outstanding contribution to charitable endeavors and artistic success, he has been awarded honorary doctorates from the University of Glasgow, the University of Stirling, and the Royal Conservatoire of Scotland.